MongoDB Performance Tuning

Optimizing MongoDB Databases and their Applications

Guy Harrison
Michael Harrison

MongoDB Performance Tuning: Optimizing MongoDB Databases and their Applications

Guy Harrison
Kingsville, VIC, Australia

Michael Harrison
Derrimut, VIC, Australia

ISBN-13 (pbk): 978-1-4842-6878-0
https://doi.org/10.1007/978-1-4842-6879-7

ISBN-13 (electronic): 978-1-4842-6879-7

Managing Director, Apress Media LLC: Welmoed Spahr
Acquisitions Editor: Jonathan Gennick
Development Editor: Laura Berendson
Coordinating Editor: Jill Balzano

Cover image designed by Freepik (www.freepik.com)

Distributed to the book trade worldwide by Springer Science+Business Media LLC, 1 New York Plaza, Suite 4600, New York, NY 10004. Phone 1-800-SPRINGER, fax (201) 348-4505, e-mail orders-ny@springer-sbm.com, or visit www.springeronline.com. Apress Media, LLC is a California LLC and the sole member (owner) is Springer Science + Business Media Finance Inc (SSBM Finance Inc). SSBM Finance Inc is a **Delaware** corporation.

For information on translations, please e-mail booktranslations@springernature.com; for reprint, paperback, or audio rights, please e-mail bookpermissions@springernature.com.

Apress titles may be purchased in bulk for academic, corporate, or promotional use. eBook versions and licenses are also available for most titles. For more information, reference our Print and eBook Bulk Sales web page at http://www.apress.com/bulk-sales.

Any source code or other supplementary material referenced by the author in this book is available to readers on GitHub via the book's product page, located at www.apress.com/9781484268780. For more detailed information, please visit http://www.apress.com/source-code.

Printed on acid-free paper

Dedicated to my darling Jenny, who makes my life joyful.

—Guy

Dedicated to Oriana, without whom this book would have been completed much sooner.

—Mike

Table of Contents

About the Authors

Guy Harrison is CTO at ProvenDB, a partner at Toba Capital, and a software professional with more than 20 years of experience in database design, development, administration, and optimization. He is the author of *Next Generation Databases* (Apress) and many other books and articles on database technology. Guy writes monthly columns for *Database Trends on Applications* (dbta.com) on MongoDB and emerging technologies. He can be found on the internet at `http://guyharrison.net`.

Michael Harrison is the lead developer at ProvenDB, working intimately with MongoDB from both an application and a database perspective. He is a coauthor of *The MongoDB Workshop* as well as senior developer of dbKoda, an open source development environment for MongoDB.

About the Technical Reviewer

 **Michael Grayson** is a Database Engineer working at Percona with nearly 15 years of experience with databases and over 6 years of experience with MongoDB. He has spoken at MongoDB World, SQL PASS Summit, and lots of regional events (SQL Saturdays, Oracle User Groups, MongoDB User Groups [MUGs]) about MongoDB and Apache Kafka. He has previously worked at companies such as Paychex and Thomson Reuters and holds certifications in both AWS and Azure. He has a bachelor's degree from Drexel University. He lives in the Rochester, NY, area with his wife and four children and can be found on Twitter at @mikegray831. He blogs occasionally at `https://mongomikeblog.wordpress.com/blog/` but now more often on the Percona Blog, `www.percona.com/blog/`.

Acknowledgments

We'd like to thank everyone in Apress who helped in the production of this book, in particular lead editor Jonathan Gennick, coordinating editor Jill Balzano, and development editor Laura Berendson. We'd also like to thank Michael Grayson for his thorough technical review.

Guy would like to thank his wife Jenny for her love, support and chocolate. He'd also like to thank Mike for giving him something to keep him sane during Melbourne's 112-day COVID-19 lockdown.

Mike would like to thank Jessica for the love and support, but more importantly, for providing a steady flow of coffee. Additionally, Mike would like to thank Guy for taking the lead when creating this title and dragging him along the way.

This book is dedicated to the newest member of the Harrison family: Oriana, without whom this book would have been completed much earlier.

Guy Harrison

Michael Harrison

Melbourne, Australia

December 2020

Introduction

When MongoDB emerged in 2009, database technologies were at a crossroads. For more than 20 years, relational databases such as Oracle, SQL Server, and MySQL had dominated the database market. These databases, which combined the relational data model, SQL language, and "ACID" transactions, had been the foundation for applications that transformed modern business and which powered the Internet revolution. But by the middle of the first decade of the new century, it was clear that the relational database was failing to meet the demands of a new breed of always-on, globally scalable, web applications. These new "Web 2.0" applications demanded new breeds of database management systems.

By 2010, a plethora of non-relational "NoSQL" systems had emerged – Hadoop, HBase, Cassandra, and many others. Of these non-relational upstarts, MongoDB has been by almost any measure the most successful. As we write this, MongoDB ranks as one of the top five database management systems.[1] Of these top five, only MongoDB is based on 21st-century technologies. The other four (Oracle, MySQL, SQL Server, and Postgres) all have their origins in the 1980s and 1990s.

MongoDB's success can be ascribed to many factors – such as alignment with object-oriented programming paradigms and compatibility with modern DevOps practices. In the main, MongoDB has thrived because it made life easier for developers. However, in the past few years, we've seen MongoDB graduate from a "by developers for developers" database to a platform supporting a new generation of mission-critical systems across an increasingly broad range of enterprises.

As MongoDB has matured and expanded its enterprise footprint, performance management has become increasingly important. As we know, poorly performing customer-facing applications can be fatal for today's online enterprise. For instance, when the load time for a web page increases from 1 second to 5 seconds, the probability of a user abandoning the page rises by 90%[2] – directly impacting online revenue. And because databases perform so much disk IO and data crunching, the database is often the root cause of that poor performance.

---

[1] See https://db-engines.com/en/ranking
[2] https://tinyurl.com/yyyeckw8

Furthermore, in the cloud, performance management is cost management: poorly performing databases consume unnecessary CPU, memory, and IO resources that cost real money. A couple of days spent tuning a large-scale MongoDB-based cloud application could potentially save hundreds of thousands of dollars in hosting fees.

Indeed, we could even argue that performance management is an environmental imperative. The electricity that powers busy database servers costs more than just money – it's also associated with greenhouse gas production. Reducing energy consumption in the home is a social responsibility; reducing energy consumption in the data center is as important. A badly tuned MongoDB database is like a poorly tuned car that backfires and belches smoke: it may get you from A to B, but it will cost you more in gas and exact a heavier toll on the environment.

This book is our attempt to produce a coherent and comprehensive MongoDB tuning manual. To that end, we set out with the following objectives:

- To provide a methodology for MongoDB performance tuning that addresses performance issues systematically and efficiently. In particular, this methodology attempts to address *causes* before *symptoms*.

- To address all aspects of MongoDB performance management, from database design through to the tuning of application code and on to server and cluster optimization.

- To maintain a strong focus on tuning *fundamentals*. Fundamentals are usually where the most significant performance gains can be achieved and – if not addressed – usually limit the benefits gained through the application of advanced techniques.

How This Book Is Structured

The chapters of this book fall into the following broad parts:

- Chapters 1–3 cover methods and techniques. In these chapters, we describe a performance tuning methodology that we believe provides the most effective means of tuning MongoDB databases. We also offer some background on MongoDB architecture and on the tools that MongoDB provides for investigating, monitoring, and diagnosing MongoDB performance.

- Chapters 4 and 5 cover application and database design. Here, we cover the basics of developing an efficient document model and of indexing MongoDB collections.

- Chapters 6–10 cover the optimization of application code. Tuning your application code usually offers the most significant database performance opportunities and should be addressed before adjusting your server or cluster configuration. We'll look at how to optimize MongoDB find() statements, aggregation pipelines, and data manipulation statements.

- Chapters 11–14 discuss the optimization of the MongoDB server and the hardware on which it runs. We'll explain how to optimize memory to avoid IO, how to optimize the IO you can't prevent, and finally how to configure an efficient MongoDB cluster.

Who Should Read This Book

This book is for anyone who is interested in improving the performance of a MongoDB database or the applications that depend on that database. This includes application architects, developers, and database administrators.

Although the book presents a coherent and logical ceiling-to-floor approach to database tuning, not all sections of the book will appeal equally to all readers. For instance, developers may find the sections on application code more helpful than the sections on IO optimization. Likewise, database administrators who have no access to application code will probably find the sections on server optimization more useful.

Each of these groups may choose to skip sections of the book covering aspects of performance over which they have no control. However, we would emphasize that the philosophy of this book advocates addressing the root causes of performance issues *before* alleviating symptoms. It is assumed in later chapters (Chapter 12, for instance) that you have performed the activities outlined in earlier chapters (e.g., Chapter 5).

We intend this book to be accessible to those who are relatively new to the MongoDB database, so we at least briefly explain and define key concepts and MongoDB architecture. However, some familiarity with MongoDB and the JavaScript programming language is assumed.

Scripts and Sample Data

This book utilizes various scripts to report on MongoDB performance. All of these scripts are available on GitHub at https://github.com/gharriso/MongoDBPerformanceTuningBook.

The master script mongoTuning.js provides access to all these scripts from within a MongoDB shell session. To use these scripts from within a MongoDB shell, simply issue the Mongo command with the script name as an argument and add the "--shell" option, for example:

```
$ mongo --shell mongoTuning.js
MongoDB shell version v4.2.0
connecting to: mongodb://127.0.0.1:27017/?compressors=disabled&gssapi
ServiceName=mongodb

MongoDB server version: 4.2.0

rs0:PRIMARY>
```

The examples can also be found in our GitHub repository under the Examples folder. The data that these examples use can be found in the sampleData folder as a compressed dump file. Instructions on how to load the data can be found in the same folder.

PART I

Methods and Tools

CHAPTER 1

Methodical Performance Tuning

Performance is a critical success factor for any application. If you think about the apps you use every day, it's evident that you only use the apps that perform well. Would you use Google if Google searches took 2 minutes while Bing was almost instantaneous? Of course not. Indeed, research has shown that about half the population abandons a website if a page takes longer than 3 seconds to load.[1]

Application performance can depend on many factors, but the most frequent avoidable cause of poor performance is the database. Moving data from disk into the database and then from the database to the application involves the slowest components of the application infrastructure – the disk drives and the network. It's therefore critical that the application code that interacts with the database and the database itself be tuned for premium performance.

A Cautionary Tale

Your MongoDB tuning methodology is critical to the ultimate success of your tuning endeavor. Consider the following cautionary tale.

A significant website backed by a MongoDB database is exhibiting unacceptable performance. As an experienced MongoDB professional, you are called in to diagnose the problem. When you look at the critical operating system performance metrics, two things stick out: both CPU and IO on the replica set primary are high. Both the CPU load average and the disk IO latencies suggest that the MongoDB system needs more CPU and IO capacity.

---

[1]https://developers.google.com/web/fundamentals/performance/why-performance-matters

G. Harrison and M. Harrison, *MongoDB Performance Tuning*, https://doi.org/10.1007/978-1-4842-6879-7_1

After a quick calculation, you recommend sharding MongoDB to spread the load across four servers. The dollar cost is substantial, as is the downtime required to redistribute data across the shards. Nevertheless, something has to be done, so management approves the expense and the downtime. Following the implementation, website performance is acceptable, and you modestly take the credit.

A successful outcome? You think so, until

- Within a few months performance is again a problem – each shard is now running out of capacity.

- Another MongoDB expert is called in and reports that a single indexing change would have fixed the original problem with no dollar cost and no downtime. Furthermore, she notes that the sharding has actually harmed the performance of specific queries and recommends de-sharding several collections.

- The new index is implemented, following which the database workload is reduced to one-tenth of that observed during your initial engagement. Management prepares to sell the now-surplus hardware on eBay and marks your consulting record with a "do not re-engage" stamp.

- Your significant other leaves you for a PHP programmer, and you end up shaving your head and becoming a monk.

After months of silent meditation, you realize that while your tuning efforts correctly focused on the activities consuming the most time within the database, they failed to differentiate between *causes* and *effects*. Consequently, you mistakenly dealt with an *effect* – the high CPU and IO rates – while neglecting the *cause* (a missing index).

Symptomatic Performance Tuning

The approach outlined above might be called *symptomatic performance tuning*. As a performance tuning doctor, we ask the application "Where does it hurt" and then do our best to relieve that pain.

Symptomatic performance tuning has its place: if you are in "firefighting" mode – in which an application is virtually unusable because of performance problems – it may be the best approach. But in general, it can have several undesirable consequences:

- We may treat the *symptoms*, rather than the *causes* of poor performance.

- We may be tempted to seek hardware-based solutions when configuration or application changes would be more cost-effective.

- We might deal with today's pain, but fail to achieve a permanent or scalable solution.

Systematic Performance Tuning

The best way to avoid mistakenly focusing on a cause rather than an effect is to tune your database system in a top-down manner. This approach is sometimes referred to as "tuning by layers," but we like to call it "systematic performance tuning."

Anatomy of a Database Request

To avoid the pitfalls of a symptomatic approach, we need our tuning activities to follow well-defined stages. These stages are dictated by the reality of how applications, databases, and operating systems interact. At a very high level, database processing occurs in "layers" as follows:

1. Applications send requests to MongoDB in the form of calls to the MongoDB API. The database responds to these requests with return codes and arrays of data.

2. Then, the database must *parse* the request. The database must work out what resources the user intends to access, check that the user is authorized to perform the requested activities, determine the exact access mechanisms to be employed and acquire relevant locks and resources. These operations use operating system resources (CPU and memory) and may create contention with other concurrently executing database sessions.

3. Eventually, the database request will need to process (create, read, or change) some of the data in the database. The exact amount of data that will need to be processed can vary depending on the database design (the document schema model and indexes) and the precise coding of the application request.

4. Some of the required data will be in memory. The chance that
    the data will be in memory will be determined mainly by the
    frequency with which the data is accessed and the amount of
    memory available to cache the data. When we access database
    data in memory, it's called a *logical read*.

5. If the data is not in memory, it must be accessed from disk,
    resulting in a *physical read*. Physical disk IO is by far the most
    expensive of all operations. Therefore, the database goes to a lot of
    effort to avoid these physical reads. However, some disk activity is
    inevitable.

Activity in each of these layers influences the demand placed on the subsequent
layer. For instance, if a request is submitted that somehow fails to exploit an index, it will
require an excessive number of logical reads, which in turn will eventually involve a lot
of physical reads.

Tip   It's tempting when you see a lot of IO or contention to deal with the symptom
directly by tuning the disk layout. However, if you sequence your tuning efforts so
as to work through the layers in order, you have a much better chance of fixing root
causes and relieving performance at lower layers.

Here are the three steps of systematic performance tuning in a nutshell:

1. Reduce application demand to its logical minimum by tuning
    database requests and by optimizing database design (indexing
    and document modelling).

2. Having reduced demand on the database in the previous step,
    optimize memory to avoid as much physical IO as possible.

3. Now that the physical IO demand is realistic, configure the
    IO subsystem to meet that demand by providing adequate IO
    bandwidth and evenly distributing the resulting load.

The Layers of a MongoDB Database

MongoDB – and indeed, almost all database management systems – consists of multiple
layers of code, as shown in Figure 1-1.

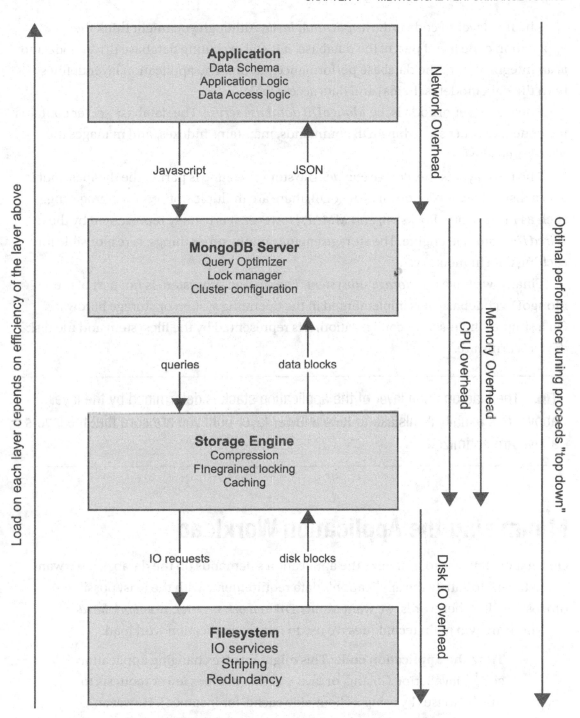

Figure 1-1. *The critical layers of a MongoDB application*

The first layer of code is the *application layer*. Although you might think the application code is not part of the database, it is still executing database driver code and is an integral part of the database performance picture. The application layer defines both the data model (schema) and data access logic.

The next layer of code is the *MongoDB database server*. The database server contains the code that processes MongoDB commands, maintains indexes, and manages the distributed cluster.

The next layer is the *storage engine*. The storage engine is part of the database but is also a distinct layer of code. In MongoDB, there are multiple options for storage engines, such as in-memory, RocksDB, and MMAP. However, it is usually represented by the *WiredTiger* storage engine. The storage engine, among other things, is responsible for caching data in memory.

Finally, we have the *storage subsystem*. The storage subsystem is not part of the MongoDB codebase: it is implemented in the operating system or storage hardware. On a simple single-server configuration, it is represented by the filesystem and the disk device's firmware.

Tip   The load on each layer of the application stack is determined by the layer above. It is usually a mistake to tune a lower layer until you are sure that the layers above are optimized.

Minimizing the Application Workload

Our first objective is to minimize the application's demands on the database. We want the database to satisfy the application's data requirements with the least possible processing. In other words, we want MongoDB to *work smarter*, not *work harder*.

There are two main techniques we use to reduce application workload:

- **Tune the application code**: This might involve changing application code – JavaScript, Golang, or Java – so that it issues fewer requests to the database (by using a client-side cache, for instance). However, more often this will involve re-writing application MongoDB-specific database calls such as find() or aggregate().

- **Tune the database design**: The database design is the physical implementation of the application's databases. Tuning the database design might involve modifying indexes or making changes to the document model used within individual collections.

Chapters 4 through 9 cover in detail the various techniques we can use to minimize application workload, specifically:

- **Structuring an application to avoid overloading the database**: Applications can avoid making needless requests of the database and can be architected to minimize locks, hot spots, and other contention. The programs that interact with MongoDB can be designed and implemented to minimize database round trips and unnecessary requests.

- **Optimizing the physical database design**: This includes indexing and structuring the document schema model to reduce the work required to execute MongoDB requests.

- **Writing efficient database requests**: This involves understanding how to write and optimize find(), update(), aggregate(), and other commands.

These techniques not only represent the logical place to start in our tuning efforts, they also represent the techniques that provide the most dramatic performance improvements. It's not at all uncommon for application tuning to result in performance improvements of 100 or even 1000 times: improvements that you rarely see when optimizing memory or adjusting physical disk layout.

Reducing Physical IO

Now that the application demand has been minimized, we turn our attention to reducing the time spent waiting for IO. In other words, before trying to reduce the time taken for each IO (IO latency), we try to reduce the number of IO requests. As it turns out, reducing the amount of IO almost always reduces the IO latency anyway, so attacking the volume of IO first is doubly effective.

Most physical IO in a MongoDB database occurs either because an application session requests data to satisfy a query or data modification request. Allocating sufficient memory to the WiredTiger cache and other memory structures is the most important step toward reducing physical IO. Chapter 11 is dedicated to this topic.

Optimizing Disk IO

At this point, we've normalized the application workload – in particular, the amount of logical IO demanded by the application. We've also configured available memory to minimize the amount of logical IO that ends up causing physical IO. Now – and only now – it makes sense to make sure that our disk IO subsystem is up to the challenge.

To be sure, optimizing disk IO subsystems can be a complex and specialized task; but the basic principles are straightforward:

- Ensure the IO subsystem has enough bandwidth to cope with the physical IO demand. This is determined by the number of distinct disk devices you have allocated and the types of the disk devices.

- Spread your load evenly across the disks you have allocated – the best way to do this is RAID 0 (striping). The worst way – for most databases – is RAID 5 or similar, which incurs a hefty penalty on write IO.

- In cloud-based environments, you usually don't have to worry about the mechanics of striping. However, you will still need to ensure that the total IO bandwidth you have allocated is sufficient.

The obvious symptom of an overly stressed IO subsystem is excessive delays responding to IO requests. For example, you may have an IO subsystem capable of supporting 1000 requests per second, but you may only be able to push it to 500 requests per second before response time for individual requests degrades. This throughput/response time trade-off is an essential consideration when configuring IO subsystems.

Chapters 12 and 13 cover the process of optimizing disk IO in detail.

Cluster Tuning

All of the preceding factors apply equally to single instance MongoDB deployments and to MongoDB clusters. However, clustered MongoDB involves additional challenges and opportunities, for instance:

- In a standard replica set configuration – in which there is a single master node and multiple secondary nodes – we need to choose the trade-off between performance, consistency, and data integrity. The *read concern* and *write preference* parameters control how data is written and read from secondary nodes. Tweaking these can improve performance but open up the possibility of data loss during a failover or the reading of stale data.

- In a sharded replica set, there are multiple master nodes, which allow for greater scalability and better performance for very large databases with high transaction rates. However, sharding may not be the most cost-effective way to achieve a performance result and does involve performance trade-offs. If you do shard, the selection of the shard key and determining the collections to be sharded are going to be critical to your success.

We will discuss cluster configuration and tuning in detail in Chapters 13 and 14.

Summary

When faced with an IO-bound database, it is tempting to deal with the most obvious symptom – the IO subsystem – immediately. Unfortunately, this usually results in treating the symptom rather than the cause and is often expensive and, frequently, ultimately futile. Because problems in one database layer can be caused or cured by configuration in the higher layer, the most efficient and effective way to optimize a MongoDB database is to tune upper layers before tuning the lower layers:

1. Reduce application demand to its logical minimum by optimizing database requests and by tuning database design (indexing and document modelling).

2. Having reduced demand on the database in the previous step, optimize memory to avoid as much physical IO as possible.

3. Now that the physical IO demand is realistic, configure the IO subsystem to meet that demand by providing adequate IO bandwidth and evenly distributing the resulting load.

CHAPTER 2

MongoDB Architecture and Concepts

This chapter aims to equip you with an understanding of MongoDB architecture and internals referenced in subsequent chapters, which are necessary for MongoDB performance tuning.

A MongoDB tuning professional should be broadly familiar with these main areas of MongoDB technology:

- The MongoDB document model

- The way MongoDB applications interact with the MongoDB database server through the MongoDB API

- The MongoDB *optimizer*, which is the software layer concerned with maximizing the performance of MongoDB requests

- The MongoDB server architecture, which comprises the memory, processes, and files that interact to provide database services

Readers who feel thoroughly familiar with this material may wish to skim or skip this chapter. However, we will be assuming in subsequent chapters that you are familiar with the core concepts presented here.

The MongoDB Document Model

As you are no doubt aware, MongoDB is a *document database*. Document databases are a family of non-relational databases which store data as structured documents – usually in *JavaScript Object Notation* (*JSON*) format.

13

© Guy Harrison, Michael Harrison 2021
G. Harrison and M. Harrison, *MongoDB Performance Tuning*, https://doi.org/10.1007/978-1-4842-6879-7_2

JSON-based document databases like MongoDB have flourished over the past decade for many reasons. In particular, they address the conflict between object-oriented programming and the relational database model which had long frustrated software developers. The flexible document schema model supports agile development and DevOps paradigms and aligns closely with dominant programming models – especially those of modern, web-based applications.

JSON

MongoDB uses a variation of *JavaScript Object Notation* (JSON) as its data model, as well as for its communication protocol. JSON documents are constructed from a small set of elementary constructs – *values*, *objects*, and *arrays*:

- **Arrays** consist of lists of values enclosed by square brackets ("["and "]") and separated by commas (",").

- **Objects** consist of one or more name-value pairs in the format "name":"value", enclosed by braces ("{"and :}") and separated by commas (",").

- **Values** can be Unicode strings, standard format numbers (possibly including scientific notation), Booleans, arrays, or objects.

The last few words in the preceding definition are critical. Because values may include objects or arrays, which themselves contain values, a JSON structure can represent an arbitrarily complex and nested set of information. In particular, arrays can be used to represent repeating groups of documents which in a relational database would require a separate table.

Binary JSON (BSON)

MongoDB stores JSON documents internally in the *Binary JSON* (*BSON*) format. BSON is designed to be a more compact and efficient representation of JSON data and uses more efficient encoding for numbers and other data types. For instance, BSON includes field length prefixes that allow scanning operations to "skip over" elements and hence improve efficiency.

BSON also provides a number of extra data types not supported in JSON. For example, a numeric value in JSON could be a Double, Int, Long, or Decimal128 in BSON. Additional types such as ObjectID, Date, and BinaryData are also commonly used. However, most of the time, the differences between JSON and BSON are unimportant.

Collections

MongoDB allows you to organize "similar" documents into *collections*. Collections are analogous to tables in a relational database. Usually, you'll store only documents with a similar structure or purpose within a specific collection, though by default the structure of the documents in a collection is not enforced.

Figure 2-1 shows the internal structure of JSON documents and how documents are organized into collections.

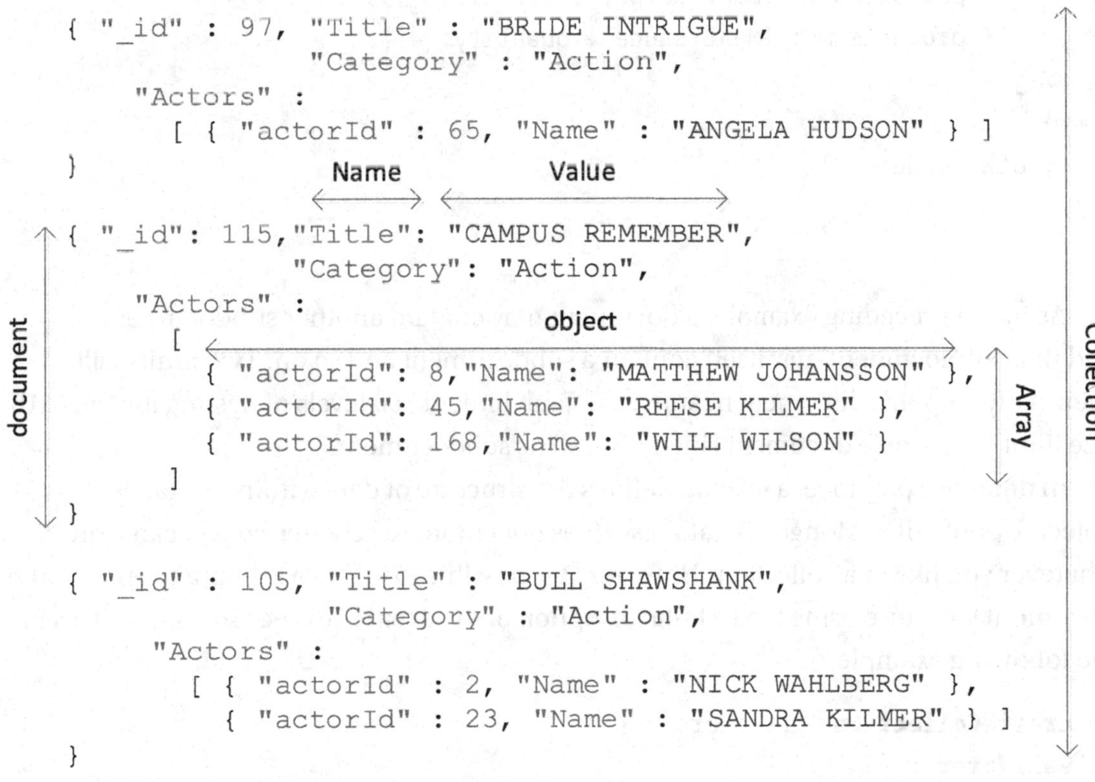

```
{ "_id" : 97, "Title" : "BRIDE INTRIGUE",
            "Category" : "Action",
    "Actors" :
       [ { "actorId" : 65, "Name" : "ANGELA HUDSON" } ]
}
                    Name           Value

{ "_id": 115,"Title": "CAMPUS REMEMBER",
            "Category": "Action",
    "Actors" :
       [                          object
          { "actorId": 8,"Name": "MATTHEW JOHANSSON" },
          { "actorId": 45,"Name": "REESE KILMER" },
          { "actorId": 168,"Name": "WILL WILSON" }
       ]
}

{ "_id" : 105, "Title" : "BULL SHAWSHANK",
            "Category" : "Action",
    "Actors" :
       [ { "actorId" : 2, "Name" : "NICK WAHLBERG" },
         { "actorId" : 23, "Name" : "SANDRA KILMER" } ]
}
```

Figure 2-1. JSON document structure

MongoDB Schemas

The MongoDB document model allows for objects that would require many tables in a relational database to be stored within a single document.

Consider the following MongoDB document:

```
{
  _id: 1,
  name: 'Ron Swanson',
  address: 'Really not your concern',
  dob: ISODate('1971-04-15T01:03:48Z'),
  orders: [
    {
      orderDate: ISODate('2015-02-15T09:05:00Z'),
      items: [
        { productName: 'Meat damper', quantity: 999 },
        { productName: 'Meat sauce', quantity: 9 }
      ]
    },
    { otherorders  }
  ]
};
```

As in the preceding example, a document may contain another subdocument, and that subdocument may itself contain a subdocument and so on. Two limits will eventually stop this document nesting: a default limit of 100 levels of nesting and a 16MB size limit for a single document (including all its subdocuments).

In database parlance, a *schema* defines the structure of data within a database object. By default, a MongoDB database does not enforce a schema, so you can store whatever you like in a collection. However, it is possible to create a schema to enforce the document structure using the validator option of the createCollection method, as in the following example:

```
db.createCollection("customers", {
  "validator": {
      "$jsonSchema": {
          "bsonType": "object",
```

```
"additionalProperties": false,
"properties": {
    "_id": {
        "bsonType": "objectId"
    },
    "name": {
        "bsonType": "string"
    },
    "address": {
        "bsonType": "string"
    },
    "dob": {
        "bsonType": "date"
    },
    "orders": {
        "bsonType": "array",
        "uniqueItems": false,
        "items": {
            "bsonType": "object",
            "properties":  {
                "orderDate": { "bsonType": "date"},
                "items": {
                    "bsonType": "array",
                    "uniqueItems": false,
                    "items": {
                        "bsonType": "object",
                        "properties": {
                            "productName": {
                                "bsonType": "string"
                            },
                            "quantity": {
                                "bsonType": "int"
                            }
                        }
                    }
                }
            }
```

```
                    }
                 }
              }
           }
        }
     }
  },
  "validationLevel": "strict",
  "validationAction": "warn"
});
```

The validator is in the *JSON schema* format – which is an open standard that allows for JSON documents to be annotated or validated. A JSON schema document will generate warnings or errors if a MongoDB command results in a document that does not match the schema definition. JSON schemas can be used to define mandatory attributes, restrict other attributes, and define the data types or data ranges that a document attribute can adopt.

The MongoDB Protocol

The MongoDB protocol defines the communication mechanism between the client and the server. Although the fine details of the protocol are outside the scope of our performance tuning efforts, it is important to understand the protocol, since many of the diagnostic tools will display data in the MongoDB protocol format.

Wire Protocol

The protocol for MongoDB is also known as the MongoDB *wire protocol*. This is the structure of the MongoDB packets which are sent to and received from the MongoDB server. The wire protocol runs over a TCP/IP connection – by default over port 27017.

The actual packet structure of the wire protocol is beyond our scope, but the essence of each packet is a JSON document containing a request or a response. For instance, if we send a command to MongoDB from the shell like this:

```
db.customers.find({FirstName:'MARY'},{Phone:1}).sort({Phone:1})
```

then the shell will send a request across the wire protocol that looks something like this:

```
{ "find" : "customers",
  "filter" : { "FirstName" : "MARY" },
  "sort" : { "Phone" : 1.0 },
  "projection" : { "Phone" : 1.0},
  "$db" : "mongoTuningBook",
  "$clusterTime" : { "clusterTime" : {
        "$timestamp" : { "t" : 1589596899, "i" : 1 } },
   "signature" : { "hash" : { "$binary" : { "base64" : ]
                "4RGjzZI5khOmM9BBWLz6y9xLZ9w=", "subType" : "00" } },
    "keyId" : 6826926447718825986 } },
    "lsid" : { "id" : { "$binary" : { "base64" :
    "JI3lUrOMRQmOY6Pr3iQ8EQ==", "subType" : "04" } } } }
```

MongoDB Drivers

A MongoDB driver translates requests from a programming language into wire protocol format. Each driver can have subtle syntax differences. For instance, in NodeJS the preceding MongoDB shell request is subtly different:

```
const docs = await db.collection('customers').
        find({'FirstName': 'MARY'},
            {'Phone': 1}).
        sort({Phone: 1}).toArray();
```

Because NodeJS is a JavaScript platform, the syntax is still similar to the MongoDB shell. But in other languages, the differences can be more marked. For instance, here is the same query in the Go language:

```
collection := client.Database("MongoDBTuningBook").
            Collection("customers")
filter := bson.D{{"FirstName", "MARY"}}
findOptions := options.Find()
findOptions.SetSort(map[string]int{"Phone": 1})
findOptions.SetProjection(map[string]int{"Phone": 1})
```

```
cursor, err := collection.Find(ctx, filter, findOptions)
var results []bson.M
cursor.All(ctx, &results)
```

However, regardless of the syntax required by a MongoDB driver, the MongoDB server always receives packets which are in the standard wire protocol format.

MongoDB Commands

Logically MongoDB commands break down into the following categories:

- **Query commands**, such as find() and aggregate(), which return information from the databases

- **Data manipulation commands**, such as insert(), update(), and delete(), which modify data within the database

- **Data definition commands**, such as createCollection() and createIndex(), which define the structure of data in the database

- **Administration commands**, such as createUser() and setParameter(), which control the operations of the database

Database performance management is mainly concerned with the overhead and throughput of query and data manipulation statements. However, administration and data definition commands include some of the "tools of the trade" that we use to resolve performance problems (see Chapter 3).

The find Command

The find command is the workhorse of MongoDB data access. It has a quick and easy syntax and has a flexible and powerful filtering capability. The find() command has the following high-level syntax:

```
db.collection.find(
        {filter},
        {projection})
   sort({sortCondition}),
   skip(skipCount),
   limit(limitCount)
```

The preceding syntax is shown for the Mongo shell; the syntax for language-specific drivers can vary slightly.

The key parameters to the find() command are as follows:

- **Filter** is a JSON document that defines the documents to be returned.

- **Projection** defines the attributes from each document which will be returned.

- **Sort** defines the order in which documents will be returned.

- **Skip** allows some initial documents in the output to be skipped.

- **Limit** restricts the total number of documents to be returned.

In the wire protocol, a find() command returns just the first batch of documents (usually 1000), and subsequent batches are fetched by a getMore command. The MongoDB drivers generally handle getMore processing statements on your behalf, but you can vary the batch size to optimize performance in many cases (see Chapter 6).

The aggregate Command

find() can perform a wide variety of queries, but it lacks many of the capabilities of the relational database's SQL command. For instance, a find() operation cannot join data from multiple collections and cannot aggregate data. When you need more functionality than find(), you will generally turn to aggregate().

At a high level, the syntax for aggregate is deceptively simple:

```
db.collection.aggregate([pipeline]);
```

where *pipeline* is an array of instructions to the aggregate command. Aggregate supports more than two dozen pipeline operators, and most are beyond the scope of this book. However, the most commonly used operators are

- **$match**, which filters documents within a pipeline using a syntax similar to the find() command

- **$group**, which aggregates multiple documents into a smaller aggregated set

- **$sort**, which sorts documents within the pipeline

- **$project**, which defines the attributes to be returned from each document

- **$unwind**, which returns one document for each element in an array

- **$limit**, which restricts the number of documents to be returned

- **$lookup**, which joins documents from another collection

Here's an example of aggregate that uses most of these operations to return a count of movie views by category:

```
db.customers.aggregate([
  { $unwind:  "$views" },
  { $project: {
        "filmId": "$views.filmId"
      }
  },
  { $group:{     _id:{ "filmId":"$filmId"  },
            "count":{$sum:1}
    }
  },
  { $lookup:
    { from:          "films",
      localField:   "_id.filmId",
      foreignField: "_id",
      as:           "filmDetails"
    }
  },
  { $group:{      _id:{
            "filmDetails_Category":"$filmDetails.Category"},
            "count":{$sum:1},
            "count-sum":{$sum:"$count"}
    }
  },
```

```
{ $project: {
        "category": "$_id.filmDetails_Category"   ,
        "count-sum": "$count-sum"
        }
},
{ $sort:{   "count-sum":-1 }},
]);
```

Aggregation pipelines can be hard to write and hard to optimize. We'll look in detail at aggregation pipeline optimization in Chapter 7.

Data Manipulation Commands

insert(), update(), and delete() allow documents to be added, changed, or removed from a collection.

Both update() and delete() take a filter argument that defines the documents to be processed. The filter condition is identical to that from the find() command.

Optimization of the filter condition is usually the most important factor when optimizing updates and deletes. Their performance is also affected by the configuration of *write concern* (see the following section).

Here is an example of insert, update, and delete commands:

```
db.myCollection.insert({_id:1,name:'Guy',rating:9});
db.myCollection.update({_id:1},{$set:{rating:10}});
db.myCollection.deleteOne({_id:1});
```

We discuss the optimization of data manipulation statements in Chapter 8.

Consistency Mechanisms

All databases have to make trade-offs between consistency, availability, and performance. Relational databases like MySQL are regarded as *strongly consistent* databases because all users always see a consistent view of data. Non-relational databases such as Amazon Dynamo are often called *weakly consistent* or *eventually consistent* databases because users are not guaranteed to see such a consistent view.

MongoDB is – within limitations – strongly consistent by default, although it can be made to behave like an eventually consistent database through the configuration of *write concern* and *read preference*.

Read Preference and Write Concern

A MongoDB application has some control over the behavior of read and write operations, providing a degree of tunable consistency and availability.

- The **write concern** setting determines when MongoDB regards a write operation as having completed. By default, write operations complete once the primary has received the modification. Consequently, if the primary should fail irrecoverably, then data might be lost.

- However, if the write concern is set to "*majority*", then the database will not complete the write operation until a majority of secondaries receive the write. We can also set the write concern to wait until all secondaries or a specific number of secondaries receive the write operation.

- Write concern can also determine if write operations proceed to the on-disk *journal* before being acknowledged. This is true by default.

- The **read preference** determines where a client sends read requests. By default, read requests are sent to the primary. However, the client driver can be configured to send read requests to the secondary by default, to a secondary only if the primary is not available, or to whichever server is "nearest." The later setting is intended to favor low latency over consistency.

The default settings for the read preference and write concern result in MongoDB behaving as a strictly consistent system: everybody will see the same version of a document. Allowing reads to be satisfied from a secondary node results in a more eventually consistent behavior.

Read preference and write concern have definite performance impacts that we will discuss in Chapters 8 and 13.

Transactions

Although MongoDB started its life as a non-transactional database, since version 4.0 it has been possible to perform atomic transactions across multiple documents. For instance, in this example we atomically reduce the balance of one account by 100 and increment another account by the same amount:

```
session.startTransaction();
mycollection.update({userId:1},{$inc:{balance:100}});
mycollection.update({userId:2},{$inc:{balance:-100}});
session.commitTransaction();
```

The two updates will either both succeed or both fail.

In practice, coding transactions require some error handling logic, and the design of transactions can significantly affect performance. We discuss these considerations in Chapter 9.

Query Optimization

Like most databases, MongoDB commands represent a logical request for data, rather than a series of instructions for retrieving that data. For instance, a find() operation specifies the data that will be returned, but does not explicitly specify the indexes or other access methods to be employed in retrieving the data.

As a result, the MongoDB code must determine the most efficient way to process data requests. The *MongoDB optimizer* is the MongoDB code that makes these determinations. The decision that the optimizer makes for each command is referred to as the *query plan*.

When a new query or command is sent to MongoDB, the optimizer performs the following steps:

1. The optimizer looks for a matching query in the MongoDB *plan cache*. A matching query is one in which all of the filter and operation attributes match, even if the values do not. Such queries are said to have the same *query shape*. For instance, if you issue the same query against the customers collection for different customer names, MongoDB will consider these to have the same query shape.

2. If the optimizer cannot find a matching query, then the optimizer
    will consider all the possible ways of executing the query. The
    query that has the lowest number of *work units* will be successful.
    Work units are specific operations that MongoDB must perform –
    correlating mostly with the number of documents that must be
    processed.

3. MongoDB will select the plan that has the lowest number of work
    units, use that plan to execute the query, and store that query plan
    in the plan cache.

In practice, MongoDB tends to use index-based plans whenever possible and will
usually choose the index that is the most *selective* (see Chapter 5).

MongoDB Architecture

You can do a lot of performance optimization without any reference to MongoDB
architecture. However, if we do our job well and completely optimize the workload,
eventually the limiting factor on performance will become the database server itself. At
this point, we need to understand the MongoDB architecture if we want to optimize its
internal efficiency.

Mongod

In a simple MongoDB implementation, a MongoDB client sends wire protocol messages
to the MongoDB daemon process *mongod*. For instance, if you install MongoDB on
your laptop, a single mongod process will respond to all of the MongoDB wire protocol
requests.

Storage Engines

A *storage engine* abstracts database storage from the underlying storage medium and
format. For instance, one storage engine might store data in memory, while another
might be designed to store data in cloud object stores, while a third might store data on a
local disk.

MongoDB can support multiple storage engines. Initially, MongoDB shipped with a relatively simple storage engine which stored data as memory-mapped files. This storage engine was known as the *MMAP* engine.

In 2014 MongoDB acquired the *WiredTiger* storage engine. WiredTiger has many advantages over MMAP and became the default storage engine from MongoDB 3.6. We'll be focusing predominantly on WiredTiger within this book.

WiredTiger provides MongoDB with a high-performance disk access layer which includes caching, consistency, and concurrency management and other modern data access facilities.

Figure 2-2 illustrates the architecture of a simple MongoDB deployment.

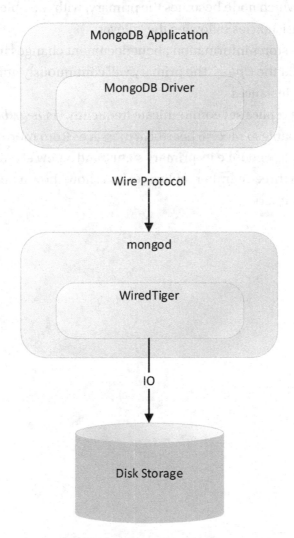

Figure 2-2. *Simple MongoDB deployment architecture*

Replica Sets

MongoDB achieves fault tolerance through the use of *replica sets*.

A replica set consists of a *primary node* together with two or more *secondary nodes*. The primary node accepts all write requests which are propagated synchronously or asynchronously to the secondary nodes.

The primary node is selected by an election involving all available nodes. To be eligible to become primary, a node must be able to contact more than half of the replica set. This approach ensures that if a network partition splits a replica set into two partitions, only one of the partitions will attempt to elect a primary. The *RAFT protocol*[1] is used to determine which node becomes the primary, with the objective of minimizing any data loss or inconsistencies following the failover.

The primary node stores information about document changes in a collection within its local database called the *Oplog*. The primary will continuously attempt to apply these changes to secondary instances.

Members within a replica set communicate frequently via *heartbeat* messages. If a primary finds it is unable to receive heartbeat messages from more than half of the secondaries, then it will renounce its primary status, and a new election will be called. Figure 2-3 illustrates a three-member replica set and shows how a network partition leads to a change of primary.

---

[1]https://en.wikipedia.org/wiki/Raft_(computer_science)

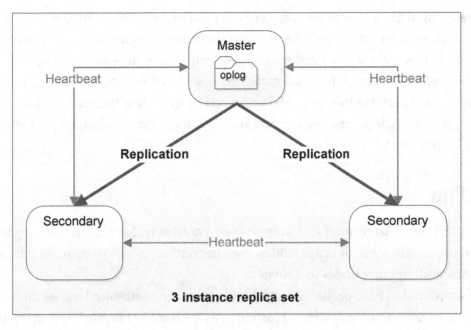

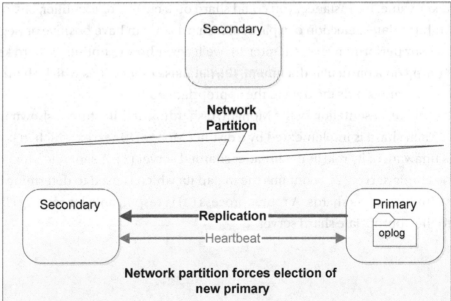

Figure 2-3. *MongoDB replica set election*

MongoDB replica sets primarily exist to support high availability – allowing a MongoDB cluster to survive a failure in an individual node. However, they can also provide performance advantages or disadvantages.

If the MongoDB *write concern* is greater than 1, then every MongoDB write operation (inserts, updates, and deletes) will need to be confirmed by more than one member of the cluster. This will result in a cluster which performs more slowly than a single node cluster. On the other hand, if the *read preference* is set to allow reads from secondary nodes, then read performance might be improved by spreading the read load across multiple servers. We'll discuss the performance impact of read preference and write concern in Chapter 13.

Sharding

While replica sets exist primarily to support high availability, MongoDB *sharding* is intended to provide scale-out capabilities. "Scaling out" allows us to increase database capacity by adding more nodes to a cluster.

In a sharded database cluster, selected collections are partitioned across multiple database instances. Each partition is referred to as a "shard." This partitioning is based on a *shard key* value; for instance, you could shard on a customer identifier, customer ZIP code or birth date. Selection of a particular shard key can have positive or negative impacts on your performance; in Chapter 14, we'll cover how to optimize shard keys. When operating on a particular document, the database determines which shard should contain the data and sends the data to the appropriate node.

A high-level representation of the MongoDB sharding architecture is shown in Figure 2-4. Each shard is implemented by a distinct MongoDB server, which in most respects is unaware of its role in the broader sharded server (1). A separate MongoDB server – the config server (2) – contains the metadata which is used to determine how data is distributed across shards. A router process (3) is responsible for routing client requests to the appropriate shard server.

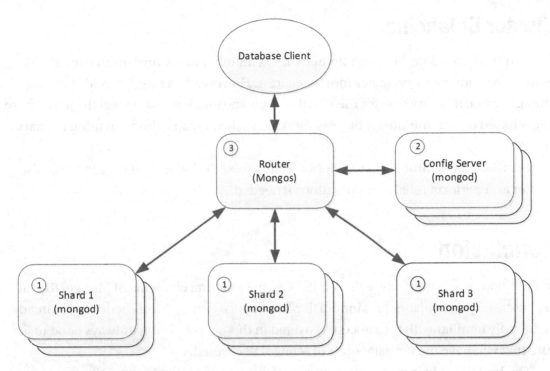

Figure 2-4. *MongoDB sharding*

To shard a collection, we choose a *shard key*, which are one or more indexed attributes that will be used to determine the distribution of documents across shards. Note that not all collections need be sharded. Traffic for unsharded collections will be directed to a single shard.

Sharding Mechanisms

Distribution of data across shards can be either *range-based* or *hash-based*. In range-based partitioning, each shard is allocated a specific range of shard key values. MongoDB consults the distribution of key values in the index to ensure that each shard is allocated approximately the same number of keys. In hash-based sharding, keys are distributed based on a hash function applied to the shard key.

See Chapter 14 for more details of range- and hash-based sharding.

Cluster Balancing

When hash-based sharding is implemented, the number of documents in each shard tends to remain balanced under most scenarios. However, in a range-based sharding configuration, it is very easy for the shards to become unbalanced, especially if the shard key is based on a continuously increasing value such as an auto-incrementing primary key ID.

For this reason, MongoDB will periodically assess the balance of shards across the cluster and perform rebalance operations if needed.

Conclusion

In this chapter, we've briefly reviewed the key architectural elements of MongoDB that are essential prerequisites for MongoDB performance tuning. Most readers will already be broadly familiar with the concepts covered in this chapter, but it's always good to be sure that you have the fundamentals of MongoDB covered.

The best place to learn more about any of these topics is the MongoDB documentation set – available online at `https://docs.mongodb.com/`.

In the next chapter, we'll deep dive into the essential tools provided with MongoDB that should be your constant companions during your tuning endeavors.

CHAPTER 3

Tools of the Trade

They say a tradesman is only as good as his or her tools. Luckily, you don't need expensive or hard-to-find tools to tune a MongoDB application or database. However, you should be thoroughly familiar with the tools that MongoDB makes available to you free of charge within the MongoDB server.

In this chapter, we'll review the components that make up the essential toolkit for MongoDB performance tuning, in particular:

- The explain() method, which reveals the steps that MongoDB undertakes when executing a command

- The *profiler*, which allows you to capture and analyze the workload on the MongoDB server

- The commands that reveal the global state of the MongoDB server – ServerStatus() and CurrentOp() in particular

- The graphical MongoDB *Compass* tool, which provides a user-friendly graphical alternative to the mostly command-line utilities listed previously

Introduction to explain()

The explain() method allows you to examine query plans. It's an essential tool for tuning MongoDB performance.

For almost all operations, there is more than one way for MongoDB to retrieve and process the documents involved. When MongoDB prepares a statement for execution, it must decide which approach will be fastest. The process of determining this "optimal" path to the data is the process of *query optimization*, which we introduced in Chapter 2.

33

G. Harrison and M. Harrison, *MongoDB Performance Tuning*, https://doi.org/10.1007/978-1-4842-6879-7_3

For instance, consider the following query:

```
db.customers.
  find(
    {
      FirstName: "RUTH",
      LastName: "MARTINEZ",
      Phone: 496523103
    },
    { Address: 1, dob: 1 }
  ).
  sort({ dob: 1 });
```

For this example, suppose there are indexes on FirstName, LastName, Phone, and dob. These indexes give MongoDB the following choices for resolving the query:

- Scan the entire collection looking for documents matching the name and phone number filter conditions, and then sort those documents by dob.

- Use the index on FirstName to find all the "RUTH"s, then filter those documents based on LastName and Phone, and then sort the remainder on dob.

- Use the index on LastName to find all the "MARTINEZ"s, then filter those documents based on FirstName and Phone, and then sort the remainder on dob.

- Use the index on Phone to find all documents with a matching phone number. Then eliminate any who are not RUTH MARTINEZ, and then sort by dob.

- Use the index on dob to sort the documents in order of date of birth, and then eliminate documents that don't match the query criteria.

Each of these approaches will return the correct results, but each will have different performance characteristics. It's the job of the MongoDB optimizer to decide which approach will be quickest.

The explain() method reveals the query optimizer's decision and – in some cases – lets you examine its reasoning.

Getting Started with explain()

To examine the optimizer's decisions, we use the explain() method of the collection object and pass a find(), update(), insert(), or aggregate() operation to that method. For instance, to explain the query we introduced earlier, we could issue this command[1]:

```
var explainCsr=db.customers.explain().
  find(
    {
      FirstName: "RUTH",
      LastName: "MARTINEZ",
      Phone: 496523103
    },
    { Address: 1, dob: 1 }
  ).
  sort({ dob: 1 });
var explainDoc=explainCsr.next();
```

explain() emits a cursor that returns a JSON document containing information about the query's execution. Because it's a cursor, we need to fetch the explain output by calling next() after we call explain().

The part of the explain output that is most important initially is the winningPlan section, which we can extract like this:

```
mongo> printjson(explainDoc.queryPlanner.winningPlan);
{
  "stage": "PROJECTION_SIMPLE",
  "transformBy": {
    "Address": 1,
    "dob": 1
  },
  "inputStage": {
    "stage": "SORT",
    "sortPattern": {
```

---

[1]It's also possible to place the explain() operation last: db.collection.find().explain() instead of db.collection.explain().find(). However, the former syntax is deprecated and not recommended.

```
      "dob": 1
    },
    "inputStage": {
      "stage": "SORT_KEY_GENERATOR",
      "inputStage": {
        "stage": "FETCH",
        "filter": {
          "$and": [
            <snip>
          ]
        },
        "inputStage": {
          "stage": "IXSCAN",
          "keyPattern": {
            "Phone": 1
          },
          "indexName": "Phone_1",
          "isMultiKey": false,
          "multiKeyPaths": {
            "Phone": [ ]
          },
          "isUnique": false,
          "isSparse": false,
          "isPartial": false,
          "indexVersion": 2,
          "direction": "forward",
          "indexBounds": {
            "Phone": [
              "[496523103.0, 496523103.0]"
            ]
          }
        }
      }
    }
  }
}
```

It's still pretty complex – and we removed some stuff to simplify it. However, you can see it lists the multiple stages of query execution with the input to each stage (the previous step) nested as inputStage. In order to decipher the output, you start with the most deeply nested inputStage – reading the JSON from the inside out – to get the plan.

If you prefer, you can use the mongoTuning.quickExplain function from our utility scripts to print out the steps in the order in which they are executed:

```
Mongo Shell>mongoTuning.quickExplain(explainDoc)
1       IXSCAN Phone_1
2       FETCH
3     SORT_KEY_GENERATOR
4    SORT
5  PROJECTION_SIMPLE
```

This script prints the execution plan in a very concise format. Here's an explanation of each step:

1. **IXSCAN Phone_1**: MongoDB uses the Phone_1 index to find documents with a matching value for the Phone attribute.

2. **FETCH**: MongoDB filters out documents returned from the index that don't have the correct values for FirstName and LastName.

3. **SORT_KEY_GENERATOR**: MongoDB extracts dob values from the FETCH operation in preparation for the subsequent SORT operation.

4. **SORT**: MongoDB sorts the documents based on the values of dob.

5. **PROJECTION_SIMPLE**: MongoDB emits the address and dob attributes into the output stream (these were the only attributes requested by the query).

There's a wide variety of possible execution plans, and we'll look at a lot of them in the subsequent chapters.

Getting familiar with the possible execution steps that MongoDB can employ is essential to understanding what MongoDB is doing. You can find an explanation of the different steps on this books Github repository at https://github.com/gharriso/MongoDBPerformanceTuningBook/blob/master/ExplainPlanSteps.md. You'll also find a wealth of information within the MongoDB documentation at https://docs.mongodb.com/manual/reference/explain-results/.

The sheer number of explain() operations might seem daunting, but most of the time, you'll be dealing with combinations of a few fundamental procedures, such as

- COLLSCAN: The entire collection scanned without utilizing an index

- IXSCAN: The use of an index to find documents (see Chapter 5 for details on indexing)

- SORT: The sorting of documents without the use of an index

Alternate Plans

explain() can tell you not just which plan was used but which other plans were rejected. The rejected plans are found within the array rejectedPlans within the queryPlanner section. Here, we use quickExplain to examine one of the rejected plans:

```
Mongo> mongoTuning.quickExplain
        (explainDoc.queryPlanner.rejectedPlans[1])
1        IXSCAN LastName_1
2        IXSCAN Phone_1
3      AND_SORTED
4     FETCH
5    SORT_KEY_GENERATOR
6   SORT
7  PROJECTION_SIMPLE
```

This rejected plan merged two indexes – one on LastName and one on Phone – to retrieve the results. Why was it rejected? The first time this query was executed, the MongoDB query optimizer estimated the amount of work required to execute each of the candidate plans. The plan with the lowest work estimate – generally the plan that has to process the smallest number of documents – wins. queryPlanner.rejectedPlans lists the rejected plans.

Execution Statistics

If you pass the argument "executionStats" to explain(), then explain() will execute the entire request and report on the performance of each step in the plan. Here's an example of using executionStatistics:

```
var explainObj = db.customers.
  explain('executionStats').
  find(
    {FirstName: "RUTH",
      LastName: "MARTINEZ",
      Phone: 496523103},
    { Address: 1, dob: 1 }
  ).sort({ dob: 1 });

var explainDoc = explainObj.next();
```

The execution statistics are included in the executionStages section of the resulting plan document:

```
mongo> explainDoc.executionStats
{
  "executionSuccess": true,
  "nReturned": 1,
  "executionTimeMillis": 0,
  "totalKeysExamined": 1,
  "totalDocsExamined": 1,
  "executionStages": {
    "stage": "PROJECTION_SIMPLE",
    "nReturned": 1,
    "executionTimeMillisEstimate": 0,
    "works": 6,
    "advanced": 1,
    "needTime": 3,
    "needYield": 0,
    "saveState": 0,
    "restoreState": 0,
    "isEOF": 1,
    "transformBy": {
      "Address": 1,
      "dob": 1
    },
```

```
    "inputStage": {
      "stage": "SORT",
// Many, many more lines of output
            }}
}
```

Note   In order to obtain the execution statistics, explain("executionStats")
will fully execute the MongoDB statement concerned. This means that it may take
much longer to complete than a simple explain() and place significant load on
the MongoDB server.

The executionSteps subdocument contains overall execution statistics – such as
executionTimeMillis – as well as an annotated execution plan in the executionStages
document. executionStages is structured just like winningPlan, but it has statistics for
each step. There are a lot of statistics, but perhaps the most significant ones are

- **executionTimeMillisEstimate**: Number of milliseconds consumed
  executing the step concerned

- **keysExamined**: Number of index keys read by the step

- **docsExamined**: Number of documents read by the step

It's hard to read the executionSteps document – so we wrote mongoTuning.
executionStats() to print out the steps and key statistics in the same format as the
mongoTuning.quickExplain script:

```
mongo> mongoTuning.executionStats(explainDoc);

1    COLLSCAN ( ms:10427 docs:411121)
2    SORT_KEY_GENERATOR ( ms:10427)
3    SORT ( ms:10427)
4   PROJECTION_SIMPLE ( ms:10428)

Totals:  ms: 12016  keys: 0  Docs: 411121
```

We'll use this function in the next section to tune a MongoDB query.

Using explain() to Tune a Query

Now that we've learned how to use explain(), let's run through a short example showing how to use it to tune a query. Here is the explain command for the query we want to tune:

```
mongo> var explainDoc=db.customers.
   explain('executionStats').
   find(
    { Country: 'United Kingdom',
      'views.title': 'CONQUERER NUTS' },
    { City:1,LastName: 1, phone: 1 }
   ).
   sort({City:1, LastName: 1 });
```

This query – against a hypothetical Netflix-style customer database – generates a list of customers in the United Kingdom who have watched the film *Conqueror Nuts*.

Let's use mongoTuning.executionStats to extract the execution statistics:

```
Mongo> mongoTuning.executionStats(explainDoc);

1     COLLSCAN ( ms:12 docs:411121)
2     SORT_KEY_GENERATOR ( ms:12)
3     SORT ( ms:12)
4   PROJECTION_SIMPLE ( ms:12)

Totals: ms: 253  keys: 0  Docs: 411121
```

The COLLSCAN step – a full scan of the entire collection – comes first and examines 411,121 documents. It only takes 253 milliseconds (about one-fourth of a second), but maybe we can do better. There's also a SORT in there, and we'd like to see if we can avoid the sort using an index. So let's create an index that has the attributes from the filter clause (Country and views.title) and the attributes from the sort operation (City and LastName):

```
db.customers.createIndex(
  { Country: 1, 'views.title': 1,
    City: 1, LastName: 1  },
  { name: 'ExplainExample' }
);
```

Now when we generate the executionStats, our output looks like this:

```
1     IXSCAN ( ExplainExample ms:0 keys:685)
2     FETCH ( ms:0 docs:685)
3     PROJECTION_SIMPLE ( ms:0)

Totals:  ms: 2  keys: 685  Docs: 685
```

With the new index in place, the query returns almost instantaneously, and the number of documents (keys) examined has reduced from 411,121 to 685. We've reduced the amount of data accessed by 97% and improved the execution time by several orders of magnitude. Note also that there is no longer a SORT step – MongoDB was able to use the index to return documents in sorted order without an explicit sort.

Explain itself doesn't tune queries, but without explain() you'll have only the vaguest indication as to what MongoDB is up to. Therefore, we'll use explain extensively throughout the book when optimizing MongoDB queries.

Visual Explain Utilities

There's plenty of options for visualizing explain output without having to read through mountains of JSON output or using our utility scripts. Visual explain utilities can be beneficial, though in our experience it remains essential to be able to debug raw explain output and to be able to get explains from the command line.

MongoDB Compass is MongoDB's own graphical user interface utility. Figure 3-1 shows how MongoDB Compass can display a visual representation of explain output.

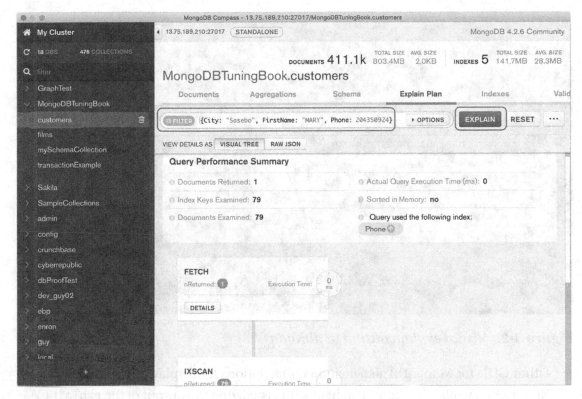

Figure 3-1. *Visual explain output in MongoDB Compass*

Figure 3-2 shows visual explain output in the open source dbKoda product.[2]

_____

[2]Full Disclosure: Both Mike and Guy worked on the dbKoda product.

Figure 3-2. *Visual explain output in dbKoda*

Other GUIs for MongoDB also include visual options for displaying explain output.

Remember, while these tools can help with visualizing the output of the explain() command, it's up to you to be able to interpret the output and take appropriate tuning action!

The Query Profiler

explain() is a great tool to tune an individual MongoDB query, but can't tell you which queries in an application might need tuning. For instance, in the example we gave in Chapter 1, we described an application in which IO was overloaded as a result of a single missing index. How do we find the statements that are generating that IO and from there identify the index required? This is where the MongoDB *profiler* comes in.

The MongoDB profiler allows you to collect information about the commands that are being run on the database. Where explain() will enable you to determine how a single command is being executed, the profiler will give you a higher-level view of what commands are running and which commands might require tuning.

By default, the query profiler is disabled and can be configured individually on each database. The profiler can be set to one of three levels:

- **0**: A setting of 0 means that profiling is disabled for the database. This is the default level.

- **1**: The profiler will only collect information about commands that take longer than `slowms` to complete.

- **2**: The profiler will collect information for all commands, whether they complete faster than `slowms` or not.

Profiling is controlled by the `db.setProfilingLevel()` command. `setProfilingLevel` has the following syntax:

```
db.setProfilingLevel(level,
    {slowms:slowMsThreshold,
     sampleRate:samplingRate});
```

`setProfilingLevel` takes the following arguments:

- `Level` corresponds to the three levels (0, 1, or 2) outlined in the preceding text. 0 disables tracing, 1 sets tracing for statements that consume more than the `slowms` threshold, while 2 sets tracing for all statements.

- `slowMsThreshold` sets the millisecond execution threshold for level 1 tracing.

- `samplingRate` determines a random sampling level. For instance, if `samplingRate` is set to 0.5, then half of all statements will be traced.

Note   The query profiler cannot be used on sharded instances. If `setProfilingLevel` is issued against a sharded cluster, it will only set the values of `slowms` and `samplerate` that determine which operations will be written to the MongoDB log.

You can check the current level of tracing with the `db.getProfilingStatus()` command.

In the following example, we check the current profiling level, then set profiling so that it captures all statements that consume more than 2 milliseconds of execution time, and finally, we check the current profiling level again to observe our new configuration:

```
mongo>db.getProfilingStatus();
{
   "was": 0,
   "slowms": 20,
   "sampleRate": 1
}
mongo>db.setProfilingLevel(1,{slowms:2,sampleRate:1});
{
   "was": 0,
   "slowms": 20,
   "sampleRate": 1,
   "ok": 1
}
mongo>db.getProfilingStatus();
{
   "was": 0,
   "slowms": 2,
   "sampleRate": 1
}
```

The system.profile Collection

Profiling information is stored in the system.profile collection. system.profile is a circular collection – the collection is fixed in size, and when that size is exceeded, older entries are removed to make way for new entries. The default size for system.profile is only 1MB, so you may wish to increase its size. You can do this by stopping profiling, dropping the collection, and recreating it with a larger size, as in this example:

```
mongo>db.setProfilingLevel(0);
{
   "was": 1,
   "slowms": 2,
   "sampleRate": 1,
   "ok": 1
}
mongo >db.system.profile.drop();
```

```
true
mongo >db.createCollection(
            "system.profile",
            {capped: true, size:10485760 } ); // 10MB
{
  "ok": 1
}
mongo >db.setProfilingLevel(1);
{
  "was": 0,
  "slowms": 2,
  "sampleRate": 1,
  "ok": 1
}
```

Analyzing Profiling Data

Our general approach for profiling is as follows:

1. Turn on profiling with an appropriate slowms level, sampleRate, and system.profile collection size.

2. Allow a representative workload to act upon the database.

3. Turn off profiling and analyze the results.

Note   We don't generally want profiling turned on all the time as it can impose a significant performance burden upon the database.

To analyze data within system.profile, we can issue MongoDB find() or aggregate() statements against that collection. There's a lot of useful information held in system.profile, but it can be confusing and difficult to analyze. There are a large number of attributes to examine, and in some scenarios, a single statement's execution statistics might be spread across multiple entries in the collection.

To get an accurate picture of the burden that specific statements impose on the database, we need to aggregate the data for all statements that are equivalent in structure, even if they are not exactly identical in text. Such statements are said to have the same *query shape*. So, for instance, the following two queries are probably from the same piece of code and will have the same tuning solution:

```
db.customers.find({"views.filmId":987}).sort({LastName:1});
db.customers.find({"views.filmId":317}).sort({LastName:1});
```

However, since each execution of this statement will have a separate entry in the `system.profile` collection, we need to aggregate statistics across all of those executions. We can do that by aggregating all statements that have the same value for the `system.profile` attribute `queryHash`.

There's also a further complication for statements that process a lot of data. For instance, a query that pulls more than 1000 documents will have an entry for the initial query and also entries for each `getMore` operation that fetches each successive batch of data. Luckily, each `getMore` operation will share a `cursorId` attribute with its parent operation so we can aggregate on that attribute as well.

Listing 3-1 shows an aggregation pipeline that performs the necessary aggregations to list the statements that are consuming the most time in the database.[3]

Listing 3-1. Aggregating statistics from system.profile

```
db.system.profile.aggregate([
  { $group:{ _id:{ "cursorid":"$cursorid"  },
             "count":{$sum:1},
             "queryHash-max":{$max:"$queryHash"} ,
             "millis-sum":{$sum:"$millis"} ,
             "ns-max":{$max:"$ns"}
    }
  },
  { $group:{ _id:{"queryHash":"$queryHash-max" ,
             "collection":"$ns-max"   },
             "count":{$sum:1},
```

---

[3]The query in Listing 3-1 is included within our tuning script as `mongoTuning.profileQuery()`.

```
                    "millis":{$sum:"$millis-sum"}
          }
    },
    { $sort:{  "millis":-1 }},
    { $limit:  10 },
]);
```

Here's the output from this aggregation:

```
{ "_id": { "queryHash": "14C08165", "collection": "MongoDBTuningBook.
customers" }, "count": 17, "millis": 6844 }
{ "_id": { "queryHash": "81BACDE0", "collection": "MongoDBTuningBook.
customers" }, "count": 13, "millis": 3275 }
{ "_id": { "queryHash": "1215D594", "collection": "MongoDBTuningBook.
customers" }, "count": 13, "millis": 3197 }
{ "_id": { "queryHash": "C05DC5D9", "collection": "MongoDBTuningBook.
customers" }, "count": 14, "millis": 2821 }
{ "_id": { "queryHash": "B3A7D0DB", "collection": "MongoDBTuningBook.
customers" }, "count": 12, "millis": 2525 }
{ "_id": { "queryHash": "F7B164E4", "collection": "MongoDBTuningBook.
customers" }, "count": 12, "millis": 43 }
```

We can see that the query with queryHash "14C08165" consumed the most time during our tuning run. We can get details about this query by looking for entries in the system.profile collection with a matching hash value:

```
mongo>db.system.profile.findOne(
...    { queryHash: '14C08165' },
...    { ns: 1, command: 1, docsExamined: 1,
...      millis: 1, planSummary: 1 }
... );
{
  "ns": "MongoDBTuningBook.customers",
  "command": {
    "find": "customers",
    "filter": {
      "Country": "Yugoslavia"
    },
```

```
    "sort": {
      "phone": 1
    },
    "projection": {

    },
    "$db": "MongoDBTuningBook"
  },
  "docsExamined": 101,
  "millis": 31,
  "planSummary": "IXSCAN { Country: 1, views.title: 1, City: 1, LastName:
1, phone: 1 }"
}
```

This query is included in our mongoTuning package within the function
mongoTuning.getQueryByHash.

This query retrieves the command, execution time, documents examined, and
an execution plan summary for a given queryHash. system.profile includes a lot of
additional attributes, but the limited set earlier should be enough to get started with your
optimization efforts. A probable next step would be to generate full execution plans for
that command – including executionStats – and determine if a better execution plan
could be achieved (hint: we may want to do something about the sort operation).

Remember: explain() can help you tune an individual command, while the profiler
can help you find commands that need tuning. You are now well equipped to identify
and optimize problematic MongoDB commands.

Tuning with MongoDB Logs

The query profiler isn't the only way to find out what queries are running behind the
scenes. Command executions can also be found within the MongoDB logs. The location
of these logs depends on your server configuration. You can usually determine your log
file location with the following command:

```
db.getSiblingDB("admin").
  runCommand({ getCmdLineOpts: 1 } ).parsed.systemLog;
```

Let's assume that we have pushed our logs to a file, using the `--logpath` parameter such as in the following example:

```
User> mongod --port 27017 --dbpath ./data --logpath ./mongolog.txt
```

We can view our logs with operating system commands like `tail` or even with a text editor of choice. However, if we run a query and then look in our log file, we might not see any log entries recording the query execution. This is because, by default, only commands which exceed the slow operations threshold will be logged. This slow operations threshold is the same as the `slowms` parameter we introduced in the previous section on the query profiler.

There are two ways we can ensure that our executed query will show up in the log file:

1. We can reduce the value of `slowms` using the `db.setProfilingLevel` command. If `db.setProfilingLevel` is set to 0, then commands meeting the `slowms` criteria will be written to the logs. For instance, if we issue `db.setProfilingLevel(0, {slowms: 10})`, any command that takes more than 10 milliseconds to execute will be output to the logs.

2. We can use the `db.setLogLevel` command to force logging of all queries of a specified type.

`db.setLogLevel` can be used to control the verbosity of the log output. The command has the following syntax:

```
db.setLogLevel(Level,Component)
```

where

- **Level** is the verbosity of logging from 0 to 5. Generally, a level of 2 is sufficient for command monitoring.

- **Component** controls the type of log messages affected. The following components are relevant here:

  - *query*: Logs all `find()` commands

  - *write*: Logs `update`, `delete`, and `insert` statements

  - *command*: Records other MongoDB commands, including `aggregate`

Normally, you would set the verbosity back to 0 when you had completed your testing – otherwise, you may generate an unacceptable level of log output.

Now that we know how to show our commands in the log, let's see it in action!

Let's set the `logLevel` to catch `find()` operations, issue the `find()`, and then restore the logging level:

```
mongo> db.setLogLevel(2,'query')
mongo> db.listingsAndReviews.find({name: "Ribeira Charming Duplex"}).
cancellation_policy;
Moderate
mongo> db.setLogLevel(0,'query');
```

Finally, let's have a look through our log file to view our operation. In this example, we use grep to get the logs from our file, but you can also open the file in an editor:

```
$ grep -i "Ribeira" /var/log/mongodb/mongo.log
```

```
2020-06-03T07:14:56.871+0000 I  COMMAND  [conn597] command sample_
airbnb.listingsAndReviews appName: "MongoDB Shell" command: find {
find: "listingsAndReviews", filter: { name: "Ribeira Charming Duplex"
}, lsid: { id: UUID("01885ece-c731-4549-8b4f-864fe527888c") }, $db:
"sample_airbnb" } planSummary: IXSCAN { name: 1 } keysExamined:1
docsExamined:1 cursorExhausted:1 numYields:0 nreturned:1 queryHash:01AEE5EC
planCacheKey:4C5AEA2C reslen:29543 locks:{ ReplicationStateTransition: {
acquireCount: { w: 1 } }, Global: { acquireCount: { r: 1 } }, Database: {
acquireCount: { r: 1 } }, Collection: { acquireCount: { r: 1 } }, Mutex: {
acquireCount: { r: 1 } } } storage:{} protocol:op_msg 0ms
```

Your log location may be different and – especially on Windows – the commands you use to filter the log may be different.

Let's break down the key elements of the log record, skipping some of the fields that are not particularly interesting. The first few elements are about the log itself:

- `2020-06-03T07:14:56.871+0000`: The timestamp of this log

- `COMMAND`: The category of this log

Next, we have some command-specific information:

- `airbnb.listingsAndReviews`: The namespace – database and collection – of the command. This attribute can be useful for finding commands that are specific to a database or collection.

- `command: find`: The type of command that was executed, for example, `find`, `insert`, `update`, or `delete`.

- `appName: "MongoDB Shell"`: The type of connection that executed this command; this is useful for filtering a particular driver or the shell.

- `filter: { name: "Ribeira Charming Duplex" }`: The filter provided to the command.

Then we have some more specific information about how the command was executed:

- `planSummary: IXSCAN`: The most significant part of the execution plan. You may remember from our discussion on `explain()` that IXSCAN indicates that an index scan was used to resolve the query.

- `keysExamined:1 docsExamined: 1 ... nreturned:1`: Statistics relating to the command execution.

- `0ms`: The execution time. In this case, the execution time was less than one millisecond, so it was rounded down to 0.

Along with these critical metrics, the log entry contains additional information on locking and storage that you may need in more specific use cases. You may be thinking that reading these logs is quite awkward compared to some of the other tools in this chapter, and you would be right. Even with the search and filter tools provided by a text editor, parsing these logs can be cumbersome.

One way to reduce the burden of the log format is to use the log management tools provided as part of the *mtools* utility kit. Mtools includes *mlogfilter*, which allows you to filter and subset log records, while *mplotqueries* creates graphical representations of log data.

You can learn more about mtools at `https://github.com/rueckstiess/mtools`.

Server Statistics

So far, we have analyzed individual query execution with `explain()` and examined the queries running on a given database with the MongoDB profiler. To zoom out even further, we can ask MongoDB for high-level information about server activity across all databases, queries, and commands. The command to retrieve this information is `db.serverStatus()`. This command generates a large number of metrics including operation counters, queue information, index usage, connections, disk IO, and memory utilization.

The `db.serverStatus()` command is a quick and powerful way to get a lot of high-level information about your MongoDB server. `db.serverStatus()` can help you identify performance problems or even just get a deeper understanding of what other factors may be at play when you are tuning. If you can't work out why a given query is running so slowly, a quick check of the CPU and memory usage may provide a vital clue. When tuning your application, you may not always have exclusive use of a database. In these cases, it is crucial that you gain a high-level understanding of the external factors affecting server performance.

Usually, this would be where we go through the output of the command in detail. However, `db.serverStatus()` outputs so much data (almost 1000 lines) that it can be overwhelming (and often impractical) to try and analyze the raw output. Usually, you will be looking for a specific value or a subset of values rather than examining every single metric that the server has recorded. As you can see from the extremely truncated output in the following, there's also a lot of extraneous information that might not be directly relevant to our performance tuning efforts:

```
mongo> db.serverStatus()
{
        "host" : "Mike-MBP-3.modem",
        "version" : "4.2.2",
        "process" : "mongod",
        "pid" : NumberLong(3750),
        "uptime" : 474921,
        "uptimeMillis" : NumberLong(474921813),
        "uptimeEstimate" : NumberLong(474921),
        "localTime" : ISODate("2020-05-13T22:04:10.857Z"),
        "asserts" : {
```

```
                "regular" : 0,
                "warning" : 0,
                "msg" : 0,
                "user" : 2,
                "rollovers" : 0
        },
        ...
        945 more lines here.
        ...
        "ok" : 1,
        "$clusterTime" : {
                "clusterTime" : Timestamp(1589407446, 1),
                "signature" : {
                        "hash" : BinData(0,"AAAAAAAAAAAAAAAAAAAAAAAAAAAA="),
                        "keyId" : NumberLong(0)
                }
        },
        "operationTime" : Timestamp(1589407446, 1)
}
```

Due to the overwhelming nature of db.serverStatus() output, it is unusual to
simply execute the command and then scroll to the relevant data. Instead, it is often
more useful to extract only the specific values you are searching for or to aggregate the
data into a more easily parsed format.

For example, to fetch just the counts of various high-level commands that have been
executed, you could do the following:

```
mongo> db.serverStatus().opcounters
{
        "insert" : NumberLong(3),
        "query" : NumberLong(1148),
        "update" : NumberLong(15),
        "delete" : NumberLong(11),
        "getmore" : NumberLong(0),
        "command" : NumberLong(2584)
}
```

The following top-level categories from `db.serverStatus()` are often useful:

- **connections**: Statistics relating to connections within the server

- **opcounters**: Totals of command executions

- **locks**: Counters relating to internal locks

- **network**: Summary of network traffic into and out of the server

- **opLatencies**: Time taken in read and write commands and transactions

- **wiredTiger**: WiredTiger storage engine statistics

- **mem**: Memory utilization

- **transactions**: Transaction statistics

- **metrics**: Miscellaneous metrics, including counts of aggregation stages and specific individual commands

We can use these high-level categories and the nested documents within to drill into statistics of interest. For instance, we can drill into the WiredTiger cache size like this:

```
mongo> db.serverStatus().wiredTiger.cache["maximum bytes configured"]
1073741824
```

However, there are two problems with using `db.serverStatus()` in this way. Firstly, these counters don't tell us much about what's happening on the server *right now*, making it difficult to identify which of the metrics may be impacting the performance of our application. Secondly, this method assumes that either you know which metrics to look for or are iterating through the metrics one at a time looking for clues.

If you are using MongoDB Atlas or Ops Manager, these two problems will likely be solved for you as these tools calculate rates for essential metrics and display them graphically. However, it is best to understand how to get these metrics from the command line, since you never know what type of MongoDB configuration you may be working with in the future.

The solution to our first problem – the need to get statistics for a recent period – is to take two samples over a given interval and calculate the difference between them. For example, let's create a simple helper function that will use two samples to find the number of find operations that ran in a ten-second interval:

```
mongo> var sample = function() {
...    var sampleOne = db.serverStatus().opcounters.query;
```

```
...     sleep(10000); // Wait for 10000ms (10 seconds)
...     var sampleTwo = db.serverStatus().opcounters.query;
...     var delta = sampleTwo - sampleOne;
...     print(`There were ${delta} query operations during the sample.`);
... }
mongo> sample()
There were 6 query operations during the sample.
```

Now we can easily see what operations were running during our sample period, and we can divide the number of operations by our sample period to figure out the rate of operations per second. Although this works, it would be better to build a helper function to fetch all the server status data and calculate the rates of change across all of the metrics of interest. We've included just such a general-purpose script within the mongoTuning package.

mongoTuning.keyServerStats takes two samples of serverStatus across a time period of interest and prints some key performance metrics. Here, we print some statistics of interest over a 60-second interval:

```
rs1:PRIMARY> mongoTuning.keyServerStats(60000)
{
        "netKBInPS" : "743.4947",
        "netKBOutPS" : 946.0005533854167,
        "intervalSeconds" : 60,
        "queryPS" : "2392.2833",
        "getmorePS" : 0,
        "commandPS" : "355.4667",
        "insertPS" : 0,
        "updatePS" : "118.4500",
        "deletePS" : 0,
        "docsReturnedPS" : "0.0667",
        "docsUpdatedPS" : "118.4500",
        "docsInsertedPS" : 0,
        "ixscanDocsPS" : "118.4500",
        "collscanDocsPS" : "32164.4833",
        "scansToDocumentRatio" : 484244,
        "transactionsStartedPS" : 0,
        "transactionsAbortedPS" : 0,
        "transactionsCommittedPS" : 0,
        "transactionAbortPct" : 0,
```

```
    "readLatencyMs" : "0.4803",
    "writeLatencyMs" : "7.0247",
    "cmdLatencyMs" : "0.0255",
```

We'll see examples of using the mongoTuning script in later chapters.

The raw amount of data output from db.serverStatus() may seem intimidating now. But don't worry, you only need to know a dozen or so key metrics to understand how MongoDB is performing, and by using helper functions like the ones included in our mongoTuning package, you can easily examine just those relevant statistics. In later chapters, we will see how to leverage db.serverStatus() metrics to tune MongoDB server performance.

Examining Current Operations

Another useful tool when tuning performance in MongoDB is the db.currentOp() command. This command works as you might imagine – it returns information about operations that are currently running on the database. Even if you are not currently running any operations against your database, the command may still return an extensive list of background operations.

Currently executing operations will be listed in an array called inprog. Here, we count the number of operations and view (truncated) details for the first operation in the list:

```
mongo> db.currentOp().inprog.length
7
mongo> db.currentOp().inprog[0]
        {
                "type" : "op",
                "host" : "Centos8:27017",
                "desc" : "conn557",
                "connectionId" : 557,
                "client" : "127.0.0.1:44036",
                "clientMetadata" : {
                        /* Info about the OS and client driver */
                },
                "active" : true,
                "currentOpTime" : "2020-06-08T07:05:12.196+0000",
                "effectiveUsers" : [
                        {
                                "user" : "root",
```

```
                    "db" : "admin"
                }
        ],
        "opid" : 27238315, /* Other ID info */
    },
    "secs_running" : NumberLong(0),
    "microsecs_running" : NumberLong(35),
    "op" : "update",
    "ns" : "ycsb.usertable",
    "command" : {
            "q" : {
                    "_id" : "user5107998579435405958"
            },
            "u" : {
                "$set":{"field4":BinData(0,"O1sxM..==")
                    }
            },
            "multi" : false,
            "upsert" : false
    },
    "planSummary" : "IDHACK",
    "numYields" : 0,
    "locks" : {
            /* Lots of lock statistics */
    },
    "waitingForFlowControl" : false,
    "flowControlStats" : {
            "acquireCount" : NumberLong(1),
            "timeAcquiringMicros" : NumberLong(1)
    }
}
```

We can see in the preceding output that there are seven operations running. If we examine one of these entries as in the preceding example, we are presented with a lot of information about the currently executing process.

As with `db.serverStatus()`, there is a lot of information in the output, and it may at first glance appear to be too much. But there are a few parts of the output that are critical:

- `microsecs_running` tells us how long the operation has been in progress.

- `ns` is the namespace – database and collection – that the operation is working with.

- `op` shows us the type of operation in progress, and `command` shows us the command that is currently being executed.

- `planSummary` lists what MongoDB thinks is the most important element in the execution plan.

In a tuning situation, we may only care about operations being sent as part of our application. Fortunately for us, the `currentOp()` command supports an additional parameter to help us filter out the operations we don't care about.

If you are trying to identify only the operations running on a given collection, we can pass in a filter for `ns` (namespace) and only operations that match this filter will be output:

```
> db.currentOp({ns: "enron.messages"})
{
        "inprog" : [
                {
                        "type" : "op",
                        "host" : "Centos8:27017",
                        "desc" : "conn213",
                        "connectionId" : 213,
                        "client" : "1.159.98.235:52456",
                        "appName" : "MongoDB Shell",
                        "clientMetadata" : {
. . .
                        "op" : "getmore",
                        "ns" : "enron.messages",
. . .
}
```

We can also filter on a specific type of operation by passing in a filter for the `op` field or combine multiple field filters to answer questions such as "What insert operations are currently running on a specific collection?":

```
> db.currentOp({ns: "enron.messages", op: "getmore"})
```

There are also two special operators we can pass into the filter for db.currentOp. The first option is $all. As you might imagine, if $all is set to true, the output will include all operations, including system and idle connection operations. Here, we count the number of total operations, including idle operations:

```
mongo> db.currentOp({$all: true}).inprog.length
25
```

Another option is $ownOps. If $ownOps is set to true, only operations for the user executing the db.currentOp command will be returned. As you can see in the following example, these options can help reduce the number of operations returned:

```
mongo> db.currentOp({$ownOps: true}).inprog.length
1
> db.currentOp({$ownOps: false}).inprog.length
7
```

After identifying a troublesome, resource-intensive, or long-running operation using currentOp, you may want to terminate that operation. You can use the opid field from currentOp to determine the process to be killed and then use db.killOp to terminate that operation.

For example, let's say we've identified a very long-running query that is using excessive resources and causing performance issues for other operations. We can use currentOp to identify this query and db.killOp to terminate it:

```
mongo> db.currentOP({$ownOps: true}).inprog[0].opid
69035
mongo> db.killOp(69035)
{ "info" : "attempting to kill op", "ok" : 1 }
mongo> db.currentOp({$ownOps: true, opid: 69035})
{ "inprog" : [ ], "ok" : 1 }
```

After issuing killOp, we can see that operation is no longer running.

Operating System Monitoring

The commands we've looked at so far illuminate the internal state of the MongoDB server or cluster. However, it's possible that a performance problem is being caused not because of excessive resource consumption within the cluster, but insufficient resource availability on the system hosting the MongoDB processes.

As we saw in Chapter 2, a MongoDB cluster may be implemented by multiple Mongo processes, and these processes may be distributed across multiple machines. Furthermore, a MongoDB process might be sharing machine resources with other processes and workloads. This is particularly true when MongoDB is running in a containerized or virtualized host.

Operating system monitoring is a big topic, and we can only scratch the surface here. However, the following considerations apply across all operating systems and types:

- To effectively utilize **CPU resources**, it's perfectly fine to have *CPU utilization* approaching 100%. However, the *CPU run queue* – the number of processes waiting for CPU to become available – should be kept as low as possible. We want MongoDB to be able to get CPU resources when required.

- MongoDB processes – and in particular the WiredTiger cache – should be fully contained in **real system memory**. Performance will degrade rapidly if MongoDB processes or memory is "swapped out" to disk.

- **Disk service times** should stay within the expected ranges for the disk device concerned. The expected service times differ between disks – particularly between Solid State Disks and older magnetic disks. However, disk response times should generally be below 5ms.

Most serious MongoDB clusters run on the Linux operating system. On Linux, the command-line utilities vmstat and iostat can retrieve high-level statistics.

On Microsoft Windows, the graphical *task manager* and *resource monitor* utility can perform some of the same functionality.

Whichever means you employ, make sure that you maintain awareness of operating system resource utilization as you examine server statistics. For instance, it may well be that increasing the WiredTiger cache size is indicated from an examination of db. serverStatus(), but if there is not enough free memory to support such an increase, then you may actually see performance decrease as you increase the cache size.

In Chapter 10, we'll look more closely at monitoring operating system resources.

MongoDB Compass

Understanding how to tune using nothing more than the MongoDB shell is an important skill. But it's not the only way.

MongoDB Compass is the official GUI (graphical user interface) for MongoDB, and it encapsulates many of the commands we've looked at here – plus some more advanced functionality. It presents these tools in an easy-to-use interface. MongoDB Compass is free and is a handy tool to have alongside the shell when performance tuning.

However, it is important to remember that the further removed you become from your core tools (the database methods we have learned in the preceding text), the less likely you are to understand what's going on under the hood. We won't walk through every part of Compass in this book, but we will take a brief look at how it can wrap and display the other tools we've learned in this chapter. You can download MongoDB Compass at `www.mongodb.com/products/compass`.

We saw how MongoDB Compass can show graphical explain plans earlier (see Figure 3-1).

MongoDB Compass will also allow you to more easily interpret the server information we retrieved from `db.serverStatus()`. In Compass, when you have a cluster selected, you can simply swap to the "Performance" tab at the top of the window. Compass will automatically start collecting and graphing key information about your server. Information about current operations will also be displayed. Figure 3-3 shows the MongoDB Compass Performance tab.

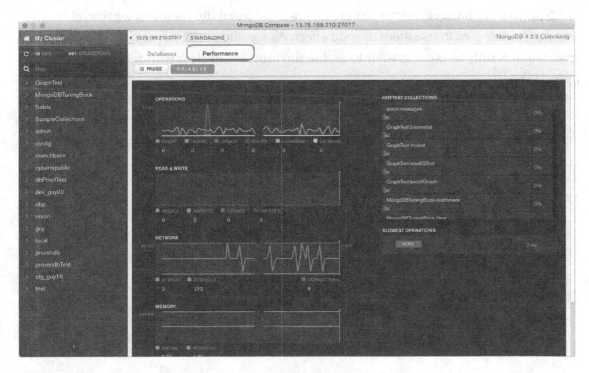

Figure 3-3. *Visual serverStatus in MongoDB Compass*

Summary

This chapter aimed to familiarize you with tools that can be leveraged across the broadest possible set of conditions when tuning the performance of your MongoDB application. Of course, we can't cover every possible tool or method in a single chapter, and not every technique described in this chapter will be a fit for every problem. These utilities and techniques may sometimes just act as a starting point and should not be depended on to solve or immediately identify any problem.

The explain() method will allow you to view, analyze, and improve how an operation will execute on the server. Examining explain() output is the first step when you believe a query needs improving. The *query profiler* identifies which queries might need tuning. The two tools used together allow you to find and fix most problematic queries and commands within your MongoDB server.

If your server is running slowly or you're unsure where to begin, the serverStatus() command can provide you with high-level insight into sever performance.

With currentOp(), you can see in real time exactly what operations are running on a given namespace, identify long-running transactions, and even kill problematic operations.

Now that we have equipped our toolbox, we can learn the underlying principles and methodologies to use them to good effect. As we said at the start of this chapter, a tradesman is only as good as their tools, but the tools are useless without the knowledge to use them.

PART II

Application and Database Design

CHAPTER 4

Schema Modelling

In databases, the *schema* defines the internal structure or organization of the data. In relational databases like MySQL or Postgres, the schema is implemented as tables and columns.

MongoDB is often described as a schema-free database, but this is somewhat misleading. By default, MongoDB does not enforce any particular document structure, but all MongoDB applications will implement some sort of document model. It's therefore more accurate to describe MongoDB as supporting *flexible* schemas.

In MongoDB, a schema is implemented by the collections   which generally represent sets of similar documents – and the structure of the documents within those collections.

The performance limits of a MongoDB application are largely determined by the document model that the application implements. The amount of work that an application needs to do to retrieve or process information is primarily dependent on how that information is distributed across multiple documents. In addition, the size of documents will determine how many documents MongoDB can cache in memory. These and many other trade-offs will determine how much physical work the database will have to do to satisfy a database request.

Although MongoDB does not have the equivalent of the expensive and time-consuming SQL ALTER TABLE statement, it remains very difficult to make fundamental changes to a document model once it has been established and deployed in production. Choosing the correct data model is, therefore, a critical early task in the design of your application.

You could fill up a book on the topic of data modelling, and indeed some have. In this chapter, we'll try to cover the core tenants of data modelling from a performance perspective.

© Guy Harrison, Michael Harrison 2021
G. Harrison and M. Harrison, *MongoDB Performance Tuning*, https://doi.org/10.1007/978-1-4842-6879-7_4

The Guiding Principles

Ironically, schema modelling with MongoDB flexible schemas can actually be harder than in the fixed schemas of the relational database.

In relational database modelling, you model the data logically, eliminating redundancy until you achieve the *third normal form*. Simplistically, third normal form is achieved when every element in a row is dependent on the key, the whole key and nothing but the key.[1] You then introduce redundancy through *denormalization* to support performance objectives. The resulting data model usually remains roughly in third normal form but with some slight modifications to support critical queries.

You could model MongoDB documents into third normal form, but it would almost always be the wrong solution. MongoDB is designed around the idea that you should include almost all relevant information within a single document – not spread it across multiple entities as you would in the relational model. Therefore, instead of creating a model based on the structure of the data, you create a model based on the structure of your queries and updates.

Here are the key objectives of MongoDB data modelling:

- **Avoid joins**: MongoDB supports a simple join capability using the aggregation framework (see Chapter 7). However, in contrast to a relational database, joins are expected to be an exception, not the rule. Aggregation-based joins are unwieldy, and it's more typical for data to be joined within the application code. In general, we try to ensure that our critical queries can find all the data they need within a single collection.

- **Manage redundancy**: By encapsulating relevant data into a single document, we create a problem of redundancy – we may have more than one place in the database where a certain data element can be found. For instance, consider a `products` collection and an `orders` collection. The `orders` collection will probably include product names within the order details. If we need to change a product name, we'll have to change it in multiple places. This will make that update operation potentially very time-consuming.

---

[1] In honor of the creator of the relational model Edgar Codd, we would often say "the key, the whole key and nothing but the key, so help me Codd!"

- **Beware of the 16MB limit**: MongoDB has a 16MB limit on the size of an individual document. We need to make sure that we never try to embed so much information that we risk exceeding that limit.

- **Maintain consistency**: MongoDB does support transactions (see Chapter 9), but they require special programming and have significant constraints. If we want to atomically update sets of information, it can be advantageous to include those data elements in a single document.

- **Monitor memory**: We want to ensure that most operations on MongoDB documents occur in memory. However, if we make our documents very large by embedding lots of information, then we reduce the number of documents that can fit in memory and might increase IO. Therefore, we want to keep documents small when we can.

Linking vs. Embedding

There are a wide variety of MongoDB schema design patterns, but they all involve variations of these two approaches:

- *Embedding* everything in a single document.

- *Linking* collections using pointers to data in other collections. This is roughly equivalent to using a relational database's third normal form model.

A Case Study

There's much room for compromise between the linking and embedding approaches and a lot of non-performance-related reasons for choosing one over the other (atomic updates and the 16M document limit, for instance). Nevertheless, let's look at how the two extremes compare from a performance point of view – at least for a specific workload.

For this case study, we will model the classic "Orders" schema. An Orders schema includes orders, details about the customer that created the order, and the products that comprise the order. In a relational database, we'd diagram this schema as in Figure 4-1.

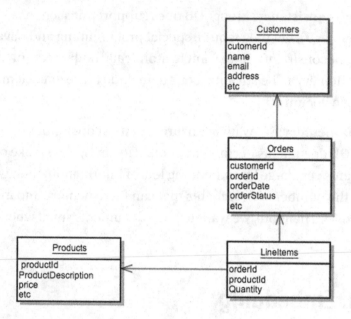

Figure 4-1. *Orders-products schema in relational form*

If we were to model this schema using only the linking paradigm, we would create a collection for each of the four logical entities. They might look something like this:

```
mongo>db.customers.findOne();
{
     "_id" : 3,
     "first_name" : "Danyette",
     "last_name" : "Flahy",
     "email" : "dflahy2@networksolutions.com",
     "Street" : "70845 Sullivan Center",
     "City" : "Torrance",
     "DOB" : ISODate("1967-09-28T04:42:22Z")
}
mongo>db.orders.findOne();
```

```
{
        "_id" : 1,
        "orderDate" : ISODate("2017-03-09T16:30:16.415Z"),
        "orderStatus" : 0,
        "customerId" : 3
}
mongo>db.lineitems.findOne();
{
        "_id" : ObjectId("5a7935f97e9e82f6c6e77c2b"),
        "orderId" : 1,
        "prodId" : 158,
        "itemCount" : 48
}
mongo>db.products.findOne();
{
        "_id" : 1,
        "productName" : "Cup - 8oz Coffee Perforated",
        "price" : 56.92,
        "priceDate" : ISODate("2017-07-03T06:42:37Z"),
        "color" : "Turquoise",
        "Image" : "http://dummyimage.com/122x225.jpg/cc0000/ffffff"
}
```

In an embedded design, we would place absolutely all information relating to an order into a single document, as follows:

```
{
  "_id": 1,
  "first_name": "Rolando",
  "last_name": "Riggert",
  "email": "rriggert0@geocities.com",
  "gender": "Male",
  "Street": "6959 Melvin Way",
  "City": "Boston",
  "State": "MA",
  "ZIP": "02119",
```

```
  "SSN": "134-53-2882",
  "Phone": "978-952-5321",
  "Company": "Wikibox",
  "DOB": ISODate("1998-04-15T01:03:48Z"),
  "orders": [
    {
      "orderId": 492,
      "orderDate": ISODate("2017-08-20T11:51:04.934Z"),
      "orderStatus": 6,
      "lineItems": [
        {
          "prodId": 115,
          "productName": "Juice - Orange",
          "price": 4.93,
          "itemCount": 172,
          "test": true
        },
```

Each customer has their own document, and inside that document, there are an array of orders. Inside each order is an array of the products included in the order (line items) and all the information about a product contained within that line item.

In our example schema, there are 1000 customers, 1000 products, 51,116 orders, and 891,551 line items. The following indexes are defined:

```
OrderExample.embeddedOrders {"_id":1}
OrderExample.embeddedOrders {"email":1}
OrderExample.embeddedOrders {"orders.orderStatus":1}

OrderExample.customers {"_id":1}
OrderExample.customers {"email":1}

OrderExample.orders {"_id":1}
OrderExample.orders {"customerId":1}
OrderExample.orders {"orderStatus":1}

OrderExample.lineitems {"_id":1}
OrderExample.lineitems {"orderId":1}
OrderExample.lineitems {"prodId":1}
```

Let's take a look at some typical operations that we might execute against these schemas and compare the performance for the two extremes.

Getting All the Data for a Customer

It's a straightforward task to get all the data for a customer when all the information is embedded in a single document. We can get all the data from the embedded version with a query like this:

```
db.embeddedOrders.find({ email: 'bbroomedr@amazon.de' })
```

With an index on email, this query completes in less than a millisecond.

Life is much harder with the four-collection version. We need to use an aggregation or custom code to achieve the same result, and we need to be sure we have indexes on the $lookup join conditions (see Chapter 7). Here's the aggregation:

```
db.customers.aggregate(
    [
        {
            $match: { email: 'bbroomedr@amazon.de' }
        },
        {
            $lookup: {
                from: 'orders',
                localField: '_id',
                foreignField: 'customerId',
                as: 'orders'
            }
        },
        {
            $lookup: {
                from: 'lineitems',
                localField: 'orders._id',
                foreignField: 'orderId',
                as: 'lineitems'
            }
        },
```

```
    {
        $lookup: {
            from: 'products',
            localField: 'lineitems.prodId',
            foreignField: '_id',
            as: 'products'
        }
    }
    ]
)
```

Not surprisingly, the aggregation/join takes way longer than the embedded solution. Figure 4-2 illustrates the relative performance – the embedded model was able to deliver more than ten times more reads per second.

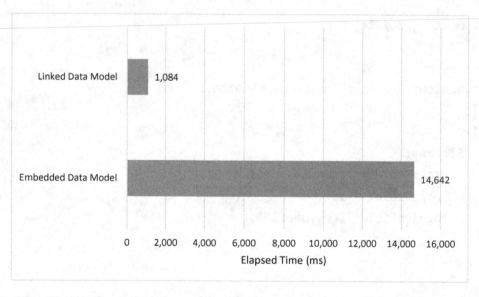

Figure 4-2. *Time taken to perform 500 customer lookups, including all order details*

Fetching All Open Orders

In a typical order processing scenario, we want to retrieve all the orders that are in an incomplete state. In our example, these orders are identified by orderStatus=0.

In the embedded case, we can get customers with open Orders like this:

```
db.embeddedOrders.find({"orders.orderStatus":0})
```

That does give us all customers with at least one open order, but if we only want to retrieve orders that are open, we are going to need to use the aggregation framework:

```
db.embeddedOrders.aggregate([
  { $match:{   "orders.orderStatus": 0 }},
  { $unwind:  "$orders" },
  { $match:{   "orders.orderStatus": 0 }},
  { $count: "count" }
] );
```

You might wonder why we have duplicate $match statements in our aggregation. The first $match gets us customers with open orders, while the second $match gets us the orders themselves. We don't need the first to get the right results, but it does improve performance (see Chapter 7).

It's far easier to get these orders in the linked data model:

```
db.orders.find({orderStatus:0}).count()
```

Not surprisingly, the simpler linked query gets the better performance. Figure 4-3 compares the performance of the two solutions.

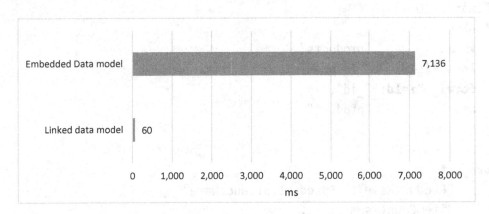

Figure 4-3. *Time taken to get a count of open orders*

Top Products

Most companies want to identify bestselling products. For the embedded model, we need to unwind the line items and aggregate by product name:

```
db.embeddedOrders.aggregate([
  { $unwind:  "$orders" },
  { $unwind:  "$orders.lineItems" },
  { $project: { "lineitems": "$orders.lineItems"   }},
  { $group:{  _id:{ "prodId":"$lineitems.prodId" ,
              " productName":"$lineitems.productName" },
              " itemCount-sum":{$sum:"$lineitems.itemCount"}} },
  { $sort:{   "lineitems_itemCount-sum":-1 }},
  { $limit:   10 },
]);
```

In the linked model, we also need to use aggregate, with $lookup joins between line items and products to get the product names:

```
db.lineitems.aggregate([
  { $group:{ _id:{ "prodId":"$prodId"  },
             "itemCount-sum":{$sum:"$itemCount"} }
  },
  { $sort:{   "itemCount-sum":-1 }},
  { $limit:   10 },
  { $lookup:
    { from:           "products",
      localField:     "_id.prodId",
      foreignField:   "_id",
      as:             "product"
    }
  },
  { $project: {
        "ProductName": "$product.productName"   ,
        "itemCount-sum": 1   ,
        "_id": 1
      }
  },
]);
```

Despite having to perform a join, the linked data model performs best. We only have to join after we get the top ten products, while in the embedded design we have to scan all of the data in the collection. Figure 4-4 compares the two approaches. The embedded data model took about twice as long as the linked data model.

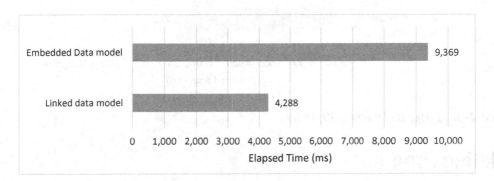

Figure 4-4. *Time taken to retrieve the top ten products*

Inserting New Orders

In this example workload, we looked at inserting a new order for an existing customer. In the embedded case, this is simply done by using a $push operation into the customer document:

```
db.embeddedOrders.updateOne(
        { _id: o.order.customerId },
        { $push: { orders: orderData } }
    );
```

In the linked data model, we have to insert into the line items collection and the orders collection:

```
var rc1 = db.orders.insertOne(orderData);
var rc2 = db.lineItems.insertMany(lineItemsArray);
```

You might think that the single update would easily outperform the multiple inserts required by the linked model. But actually, the update is a quite expensive operation – especially if there's not enough spare space in the collection to fit the new data. The linked inserts – though more numerous – are simpler operations because they don't require finding the matching document to update. Consequently, the linked model outperformed the embedded model for this example. Figure 4-5 compares the performance for 500 order inserts.

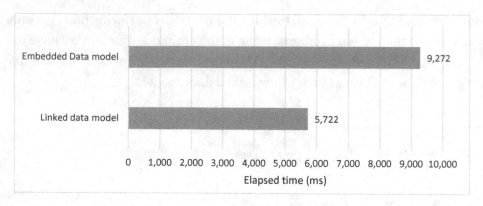

Figure 4-5. *Time to insert 500 orders*

Updating Products

What if we want to update the name of a product? In the embedded case, the product names are embedded into the line items themselves. We update the names of all the products in a single operation in MongoDB using the arrayFilters operator. Here, we update the name of product 193:

```
db.embeddedOrders.update(
        { 'orders.lineItems.prodId':193 },
        { $set: { 'orders.$[].lineItems.$[i].productName':
                'Potatoes - now with extra sugar' } },
        { arrayFilters: [{ 'i.prodId': { $eq: 193 } }], multi: true });
```

Of course, in the linked model, we can use a very simple update to the products collection:

```
db.products.update(
        { _id: 193 },
        { $set: { productName:   'Potatoes - now with extra sugar' } }
);
```

The embedded model requires us to touch many more documents than in the linked model. Consequently, ten product code price updates took hundreds of times longer in the embedded data model. Figure 4-6 illustrates the performance.

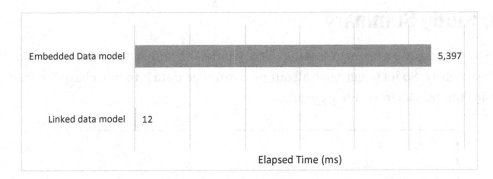

Figure 4-6. *Time to update ten product names*

Deleting a Customer

If we want to delete all data for a single customer in the four-collection model, we need to iterate through line items, orders, and customers collections. The code would look something like this:

```
db.orders.find({customerId:customerId},{_id:1}).forEach((order)=>{
        db.lineitems.deleteMany({orderId:order._id});
});
db.orders.deleteMany({customerId:1});
db.customers.deleteOne({_id:1});
```

Of course, in the embedded case, things are a lot easier:

```
db.embeddedOrders.deleteOne({_id:1});
```

The linked example performs very poorly – Figure 4-7 compares the performance for deleting 50 customers.

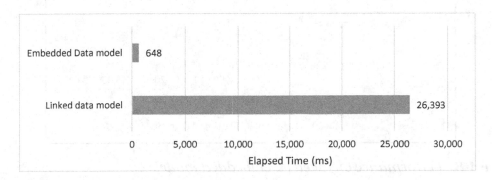

Figure 4-7. *Time to delete 50 customers*

Case Study Summary

We've looked at quite a few scenarios, and we wouldn't blame you if your head was spinning slightly. So let's aggregate all our performance data into one chart. Figure 4-8 combines the results from our six examples.

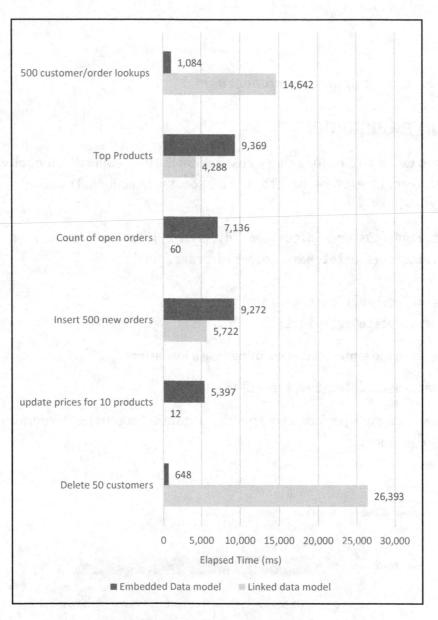

Figure 4-8. *Performance of linked vs. embedded models*

As you can see while the embedded model is pretty good at fetching all the data for a single customer or for deleting a customer, it's not superior to the linked alternative in other situations.

Tip   The answer to the question "What is the best data model for my application" is – and always has been – "it depends."

The embedded model provides many advantages when reading all of the related data for an entity, but it is generally not the fastest model for updates and for aggregate queries. Which model works best for you will depend on which aspects of your application's performance are most critical. But remember, it's hard to change the data model once your application is deployed, so any time you spend getting your data model right early in the application design process will probably pay off.

Also, remember that very few applications use an "all or nothing" approach. The best outcomes are usually achieved when we mix linking and embedding approaches to maximize the critical operations for the application.

Advanced Patterns

In the previous section, we looked at the two extremes of MongoDB data modelling: embedding everything vs. linking everything. In real life, you are likely to undertake a combination of both techniques to get the best balance between the trade-offs involved in each approach. Let's look at some of the modelling patterns that combine both approaches.

Subsetting

As we saw in the previous section, the embedded model has significant performance advantages when retrieving all data for an entity. However, there are two big risks that we need to be aware of:

- In a typical master-detail model – customers and their orders, for instance – the number of detail documents has no specific limit. But in MongoDB, a document must be no more than 16MB in size. So the embedded model can break if there are a large number of detail documents. For instance, our biggest customers might order so many products that we can't fit all the orders in a single 16MB document.

- Even if we are sure that the 16MB won't be exceeded, the effect on MongoDB memory might be undesirable. The number of documents that can fit into memory decreases as the average document size increases. Lots of large documents – potentially full of "old" data – might degrade the cache and reduce performance. We'll talk more about this in Chapter 11.

- One of the most common solutions to this conflict is a *hybrid* strategy, sometimes called *subsetting*.

- In the subsetting pattern, we embed a limited number of detail documents in the master document and store the remaining details in another collection. For instance, we might keep just the most recent 20 orders for each customer in the `customers` collection and the rest in an `orders` collection.

- Figure 4-9 illustrates the concept. Each customer has the most recent 20 orders embedded, with all orders available within the `orders` collection.

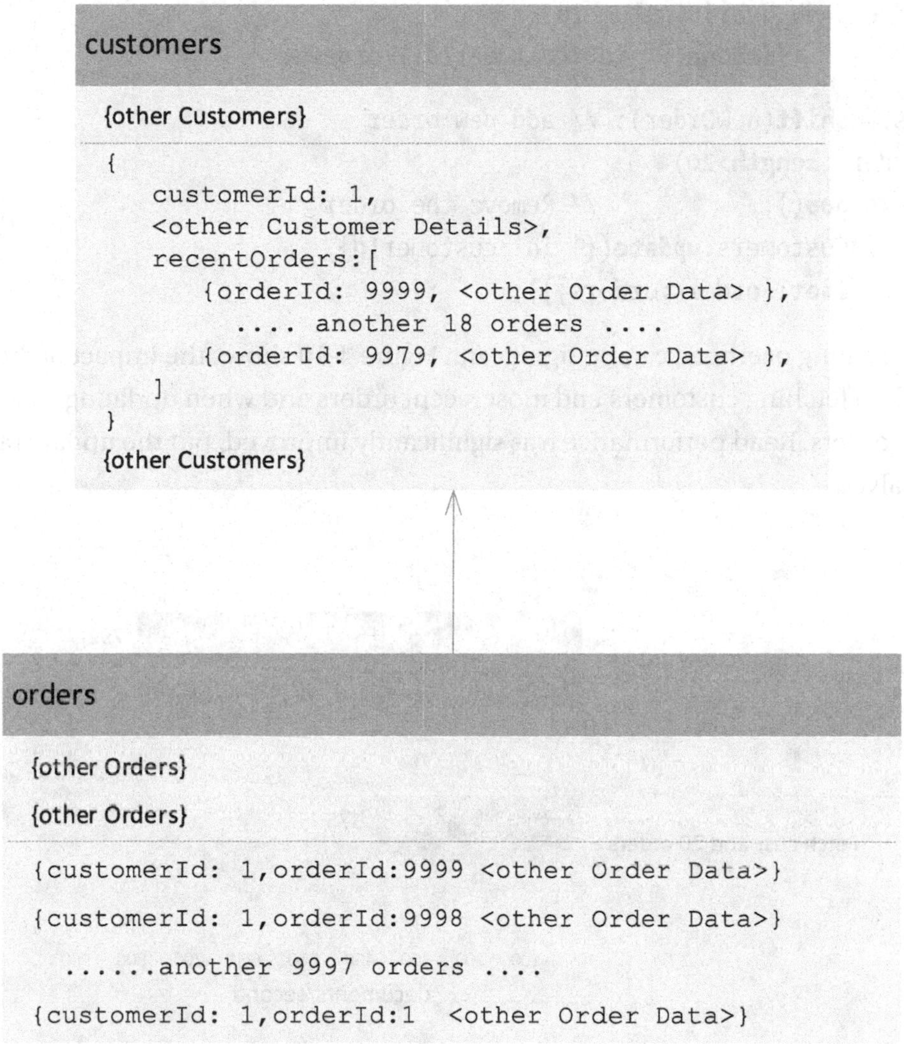

```
customers

    {other Customers}

    {
        customerId: 1,
        <other Customer Details>,
        recentOrders:[
            {orderId: 9999, <other Order Data> },
            .... another 18 orders ....
            {orderId: 9979, <other Order Data> },
        ]
    }
    {other Customers}
```

```
orders

    {other Orders}
    {other Orders}

    {customerId: 1,orderId:9999 <other Order Data>}

    {customerId: 1,orderId:9998 <other Order Data>}

        ......another 9997 orders ....

    {customerId: 1,orderId:1  <other Order Data>}
```

Figure 4-9. A hybrid "bucket" data model

If we imagine that our application displays the most recent orders for each customer on a customer lookup page, then we can see the benefits of this model. Not only have we avoided hitting the 16M document size limit, but we can now populate this customer lookup page from a single document.

However, the solution does come at a cost. In particular, we now have to shuffle orders in the embedded orders array every time we add or modify an order. Each update would need to perform additional manipulation of the embedded orders. The following code implements the shuffle of customers data in the hybrid design:

83

```
let orders=db.hybridCustomers.
            findOne({'_id':customerId}).orders;

orders.unshift(newOrder); // add new order
if (orders.length>20)
    orders.pop();              // Remove the order
db.hybridCustomers.update({'_id':customerId},
        {$set:{orders:orders}});
```

The resulting overhead can be significant. Figure 4-10 shows the impact of the hybrid model when fetching customers and most recent orders and when updating customers with new orders. Read performance was significantly improved, but the update rate was almost halved.

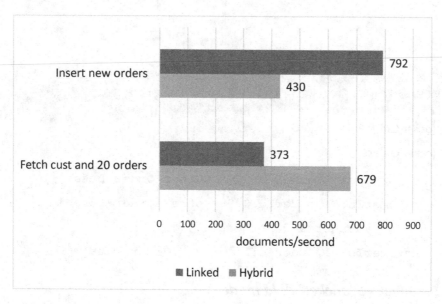

Figure 4-10. *The hybrid model can improve read performance, but slow down updates*

Vertical Partitioning

It generally makes sense to put everything relating to an entity in a single document. As we've seen previously, we can embed the multiple details relating to an entity in a JSON array, avoiding what would have required a join operation in a SQL database.

However, sometimes we can get benefits from splitting the details for an entity across multiple collections so that we can reduce the amount of data fetched in each operation. This approach is similar to the hybrid data model in that it reduces the size of the core document, but it is applied to top-level attributes, not just to arrays of details.

For instance, imagine that in each customer record we include a high-resolution photograph of the customer. These infrequently accessed images increase the overall size of the collection, degrading the time taken to perform collection scans (see Chapter 6). They also reduce the number of documents that can be held in memory which might increase the amount of IO required (see Chapter 11).

In this scenario, we can get a performance advantage if we store the binary photos in a separate collection. Figure 4-11 illustrates the arrangement.

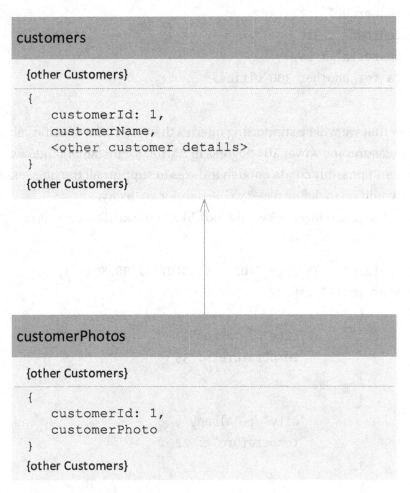

Figure 4-11. *Vertical partitioning*

The Attribute Pattern

If we have documents that include a large number of attributes of the same data type, and we know that we are going to be performing lookups using a many of these attributes, then we can reduce the number of indexes we need by using the attribute pattern.

Consider the following weather data:

```
{
        "timeStamp" : ISODate("2020-05-30T07:21:08.804Z"),
        "Akron" : 35,
        "Albany" : 22,
        "Albuquerque" : 22,
        "Allentown" : 31,
        "Alpharetta" : 24,
        <data for another 300 cities>
}
```

If we know that we will be supporting queries that search for specific values for a city (find all measurements over 100 degrees in Akron, for instance), then we have a problem. We can't possibly create enough indexes to support all the queries. A better organization would be to define name:value pair for each city.

Here's how the preceding data would look like in the attribute pattern:

```
{
        "timeStamp" : ISODate("2020-05-30T07:21:08.804Z"),
        "measurements" : [
                {
                        "city" : "Akron",
                        "temperature" : 35
                },
                {
                        "city" : "Albany",
                        "temperature" : 22
                },
                {
                        "city" : "Albuquerque",
```

```
                    "temperature" : 22
        },
        {
                    "city" : "Allentown",
                    "temperature" : 31
        },
         <data for another 300 cities>

}
```

We now have the option to define a single index on `measurements.city`, rather than attempting the impossible task of creating hundreds of indexes which would have been needed in the first design.

In some cases, you can use wildcard indexes rather than the attribute pattern – see Chapter 5. Nevertheless, the attribute pattern provides a flexible way to provide fast access to arbitrary data items.

Summary

Although MongoDB supports very flexible schema modelling, your data model design remains absolutely critical to application performance. The data model determines the amount of logical work that MongoDB needs to perform to satisfy database requests and can be very difficult to change once deployed to production.

The two "meta-patterns" in MongoDB modelling are *embedding* and *linking*. Embedding involves including all information about a logical entity in a single document. Linking involves storing related data in separate collections in a manner reminiscent of relational databases.

Embedding improves read performance by avoiding joins but can create challenges involving data consistency, update performance, and the 16MB document limit. Most applications mix embedding and linking judiciously to achieve a "best of both worlds" solution.

CHAPTER 5

Indexing

An index is a database object with its own storage that provides a fast access path into a collection. Indexes exist primarily to enhance performance, so understanding and using indexes effectively is of paramount importance when optimizing MongoDB performance.

B-Tree Indexes

The B-tree ("balanced tree") index is MongoDB's default index structure. Figure 5-1 shows a high-level overview of the B-tree index structure.

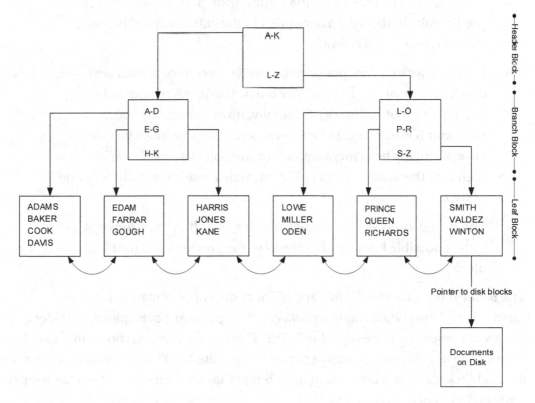

Figure 5-1. *B-tree index structure*

© Guy Harrison, Michael Harrison 2021
G. Harrison and M. Harrison, *MongoDB Performance Tuning*, https://doi.org/10.1007/978-1-4842-6879-7_5

The B-tree index has a hierarchical tree structure. At the top of the tree is the header block. This block contains pointers to the appropriate branch block for any given range of key values. The branch block will usually point to the appropriate leaf block for a more specific range or, for a larger index, point to another branch block. The leaf block contains a list of key values and pointers to the location of documents on disk.

Examining Figure 5-1, let's imagine how MongoDB would traverse this index. Should we need to access the record for "BAKER", we would first consult the header block. The header block would tell us that key values starting with A through K are stored in the left-most branch block. Accessing this branch block, we find that key values starting with A through D are stored in the left-most leaf block. Consulting this leaf block, we find the value "BAKER" and its associated disk location, which we would then use to get to the document concerned.

Leaf blocks contain links to both the previous and the next leaf block. This allows us to scan the index in either ascending or descending order and allows range queries using $gt or $lt operators to be processed using the index.

B-tree indexes have the following advantages over other indexing strategies:

- Because each leaf node is at the same depth, performance is very predictable. In theory, no document in the collection will be more than three or four IOs away.

- B-trees offer excellent performance for large collections because the depth is at most four (one header block, two levels of branch blocks, and one level of leaf block). Generally, no document will take more than four IOs to locate. In fact, because the header block will almost always already be in memory, and branch blocks usually are in memory, the actual number of physical disk reads is mostly only one or two.

- The B-tree index supports range queries as well as exact lookups. This is possible because of the links to the previous and next leaf blocks.

The B-tree index provides flexible and efficient query performance. However, maintaining the B-tree when changing data can be expensive. For instance, consider inserting a document with the key value "NIVEN" into the collection shown in Figure 5-1. To insert the document, we must add a new entry into the "L-O" block. If there is free space within this block, then the cost is substantial, but perhaps not excessive. But what happens if there is no free space in the block?

If there is no free space within a leaf block for a new entry, then an *index split* is required. A new block is allocated, and half of the entries in the existing block moved into the new block. Additionally, there is a requirement to add a new entry in the branch block pointing to the newly created leaf block. If there is no free space in the branch block, then the branch block must also be split.

These index splits are an expensive operation: new blocks are allocated, and index entries moved from one block to another. For this reason, indexes significantly slow down insert, update, and delete operations.

Caution   Indexes speed up data retrieval, but impose a burden on insert, update, and delete operations.

Index Selectivity

The *selectivity* of an index is a measure of how many documents are associated with a particular index key value. Attributes or indexes are selective if they have a large number of unique values and few duplicate values. For instance, a dateOfBirth attribute will be very selective (a large number of possible values with relatively few duplicates), while a gender attribute will not be selective (a small number of possible values with a high number of duplicates).

Selective indexes are more efficient than non-selective indexes because they point more directly to specific values. Consequently, MongoDB will try to use the most selective index.

Unique Indexes

A *unique index* is one that prevents any duplicate values for the attributes that make up the index. If you try to create a unique index on a collection that contains such duplicate values, you will receive an error. Similarly, you will also receive an error if you try and insert a document that contains duplicate unique index key values.

A unique index is typically created in order to prevent duplicate values rather than to improve performance. However, unique indexes are usually very efficient – they point to exactly one document and are therefore very selective.

All MongoDB collections have a built-in implicit unique index – on the "_id" attribute.

Index Scans

As well as being able to find specific values, indexes can also optimize partial string matches and data ranges. These *index scans* are possible because the B-tree index structure contains links to both the previous and the next leaf block. These links allow us to scan the index in either ascending or descending order.

For instance, consider this query which retrieves all customers born between two dates:

```
db.customers. find({
  $and: [
    { dateOfBirth: { $gt: ISODate('1980-01-01T00:00:00Z') } },
    { dateOfBirth: { $lt: ISODate('1990-01-01T00:00:00Z') } }
  ]
});
```

If there is an index on dateOfBirth, we can use that index to find the customers concerned. MongoDB will navigate to the index entry for the lower date and then scan through the index until it reaches an index entry where the dateOfBirth is greater than the higher date. The links between leaf blocks allow this scanning to occur efficiently.

If we examine the IXSCAN step in the explain() output for this query, we can see an indexBounds entry that shows how the index was used to scan between two values:

```
"inputStage" : {
      "keyPattern" : {
      "dateOfBirth" : 1},
      "indexName" : "dateOfBirth_1",
      . . .
      "direction" : "forward",
      "indexBounds" : {
          "dateOfBirth" : [
               "(new Date(315532800000),
                  new Date(631152000000))"
                  ]
          }
      }
```

Index scans are also executed when we do a partial match on a string condition. For instance, in the following query, the index on `LastName` is scanned for all entries where the name is greater than or equal to "HARRIS" and less than or equal to HARRIT. In practice, this only matches the names HARRIS and HARRISON, but from MongoDB's perspective, it's the same as scanning between a high and low value.

```
mongo> var explainObj=db.customers.explain('executionStats')
            .find({LastName:{$regex:/^HARRIS(.*)/}});

mongo> mongoTuning.executionStats(explainObj);

1   IXSCAN ( LastName_1 ms:0 keys:1366)
2   FETCH ( ms:0 docs:1365)

Totals:  ms: 4  keys: 1366  Docs: 1365
```

Index scans are not always a good thing. If the range is extensive, then the index scan might be worse than not using an index at all. In Figure 5-2, we see if the range of values is wide (in this example, as wide as all possible values), then it's better to do a collection scan, instead of an index lookup. However, if the range is narrow, then the index gives better performance. We'll talk more about optimizing index range scans in Chapter 6.

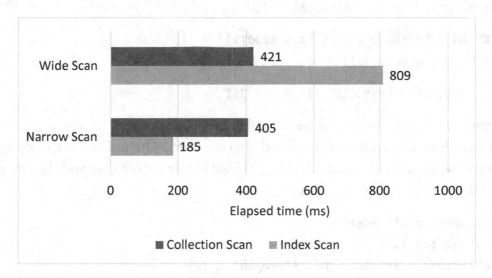

Figure 5-2. *Index scan performance and scan breadth*

Case-Insensitive Searches

It's not uncommon to search for text strings where you're not sure of the capitalization. For instance, if we don't know if a surname has been entered as "SMITH" or "Smith", we might do a case-insensitive search like this (the "i" following the regular expression specifies a case-insensitive match):

```
mongo> var e=db.customers.explain('executionStats')
               .find({LastName:/^SMITH$/i},{}) ;
mongo> mongoTuning.quickExplain(e);
1   IXSCAN LastName_1
2   FETCH
```

You might be pleasantly surprised to see that an index is used to resolve the query – so perhaps MongoDB indexes can be used for case-insensitive searches? Alas, not really. If we get executionStats, we see that although the index was used, it scanned all 410,000 keys. Yes, the index was used to find matching names, but the entire index had to be scanned.

```
mongo> var e=db.customers.explain('executionStats')
               .find({LastName:/^SMITH$/i},{}) ;
mongo> mongoTuning.executionStats(e);

1   IXSCAN ( LastName_1 ms:8 keys:410071)
2   FETCH ( ms:8 docs:711)

Totals:   ms: 293  keys: 410071  Docs: 711
```

If you want to do case-insensitive searches, then there is a trick you can use. First, create an index with a case-insensitive collation sequence. This is done by specifying a collation sequence with a strength of 1 or 2 (level 1 ignores both case and *diacritics* – special characters such as umlauts, etc.):

```
db.customers.createIndex(
  { LastName: 1 },
  { collation: { locale: 'en', strength: 2 } }
);
```

Now, if you also specify the same collation in your query, the query will return results irrespective of case. For instance, a query on "SMITH" now returns "Smith" as well:

```
mongo> db.customers.
...    find({ LastName: 'SMITH' }, { LastName: 1,_id:0 }).
...    collation({ locale: 'en', strength: 2 }).
...    limit(1);
{
  "LastName": "Smith"
}
```

And if we look at the executionStats, we see that the index is now correctly retrieving just the documents that match the criteria (in this case, there are 700-odd "Smiths" and "SMITHS):

```
 mongo> var e = db.customers.
...    explain('executionStats').
...    find({ LastName: 'SMITH' }).
...    collation({ locale: 'en', strength: 2 });
mongo> mongoTuning.executionStats(e);

1   IXSCAN ( LastName_1 ms:0 keys:711)
2  FETCH ( ms:0 docs:711)

Totals:   ms: 2   keys: 711   Docs: 711
```

Compound Indexes

A *compound index* is simply an index comprising more than one attribute. The most significant advantage of a compound index is that it is usually more *selective* than a single key index. The combination of multiple attributes will point to a smaller number of documents than indexes composed of singular attributes. A compound index that contains all of the attributes contained within the find() or $match clauses will be particularly effective.

If you frequently query on more than one attribute within a collection, then creating a compound index for these attributes is an excellent idea. For instance, we may query the customers collection by LastName and FirstName. In that case, we would probably want to create a compound index including both LastName and FirstName.

Using such an index, we could rapidly find all customers matching a given LastName and FirstName combination. Such an index will be far more effective than an index on LastName alone or separate indexes on LastName and FirstName.

If a compound index could only be used when all of its keys appeared a find() or $match, then compound indexes would probably be of pretty limited use. Luckily, a compound index can be used effectively providing any of the *initial* or *leading* attributes are requested in the query. Leading attributes are those that are specified earliest in the index definition.

Compound Index Performance

In general, you'll see index performance improve as you add more attributes to the index – providing that those attributes are included in the queries filter condition.

For instance, consider the following query:

```
db.people.find(
    {
        "LastName" : "HENNING",
        "FirstName" : "ALBERTO",
        dateOfBirth: ISODate("1953-12-23T00:00:00Z")
    },
    { _id: 0, Phone: 1 }
);
```

We are retrieving a customer phone number by providing FirstName, LastName, and dateOfBirth.

Figure 5-3 shows how the number of document accesses decreases as we add attributes to the index. Without an index, we must scan all 411,121 documents. Indexing on LastName alone reduced this to 6918 documents – effectively all the "HENNING"s in the collection. Adding FirstName got the number of documents down to 15. By adding dateOfBirth, we were down to two accesses: one to read the index entry, and from there, we read the document within the collection to get the telephone number. Our final optimization is to add the telephone number ("tel") attribute to the index. Now we don't have to access the collection at all – everything we need is in the index.

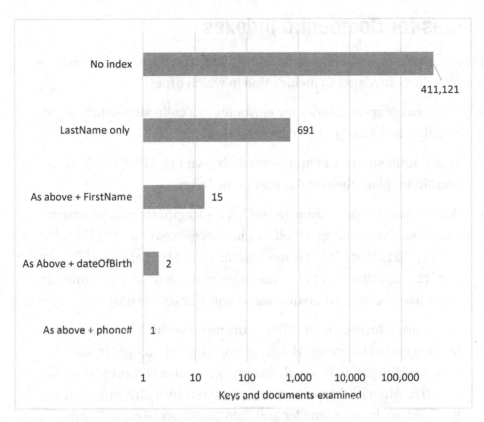

Figure 5-3. *Compound index performance (logarithmic scale)*

Compound Index Key Order

One of the great things about compound indexes is that they can support queries that don't include all of the keys in the index. A compound index can be used, providing that some of the leading attributes are included in the query.

For instance, an index specified as {LastName:1, FirstName:1, dateOfBirth:1} can be used to optimize queries on LastName alone or on LastName and FirstName. However, it would not be effective when optimizing queries against FirstName alone or on dateOfBirth. For the index to be useful, at least one of the first or *leading* keys must appear in the query.

Tip   Compound indexes can be used to accelerate queries that include any or all of the leading (first) keys in the index expression. However, they cannot optimize a query that does not at least include the first key in the index expression.

Guidelines for Compound Indexes

The following guidelines will help in deciding when to use compound indexes and how to determine which attributes to include and in which order:

- Create a compound index for attributes in a collection which appear together in a `find()` or `$match` condition.

- If attributes sometimes appear on their own in a `find()` or `$match` condition, place them at the start of the index.

- A compound index is more useful if it also supports queries where not all attributes are specified. For instance, `createIndex({"LastName":1,"FirstName":1})` is more useful than `createIndex({"FirstName":1,"LastName":1})` because queries against `LastName` only are more likely to occur than queries against `FirstName` only.

- The more selective an attribute is, the more useful it will be at the leading end of the index. However, note that WiredTiger index compression can radically shrink indexes. Index compression is most effective when leading columns are *less* selective. This might mean that such an index is smaller and therefore more likely to fit into memory. We'll talk some more about this in Chapter 11.

Covering Indexes

A *covering index* is one that can be used to completely resolve a query. Similarly, a query that can be entirely resolved by an index is called a *covered query*.

We saw an example of a covering index in Figure 5-3. An index on `LastName`, `FirstName`, `dateOfBirth`, and `Phone` was used to resolve the query without any need to retrieve data from the collection. Covering indexes are a powerful mechanism for optimizing queries. Because the index is usually far smaller than the collection, a query that does not need to bring documents from the collection into memory is highly memory and IO efficient.

Index Merges

Earlier, we emphasized that creating a compound index on *all* the conditions in a query is generally most effective.

So, for instance, in a query such as the following:

```
db.iotData.find({a:1,b:1})
```

we probably want an index on {a:1,b:1}. However, if this collection has a lot of attributes and queries have a lot of possible combinations, then it might be impractical to create all the compound indexes we need.[1]

However, if we have an index on a and another index on b, MongoDB can perform an *intersection* of the two indexes. The resulting plan looks like this:

```
1     IXSCAN a_1
2     IXSCAN b_1
3   AND_SORTED
4   FETCH
```

The AND_SORTED step indicates that an index intersection has been performed.

Index intersections for $and conditions are unusual. However, MongoDB will frequently perform an index merge for $or conditions. So, for instance, in this query:

```
db.iotData.find({$or:[{a:100},{b:100}]});
```

MongoDB will by default merge the two indexes:

```
1     IXSCAN a_1
2     IXSCAN b_1
3   OR
4   FETCH
5   SUBPLAN
```

The OR and SUBPLAN steps are indicative of an index merge.

Note   For $and conditions, a compound index is superior to an index merge. However, for an $or condition, an index merge is often the best solution.

---

[1]This might be a job for the "attribute" schema pattern which we discussed in Chapter 4.

Partial and Sparse Indexes

As we will see in Chapter 11, optimal MongoDB performance is generally achieved when all data is held in memory. However, for very large collections, it might be hard for MongoDB to hold all of an index in memory. And in some cases, we only want to use the index to scan for recent or active information. In these scenarios, we might want to create a *partial* or *sparse* index.

Partial Indexes

A partial index is one which is only maintained for a subset of information. For example, suppose we have a database of tweets and are looking for the most retweeted tweet from our account:

```
db.tweets.
  find({ 'user.name': 'Mean Magazine Bot' }, { text: 1 }).
  sort({ retweet_count: -1 }).
  limit(1);
```

An index on `user.name` and `retweet_count` will do the trick, but it will be a pretty big index. Since most tweets are not retweeted, we could create a partial index just on those tweets that have been retweeted:

```
db.tweets.createIndex(
  { 'user.name': 1, retweet_count: 1 },
  { partialFilterExpression: { retweet_count: { $gt: 0 } } }
);
```

This index will be unhelpful when we look for tweets that have never been retweeted, but providing that's not what we are trying to do, the partial index will be much smaller and more memory efficient than a full index.

Note that in order to take advantage of this index, we will need to specify a filter condition in our query that ensures that MongoDB knows that all the data we need is in the index. In our current example, we could add a condition on `retweet_count`:

```
db.tweets.find(
    { 'user.name': 'Mean Magazine Bot',
      retweet_count: { $gt: 0 } },
```

```
  { text: 1 }
).
sort({ retweet_count: -1 }).
limit(1);
```

Sparse Indexes

Sparse indexes are similar to partial indexes in that they don't index all the documents in the collection. Specifically, a sparse index doesn't include documents that don't contain the indexed attributes.

Most of the time, a sparse index is just as good as a normal index and might be significantly smaller. However, a sparse index cannot support an $exists:true search on the indexed attribute:

```
mongo>    var exp=db.customers.explain()
              .find({updateFlag:{$exists:false}});
mongo>    mongoTuning.quickExplain(exp);
1  COLLSCAN
```

However, the sparse index can search for $exists:true:

```
mongo> var exp=db.customers.explain()
                  .find({updateFlag:{$exists:true}});
mongo> mongoTuning.quickExplain(exp);
1    IXSCAN updateFlag_1
2    FETCH
```

Using Indexes for Sorting and Joining

Indexes can be used to support returning data in sorted order and can also be used to support joins between multiple collections.

Sorting

MongoDB can use an index to return data in sorted order. Because each leaf node contains links to the subsequent leaf node, MongoDB can scan index entries in sorted order, returning data without having to explicitly sort the data. We'll look at using indexes to support sorts in Chapter 6.

Using Indexes for Joins

MongoDB can join data within multiple collections using the $lookup and $graphLookup operators in the aggregation framework. For any joins of non-trivial size, these joins should be supported by index lookups to avoid exponential degradation as joins' sizes increase. This topic is covered in detail in Chapter 7.

Index Overhead

Although indexes can dramatically improve query performance, they do reduce the performance of insert, update, and delete operations. All of a collection's indexes will normally be modified when a document is inserted or deleted, and an index must also be amended when an update changes any attribute which appears in the index. Index maintenance during inserts, updates, and deletes often represents the majority of the work MongoDB must do during these operations.

It is therefore important that all our indexes contribute to query performance since these indexes will otherwise needlessly degrade insert, update, and delete performance. In particular, you should be especially careful when creating indexes on frequently updated attributes. A document can only be inserted or deleted once but may be updated many times. Indexes on heavily updated attributes or on collections that have a very high insert/delete rate will, therefore, exact a particularly high cost.

In Chapter 8, we'll look in detail at index overhead and at ways of identifying indexes that might not be pulling their weight.

Wildcard Indexes

Wildcard indexes are a particularly high-overhead index type.

A wildcard index is an index that is created on every attribute in a subdocument. So, for instance, let's say we had some data that looks like this:

```
{
 "_id" : 1,
 "data" : {
  "a" : 1728,
  "b" : 6740,
  "c" : 6481,
```

```
  "d" : 2066,
  "e" : 3173,
  "f" : 1796,
  "g" : 8112
 }
}
```

Queries might be issued against any one of the attributes in the `data` subdocument. Furthermore, there may be new attributes added by the application that we can't anticipate. To optimize performance, we need to create a separate index on each attribute:

```
db.mycollection.createIndex({"data.a":1});
db.mycollection.createIndex({"data.b":1});
db.mycollection.createIndex({"data.c":1});
db.mycollection.createIndex({"data.d":1});
db.mycollection.createIndex({"data.e":1});
db.mycollection.createIndex({"data.f":1});
db.mycollection.createIndex({"data.g":1});
```

Too many indexes! But even this won't work unless I know for sure what the attribute will be. What happens if an attribute "h" is created?

This is the sort of scenario in which *wildcard indexes* come to the rescue.[2]

As the name suggests, we can create a wildcard index by specifying a wildcard placeholder within an attribute expression, for instance:

```
db.mycollection.createIndex({"data.$**":1});
```

This statement creates an index on every attribute in the `data` document: even if new attributes are created by an application after the index is created.

That's great! But obviously, there is a cost. Let us see how wildcard indexes perform for insert, find, update, and delete statements when compared to

- No indexes at all

- A single index on a single attribute

- Separate indexes on all the attributes

---

[2]This is also a case where the attribute pattern introduced in Chapter 4 might be indicated.

For find operations, we see that wildcard indexes perform just as well as single attribute indexes – regardless of how many indexes we've created, an index provides fast access to relevant data. Figure 5-4 illustrates the results.

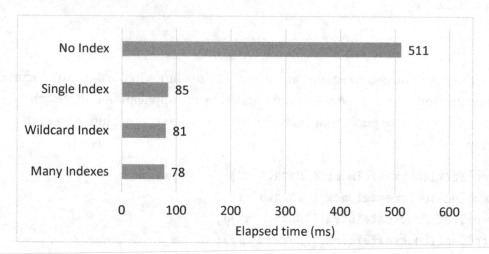

Figure 5-4. *Wildcard indexes vs. other approaches for find operations*

Although wildcard indexes have a similar profile to regular indexes, they have a very different overhead when we look at update, delete, and insert operations.

Figure 5-5 shows the time taken to perform insert, update, and delete operations when we have wildcard indexes, separate indexes on each attribute, a single index on a single attribute, or no indexes at all.

As we expect, we see a much higher overhead for multiple indexes than for a single index. However, we also see that a wildcard index imposes an overhead at least as great as that creating an individual index on every attribute.

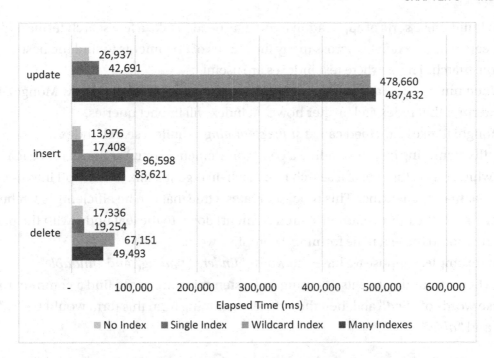

Figure 5-5. *Overhead of wildcard indexes compared with traditional indexes*

Warning   Don't create a wildcard index out of laziness. The overhead of wildcard indexes is high, and they should only be used when an alternative strategy is not available.

If some of the attributes are never searched, then the wildcard index will add an overhead that will not be worthwhile. As always, only create indexes that are necessary: all indexes impact on performance and wildcard indexes even more so.

Wildcard indexes are a really useful addition to your indexing arsenal. However, don't use them just as a programming shortcut: they impose significant overhead on insert, update, and delete performance and should only be used when the attributes to be indexed are unpredictable.

Text Indexes

It's become standard in modern applications for users to be given the ability to perform a freeform search of items, such as a list of movies, shopping items, or rental properties. Users don't want to fill in a complex form to specify which attributes to search and certainly don't want to learn MongoDB find() syntax.

To build these sorts of applications, you may need to take a few search terms and then search large text fields across many thousands of documents to find the best possible match. This is where text indexes are useful.

When tuning or creating text indexes, it's important to understand how MongoDB will interpret that index and further how that index will impact queries.

MongoDB uses a method called *suffix stemming* to build a search index.

Suffix stemming involves finding a common element (prefix) at the start of each word which forms the root of a search tree. Each divergent suffix "stems" off into its own node that may stem further. This process creates a tree that can be efficiently searched from the root (the most common shared element) down to the leaf node, with the path from the root to the leaf node forming a complete word.

For example, suppose we have the words *"finder," "finding,"* and *"findable"* somewhere in our documents. By using suffix stemming, we could find a common root in these words of *"find,"* and then the suffixes stemming from this term would be *"er," "ing,"* and *"able."*

-er

find -ing

-able

MongoDB uses this same method. When you create a text index on a given field, MongoDB will parse the text contained in that field and create an index entry for each unique stemmed term generated in a given document. This will be repeated for each indexed field and each document until all specified fields in that collection have complete text indexes.

Understanding the theory is great, but sometimes the best way to understand how text indexes work is to start interacting with them, so let's create a new text index. The command is very simple, using the same syntax as for creating any other type of index. You simply specify the field to create the index for, with the type of the index specified as "text":

```
> db.listingsAndReviews.createIndex({description: "text"})
{
```

```
        "createdCollectionAutomatically" : false,
        "numIndexesBefore" : 4,
        "numIndexesAfter" : 5,
        "ok" : 1
}
```

The text index is created as easily as that. As with our other indexes, we can create a text index on multiple attributes:

```
> db.listingsAndReviews.createIndex({summary: "text", space: "text"})
{
        "createdCollectionAutomatically" : false,
        "numIndexesBefore" : 4,
        "numIndexesAfter" : 5,
        "ok" : 1
}
```

Although you can create a text index on multiple indexes, you can only have one text index on any collection. Therefore, if you run the two commands above one after another, you will receive an error.

Note   You can only have *one* text index per collection. Therefore, to create a new text index or compound index containing a text index, you will have to first drop the old index using db.collection.**dropIndex**("index_name").

We can also create compound indexes, including a mix of text and traditional indexes:

```
> db.listingsAndReviews.createIndex({summary: "text", beds: 1})
{
        "createdCollectionAutomatically" : false,
        "numIndexesBefore" : 4,
        "numIndexesAfter" : 5,
        "ok" : 1
}
```

Another important aspect when creating text indexes is to specify the *weight* for each field. The weight of a field refers to how important that field is relative to the other indexed fields. This will be used by MongoDB when determining which results to return to use in $text queries. Weight can be specified as an option when creating your text index.

```
> db.listingsAndReviews.createIndex({summary: "text", description: "text"},
{weights: {summary: 3, description: 2}})
{
        "createdCollectionAutomatically" : false,
        "numIndexesBefore" : 4,
        "numIndexesAfter" : 5,
        "ok" : 1
}
```

Now that we have a text index on our collection, we can access it using the **$text** operator. The $text takes a $search operator which accepts a list of words (usually split by whitespace):

```
> db.listingsAndReviews.findOne({$text: {$search: "oven kettle and
microwave"}}, {summary: 1})
{
        "_id" : "6785160",
        "summary" : "Large home with that includes a bedroom with TV ,
hanging and shelf space for clothing, comfortable double bed and air
conditioning. Additional private sitting room includes sofa, kettle, bar
fridge and toaster. Exclusive use of large bathroom with shower, bath,
double sinks and toilet. LGBTQI friendly"
}
```

It is often useful when using text indexes to also project the score a given document generated during the text search. You can accomplish this using a **$meta** projection displaying the textScore field. You will usually want to sort on this projection as well, to ensure that you get the most relevant search results first.

```
mongo> db.listingsAndReviews.
...     find(
...         { $text: { $search: 'oven kettle and microwave' } },
```

```
...        { score: { $meta: 'textScore' }, summary: 1 }
...      ).
...      sort({ score: { $meta: 'textScore' } }).
...      limit(3);
{
  "_id": "25701117",
  "summary": "Totally refurbished penthouse apartment ...",
  "score": 3.5587606837606836
}
{
  "_id": "13324467",
  "summary": "Everything, absolutely EVERYTHING NEW and ... ",
  "score": 3.5549853372434015
}
```

Two other important methods you may wish to use when searching text indexes are *exclusion* and *exact matching*. Exclusions are marked using the – symbol, and exact matches are marked using double quotes. For example, the query

```
> db.listingsAndReviews.find(
      {$text: {$search:
            "\"luggage storage\" kettle and -microwave"}})
```

would search the index for an exact match of the phrase *"luggage storage"* and documents excluding the phrase *"microwave."* Using text indexes in this way can be incredibly powerful, particularly across large text heavy datasets. However, there are some limitations of text indexes to keep in mind:

- Specifying sparse for a text index has no effect. Text indexes are *always* sparse.

- If your compound index contains a *text* index, it cannot contain *multi-key* or *geospatial* fields. You will have to create separate indexes for these special index types.

- As mentioned in the example of creating a text index earlier, you can only create a single text index per collection. Additional text index creation will throw an error.

Text Index Performance

With conventional indexes, you have the ability to resolve a query using a collection scan instead of the index. However, without a text index, you cannot perform full-text searches at all. Consequently, you don't have much choice about the use of a full-text index.

However, there are some performance characteristics of full-text indexes that you should bear in mind. Firstly, you should be aware that MongoDB will perform an index scan for every term in the search criteria. For instance, here we search on five unique words and consequently perform five text index scans:

```
mongo> var exp = db.bigEnron.
...    explain('executionStats').
...    find( { $text: { $search:
       'Confirmation Rooms Credit card tax email ' } },
...    { score: { $meta: 'textScore' }, body: 1 } ).
...    sort({ score: { $meta: 'textScore' } }).
...    limit(3);

mongo> mongoTuning.executionStats(exp);

1        IXSCAN ( body_text ms:229 keys:53068)
2        IXSCAN ( body_text ms:764 keys:217480)
3        IXSCAN ( body_text ms:748 keys:229382)
4        IXSCAN ( body_text ms:1376 keys:398325)
5        IXSCAN ( body_text ms:362 keys:108996)
6        IXSCAN ( body_text ms:181 keys:93970)
7      TEXT_OR ( ms:494636 docs:843437)
8     TEXT_MATCH ( ms:494709)
9      TEXT ( body_text ms:494746)
10    SORT_KEY_GENERATOR ( ms:494795)
11    SORT ( ms:495015)
12  PROJECTION_DEFAULT ( ms:495072)
```

Consequently, as shown in Figure 5-6, the more search terms we have, the more time it takes for the text search.

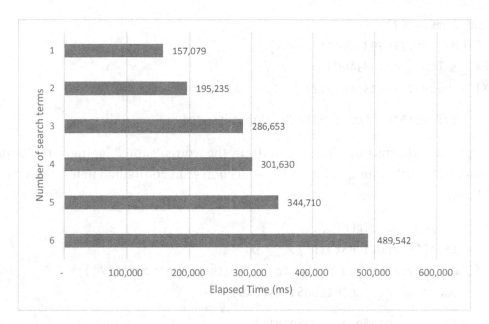

Figure 5-6. *Text index performance vs. the number of search terms*

Note   MongoDB text index performance is directly proportional to the number of terms in the search. Where necessary, limit the number of search terms to keep response time manageable.

Note that even if you search for an exact phrase, you'll still be performing one scan for each word in the phrase, because the index itself has no idea about how words are used in sequence. If you are searching for a long exact text phrase, you could be better off performing a regular expression query and a full collection scan. For instance, this query looks for the text "are you going to be at the game tonight":

```
mongo> var exp = db.bigEnron.
...    explain('executionStats').
       find( { $text: {
         $search: '"are you going to be at the game tonight"' } });
mongo>    mongoTuning.executionStats(exp);

1    IXSCAN ( body_text ms:354 keys:62838)
2    IXSCAN ( body_text ms:2136 keys:515760)
3    IXSCAN ( body_text ms:146 keys:39721)
```

```
4      OR ( ms:2767)
5    FETCH ( ms:379793 docs:563201)
6   TEXT_MATCH ( ms:383409)
7   TEXT ( body_text ms:383517)
```

Totals: ms: **414690** keys: 618319 Docs: 563201

MongoDB performs three index scans (only the words "game," "going," and "tonight" are considered worth scanning for). A full collection scan completed in less than half the elapsed time:

```
mongo> var exp = db.bigEnron.
...    explain('executionStats').
       find({body:/are you going to be at the game tonight/});
mongo>    mongoTuning.executionStats(exp);

1  COLLSCAN ( ms:102289 docs:2897816)
```

Totals: ms: **145925** keys: 0 Docs: 2897816

Tip   If you are searching for an exact phrase, you might be better off doing a collection scan–based conventional query – MongoDB text indexes are not designed for efficient multi-word phrase searches.

Here are some additional important performance considerations with text indexes:

- Due to the stemming method described earlier, text indexes can be very large and can take a long time to create.

- MongoDB recommends having enough memory on your system to keep the text index in memory, because otherwise there may be significant IO involved during the search.

When using a sort in your query, you will not be able to leverage the text index for determining order, even in compound text indexes. Keep this in mind when sorting text query results.

Text indexes are incredibly powerful and serve a wide array of modern applications, but take care when relying on them or you may find your $text queries becoming an annoying performance bottleneck.

MongoDB Atlas provides the ability to use the popular Lucene platform for text search. This facility has many advantages over MongoDB's internal text searching capability.

Geospatial Indexes

Today's location-aware applications typically need to perform searches across map data. These searches could include searching for rental properties in a region, finding nearby venues, or even categorizing photos by the location captured. Many devices today are passively capturing vast amounts of location data everywhere we go. This is often referred to as geospatial data: data about locations on Earth.

MongoDB provides both methods for querying this data as well as specific index types to optimize the queries.

Here is an example of some geospatial data:

```
{
        "_id" : ObjectId("578f6fa2df35c7fbdbaed8c4"),
        "recrd" : "",
        "vesslterms" : "",
        "feature_type" : "Wrecks - Visible",
        "chart" : "US,U1,graph,DNC H1409860",
        "latdec" : 9.3547792,
        "londec" : -79.9081268,
        "gp_quality" : "",
        "depth" : "",
        "sounding_type" : "",
        "history" : "",
        "quasou" : "",
        "watlev" : "always dry",
        "coordinates" : [
                -79.9081268,
                9.3547792
        ]
}
```

The data itself can be quite simple, although you would likely store large amounts of metadata along with the coordinates. The preceding data is in a legacy format, with the data represented as a simple coordinate pair. MongoDB also supports the *GeoJSON* format.

```
{
        "_id" : ObjectId("578f6fa2df35c7fbdbaed8c4"),
        "recrd" : "",
        "vesslterms" : "",
        "feature_type" : "Wrecks - Visible",
        "chart" : "US,U1,graph,DNC H1409860",
        "latdec" : 9.3547792,
        "londec" : -79.9081268,
        "gp_quality" : "",
        "depth" : "",
        "sounding_type" : "",
        "history" : "",
        "quasou" : "",
        "watlev" : "always dry",
        "location" : {
                "type" : "Point",
                "coordinates" : [
                        -79.9081268,
                        9.3547792
                ]
        }
}
```

The GeoJSON format specifies the type of data along with the values themselves, either a single point or an array of many coordinate pairs. GeoJSON allows you to define more complex spatial information such as lines and polygons, but for the purposes of this chapter, we will focus on simple point data in legacy format.

Here is a geospatial query that might be executed to find documents within a certain radius of the target point using the $near operator:

```
> db.shipwrecks.find(
...     {
...        coordinates:
...          { $near :
...            {
...               $geometry: { type: "Point",
```

```
                    coordinates: [ -79.908, 9.354 ] },
...              $minDistance: 1000,
...              $maxDistance: 10000
...           }
...        }
...     }
... ).limit(1).pretty();
{
        "_id" : ObjectId("578f6fa2df35c7fbdbaed8c8"),
        "recrd" : "",
        "vesslterms" : "",
        "feature_type" : "Wrecks - Submerged, dangerous",
        "chart" : "US,U1,graph,DNC H1409860",
        "latdec" : 9.3418808,
        "londec" : -79.9103851,
        "gp_quality" : "",
        "depth" : "",
        "sounding_type" : "",
        "history" : "",
        "quasou" : "depth unknown",
        "watlev" : "always under water/submerged",
        "coordinates" : [
                -79.9103851,
                9.3418808
        ]
}
```

In the preceding example, a matching geospatial index for this query already exists. In the case of the $near operator, a geospatial index is required to run the query. If you attempted to run this query without an index, MongoDB would return an error:

```
Error: error: {
        "ok" : 0,
```

```
        "errmsg" : "error processing query: ns=sample_geospatial.shipwrecks
limit=1Tree: GEONEAR  field=coordinates maxdist=10000 isNearSphere=0\nSort:
{}\nProj: {}\n planner returned error :: caused by :: unable to find index
for $geoNear query",
        "code" : 291,
        "codeName" : "NoQueryExecutionPlans"
}
```

In fact, almost all geospatial operators require an appropriate geospatial index.

In the execution plan for this query, we would see the following stage for the first time – "GEO_NEAR_2DSPHERE":

```
mongo> var exp=db.shipwrecks.explain('executionStats').
...    find(
...      {
...        coordinates:
...          { $near :
...            {
...              $geometry: { type: "Point",
                        coordinates: [ -79.908, 9.354 ] },
...              $minDistance: 1000,
...              $maxDistance: 10000
...            }
...          }
...      }
...    ).limit(1);
mongo> mongoTuning.executionStats(exp);

1    IXSCAN ( coordinates_2dsphere ms:0 keys:12)
2   FETCH ( ms:0 docs:0)
3    IXSCAN ( coordinates_2dsphere ms:0 keys:18)
4   FETCH ( ms:0 docs:1)
5   GEO_NEAR_2DSPHERE ( coordinates_2dsphere ms:0)
6  LIMIT ( ms:0)

Totals:  ms: 0  keys: 30  Docs: 1
```

This indicates we are using a 2dsphere index to help us query this geospatial data.

There are two distinct types of geospatial indexes that you may create in MongoDB:

- **2dsphere**: Used to index data that exists on a sphere like the Earth

- **2d**: Used to index data that exists on a two-dimensional plane like a traditional map

Which index you choose to use will depend on the context of the data itself. Be careful when selecting your index type. You may be able to use a 2d index on spherical data; however, the results will be warped. Think of the example of two points on opposite sides of a map; these two points may be very close on a sphere but very far on a two-dimensional plane.

To create a geospatial index, you simply specify the 2dsphere or 2d index type as the value, with the key being the field containing the location data, either as legacy coordinate data or GeoJSON data:

```
> db.shipwrecks.createIndex({"coordinates" : "2dsphere"})
```

Warning   If you attempt to create a geospatial index on a field that does not contain appropriate data in the form of GeoJSON objects or coordinate pairs, MongoDB will return an error. So check your data before creating this index.

Geospatial Index Performance

When discussing methods for ensuring your indexes are improving your performance, geospatial indexes are an outlier. Because you must have these indexes (with the exception of the $geoWithin operator), they do not necessarily grant performance boost to your queries as much as allow them to function. This makes improving your geospatial query performance a more challenging task, rather than creating or tuning the matching index; here are a few aspects you can consider in regard to geospatial indexes:

- Unlike its fellow geospatial operators, $geoWithin can be used without a geospatial index. Adding a matching index is the easiest way to improve the performance of $geoWithin.

- $near and $nearSphere will automatically sort results by distance (nearest to furthest), so if you add a sort() operation to your query, the initial sort is wasted. If you are planning on sorting your results, you may improve performance by using $geoWithin or the $geoNear aggregation stage, which does not sort the results automatically.

- When using the $near, $nearSphere, or $geoNear operators, leverage the minDistance and maxDistance parameters wherever possible. This will limit the number of documents examined by MongoDB. In the case of a query with many data points nearby, this may not affect performance. However, if there are no matching values nearby, a query within maxDistance might conceivably search the entire world!

Geospatial metadata is being added to more and more data, from images to browser logs. It is increasingly likely that somewhere in a production dataset, you may have some geospatial data. As with other index types, you should still consider whether the overhead of maintaining the index is worth the performance increase. If you don't expect the application to query the geospatial data, then a geospatial index may not be beneficial.

Geospatial Index Limitations

With both the 2dsphere and 2d index types, it is not possible to create a *covered* query. Due to the nature of geospatial operators, the documents must be examined to satisfy the query, so don't expect to create covered queries simply by creating a geospatial index.

Additionally, when working with a sharded collection (which will be covered in Chapter 14), the geospatial index cannot be used as the shard key, you won't be able to shard by GeoJSON or coordinate data. If, however, you wish to have a geospatial index on a sharded collection, you can still create it given the shard key references a different field than the index. It is also worth noting that, as was the case with text indexes, both 2d and 2dsphere indexes are always *sparse*.

The 2d index type cannot be used with more advanced GeoJSON data; it *only* supports legacy coordinate pairs.

MongoDB does allow you to create multiple geospatial indexes on a single collection. Be careful creating subsequent geospatial indexes, however, as this will affect the behavior of geospatial aggregations, and may even break existing application code. For example, if multiple geospatial ndexes exist for a query using the $geoNear aggregation pipeline stage, you must specify the key you wish to use. If multiple 2dsphere or 2d indexes exist on that collection and no key is specified, the aggregation will be unsure which index to use, causing the aggregation to fail.

Note   If you have at most one 2d index and one 2dsphere index, you will not receive an error. Instead, the query will attempt to use the 2d index if it exists; if no 2d index is found, it will attempt to use a 2dsphere index.

In practice, it is unlikely you will create many different geospatial indexes on a single collection. As always, think carefully about what queries you are likely to encounter before creating indexes.

Summary

In this chapter, we have learned what indexes are, how they work, and why they are critical. Many times, correctly identifying and creating indexes that match your queries will give you the most "bang for your buck" to improve performance. Additionally, we have learned about some more specific indexes to help with geospatial or text queries.

However, as we also learned in this chapter, indexes are not a universal band-aid for all performance problems. In some cases, an index poorly used can reduce performance. It is crucial to think about the expected load coming from your application or users and the structure of the data before deciding what sort of indexing to implement.

Indexes may be one of your most robust methods for improving MongoDB performance, but don't be lazy when creating them; a little bit of time spent on proper indexing will save you a lot of time tuning down the track.

PART III

Tuning MongoDB Code

CHAPTER 6

Query Tuning

In almost all applications, the majority of database time is spent in data retrieval. A document can only be inserted or deleted once, but will typically be read many times between updates, and even updates must retrieve the data before performing their work. Therefore, much of our MongoDB tuning efforts focus on finding data and in particular the `find()` statement, which is the workhorse of MongoDB data retrieval.

Caching Results

Back in the dim dark days when Guy worked primarily with SQL-based databases, a wise man once told him "the fastest SQL statement is the one you never send to the database." In other words, don't send requests to the database if you can avoid it. Even the simplest request involves a network round trip, and maybe an IO – so never interact with the database unless you absolutely have to.

This principle applies equally to MongoDB. We often ask the database for the same information more than once – even when we know that the information does not change.

For instance, consider the following simple function:

```
function recordView(customerId,filmId) {
  let filmTitle=db.films.findOne({_id:filmId},{Title:1}).Title;
  db.customers.update({_id:customerId},
      {$push:{views:{filmId,title:filmTitle,
                     viewDate:new ISODate()}}});
}
```

We look up the film title in the films collection – fair enough. But the film titles never change, and on any given day, some films will be viewed many times. So why go back to the database to get the film title for a film we have already processed?

© Guy Harrison, Michael Harrison 2021
G. Harrison and M. Harrison, *MongoDB Performance Tuning*, https://doi.org/10.1007/978-1-4842-6879-7_6

This admittedly more complicated code caches film titles in local memory. We never ask the database for a film title a second time:

```
var cacheDemo={};
cacheDemo.filmCache={};

cacheDemo.getFilmId=function(filmId) {
  if (filmId in cacheDemo.filmCache) {
    return(cacheDemo.filmCache[filmId]);
  }
  else
    {
      let filmTitle=db.films.findOne({_id:filmId},
                        {Title:1}).Title;
      cacheDemo.filmCache[filmId]=filmTitle;
      return(filmTitle);
    }
};

cacheDemo.recordView= function(customerId,filmId) {
  let filmTitle=cacheDemo.getFilmId(filmId);
  db.customers.update({_id:customerId},
                  {$push:{views:{filmId,title:filmTitle,
                              viewDate:new ISODate()}}});
}
```

The cached implementation is much faster. Figure 6-1 shows the elapsed time for executing each function 1000 times with random inputs.

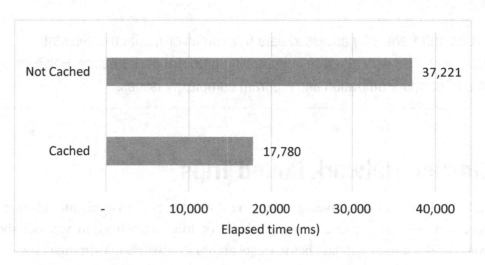

Figure 6-1. Performance improvements from simple caching

Caching is particularly suitable for small, frequently accessed collections that contain static "lookup" values.

Here are some considerations to keep in mind when implementing caching:

- Caches consume memory on the client program. In many environments, memory is abundant, and the tables considered for caching relatively small. However, for large collections and memory-constrained environments, the implementation of a caching strategy could actually degrade performance by contributing to memory shortages in the application layer or client.

- When caches are relatively small, sequential scanning (i.e., examining each entry in the cache from the first entry to the last) will probably result in adequate performance. However, if the cache is larger, the sequential scan may start to degrade performance. To maintain good performance, it may be necessary to implement advanced search techniques such as hashing or binary chop. In our preceding example, the cache was effectively indexed by film ID and would, therefore, remain efficient regardless of the number of films involved.

- If the collection being cached is updated during program execution, then the changes may not be reflected in your cache unless you implement some sophisticated synchronization mechanism. For this reason, local caching is best performed on static collections.

> **Tip**   Caching frequently accessed data from small or medium-sized static collections can be very effective in improving program performance. However, beware of memory utilization and program complexity issues.

Optimizing Network Round Trips

One of the reasons that databases are often the slowest part of an application is that they have to move data across a network link. Every time an application accesses some data from the database, that data has to travel across a network. In extreme cases (such as when your database is in a cloud server on another continent), that distance can be thousands of miles.

Network transmission takes time – usually far more time than is expended in CPU cycles. So reducing network transmissions – or network round trips – is fundamental to reducing query time.

We like to think of network transmissions as a rowboat crossing a river. We have a certain number of people on one side of the river, and we want to get them across to the other side in a boat. The more people we can get into the boat in each crossing, the fewer round trips we have to make and the sooner we'll get them all across. If the people represent documents and the boat represents a single network packet, then the same logic applies to database network traffic: our aim is to pack the greatest number of documents into each network packet.

There are two fundamental ways of "packing documents into network packets:

- By making each document as small as possible

- By making sure that network packets have no empty space

Projections

Projections allow us to specify the attributes that should be included in the results of a query. MongoDB programmers often don't bother to specify projections, because applications typically just discard the unwanted data anyway. But the impact on network round trips can be massive. Consider this query:

```
db.customers.find().forEach((customer)=>{
```

```
    if (customer.LastName in results )
        results[customer.LastName]++;
    else
        results[customer.LastName]=1;
});
```

We are getting a count of customer surnames. Notice that the only attribute we use from the `customers` collection is `LastName`. So we can add a projection to ensure that only the LastName is included in the results:

```
db.customers.find({},{LastName:1,_id:0}).forEach((customer)=>{
    if (customer.LastName in results )
        results[customer.LastName]++;
    else
        results[customer.LastName]=1;
});
```

Over a slow network, the performance difference is amazing – the projection increased throughput by ten times. Even when we run the query on the same host as the database server (thus reducing the round trip time), the performance difference is still significant. Figure 6-2 illustrates the performance improvements gained simply by adding a projection.

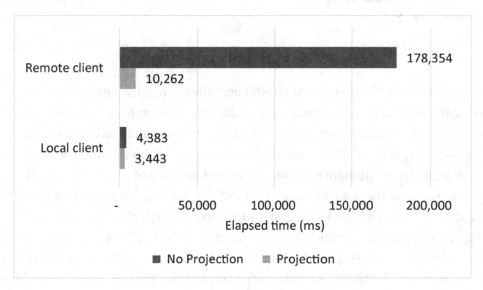

Figure 6-2. *Using projections to reduce network overhead*

Tip   Include projections in `find()` operations whenever fetching bulk data. Projections reduce the amount of data that MongoDB needs to transfer across the network and can, therefore, reduce network round trips.

Batch Processing

The number of documents that are included in each network packet in response to a query is managed automatically by MongoDB. Batches are limited to the BSON document size of 16MB, but since network packets are much smaller than this, this limitation is usually unimportant. However, by default, MongoDB will only return 101 documents in the initial batch, which means that sometimes data might be split over two network transmissions when one would be sufficient.

When retrieving data using a cursor, you can specify the number of rows fetched in each operation using the `batchSize` clause. For instance, in the following we have a cursor where the variable `batchSize` controls the number of documents retrieved from the MongoDB database in each network request:

```
var myCursor=db.millions.find({},{n:1,_id:0})
                      .batchSize(batchsize);
while (myCursor.hasNext()) {
  myCursor.next();
  count+=1;
}
```

Note that the `batchSize` operator doesn't actually change the amount of data returned to the program – it just controls the number of documents retrieved in each network round trip. This all happens "under the hood" from your program's point of view.

The effectiveness of modifying `batchSize` depends a lot on the underlying driver implementation. In the MongoDB shell, the default `batchSize` is already set as high as it can go. However, in the NodeJS driver, `batchSize` is set to a default of 1000. As a result, adjusting `batchSize` in a NodeJS program might give you a performance boost.

In Figure 6-3, we see the effect of manipulating `batchSize` for a query retrieving rows from a remote database using the NodeJS driver. Settings of `batchSize` below 1000 made performance worse – sometimes much worse! But settings greater than 1000 did improve performance.

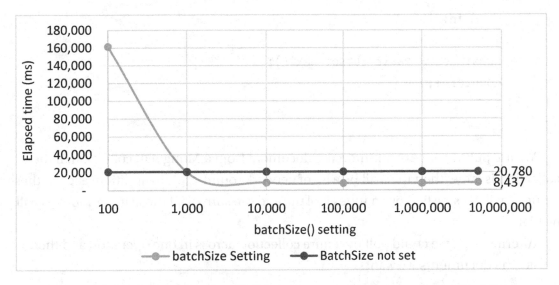

Figure 6-3. *Effect of changing* batchSize *on query performance in NodeJS*

Note that if you repeat this experiment using the MongoDB shell, you'll see no performance improvement as you increase batchSize. Each driver and client implements batchSize somewhat differently. The node driver uses a default size of 1000, while the Mongo shell uses a much higher value.

Warning   Adjusting batchSize is just as likely to degrade performance than to improve it. Only increase batchSize if you are pulling a very large number of small documents across a slow network, and always test to make sure that you are getting a performance improvement.

Avoiding Excessive Network Round Trips in Code

batchSize() helps us reduce network overhead transparently in the MongoDB driver. But sometimes the only way to optimize your network round trips is to tweak your application logic. For instance, consider this logic:

```
for (i = 1; i < max; i++) {
    //console.log(i);
    if ((i % 100) == 0) {
        cursor = useDb.collection(mycollection).find({
```

```
        _id: i
    });
    const doc = await cursor.next();
    counter++;
  }
}
```

We are pulling out every hundredth document from a MongoDB collection. If the collection is large, then that will be a lot of network round trips. In addition, each of these requests will be satisfied by an index lookup, and the sum of all those index lookups will be high.

Alternatively, we could pull the entire collection across in one operation and then extract the documents we want.

```
const cursor = useDb.collection(mycollection).find()
                    .batchSize(10000);
for (let doc = await cursor.next();
        doc != null;
        doc = await cursor.next()) {
  if (doc._id % divisor === 0) {
    counter++;
  }
}
```

Intuitively, you might think that the second approach would take much longer. After all, we are now retrieving 100 times more documents from MongoDB, right? But because the cursor pulls across thousands of documents in each batch (under the hood), the second approach is actually a lot less network-intensive. If the database is located across a slow network, then the second approach will be much faster.

In Figure 6-4, we see the performance of the two approaches for a local server (e.g., on Guy's laptop) vs. a remote (Atlas) server. When the Mongo server was on Guy's laptop, the first approach was a little faster. But when the server was remote, pulling all the data across in a single operation was far faster.

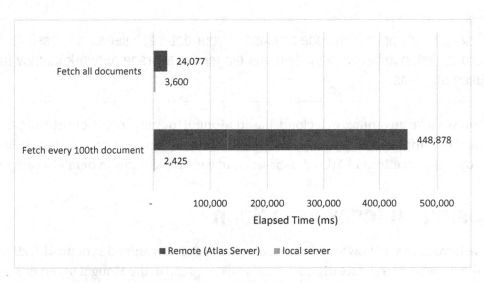

Figure 6-4. *Optimizing network round trips in client code*

Bulk Inserts

Just as we want to pull data out of MongoDB in batches, we also want to insert in batches – at least if we have lots of data to insert. Although the optimization principles are the same, the implementation is quite different. Since the MongoDB server or driver can't possibly know how many documents you are going to insert, it's up to you to structure your code to explicitly insert in bulk. We'll look at the principles and practices for bulk insert in Chapter 8.

Application Architecture

Remember our analogy of the rowboat and the river? Making sure the rowboat has a full load is how we reduce the number of trips across the river. However, the width of the river is something we usually can't control. But in an application, the distance that we have to travel is something we can control. The "distance" between the application server and the database server is the primary factor determining how much time is elapsed in each network round trip.

Therefore, the closer the application code is to the database server, the less time will be consumed in network overhead. Whenever you can, you should endeavor to locate the application server in the same data center, or even in the same network rack, as the database server.

Tip   Keep your application code as close to your database server as possible. The further the distance between the two, the higher the average network latency for database requests.

When we take advantage of a cloud-based MongoDB Atlas server, optimizing the location of our application code might seem problematic. However, we do have a lot of control over the locations of Atlas databases, and we'll look at this in detail in Chapter 13.

Choosing an Index vs. a Scan

So far, we have looked at how to reduce the amount of time consumed in network traffic. Now let's look at how we can reduce the amount of work required in the MongoDB server itself.

The most important tool we have at our disposal for query tuning is indexing. Chapter 5 was dedicated to indexing, and we spent a lot of time in that chapter learning how to create the best indexes possible.

However, an index might not always be the best option for your query.

If you are reading an entire book, you don't start by jumping to the index and then switching between each index entry and the book section it refers to. That would be silly and extremely time-consuming. You read a book by starting at the first page and reading subsequent pages in order. If you want to find a specific item in a book, that's when you use the index.

The same logic applies to MongoDB queries – if you are reading an entire collection, you don't want to use an index. If you are reading a small number of documents, then an index is preferred. But at what point does the index become more effective than the collection scan? For instance, should I use an index if I'm reading half the collection?

The answer is – unfortunately – it depends. Some of the factors which affect the "break-even" point for indexed retrieval are

- **Caching effects**: Index retrievals tend to get very good hit rates in WiredTiger cache, while full collection scans generally get a much poorer hit rate. But if all of the collection is in the cache, then a collection scan will perform closer to index speeds.

- **Document size**: Most of the time, a document will be retrieved in a single IO, so the size of the document doesn't affect index performance that much. However, larger documents mean larger collections which will push up the amount of IO needed for the collection scan.

- **Data distribution**: If documents in the collection are stored in the order of the indexed attribute (which can happen if documents are inserted in key order), then the index may need to access fewer blocks to retrieve all documents for a given key value and therefore experience a much higher hit rate. Data that is stored in sorted order is sometimes referred to as highly *clustered*.

Figure 6-5 shows the elapsed time for indexed scans and collection scans for clustered and unclustered data, plotted against the percentage of the collection being retrieved. In one test, the data was loaded into the collection in sorted order, favoring an index lookup. In another test, the data was effectively in random order.

For randomly distributed data, a collection scan completed more quickly than an index scan if more than about 8% of the collection was retrieved. However, if the data was highly clustered, the index scan outperformed the collection scan up to almost the 95% mark.

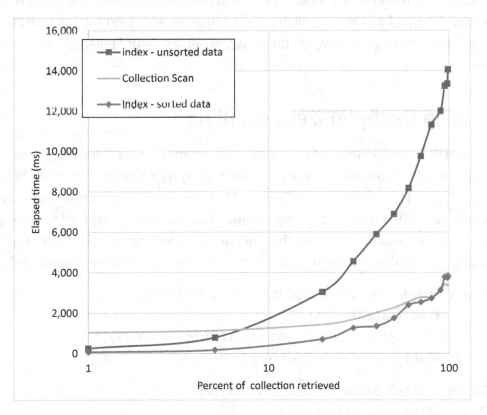

Figure 6-5. *Index and collection scan performance plotted against percent of collection accessed (logarithmic scale)*

Although it's not really possible to specify a "one-size-fits-all" cutoff point for index retrieval, the following statements are generally valid:

- **If** all documents or a large proportion of documents in the collection need to be accessed, then a full collection scan will be the quickest access path.

- **If** a single document is to be retrieved from a large collection, then an index based on that attribute will offer the quicker retrieval path.

- **Between** these two extremes, it may be difficult to predict which access path will be quicker.

Note   There is no "one-size-fits-all" break-even point for indexed vs. collection scan accesses. If only a few documents are being accessed, then the index will be preferred. If almost all the documents are being accessed, then the full collection scan will be preferred. In between these two extremes, your "mileage" will vary.

Overriding the Optimizer with Hints

The MongoDB optimizer uses a combination of heuristics – rules – and "experiments" when deciding the optimum access path. It will usually try a few different plans before settling on a plan for a specific query "shape." However, the optimizer is biased in favor of using indexes when they exist. So, for instance, the following query retrieves every document in the collection, because there are no customers born in the 1800s! However, even though all the documents are being retrieved, MongoDB chooses an indexed path.

```
mongo> var exp=db.customers.explain('executionStats').
          find({dateOfBirth:{
              $gt:new Date("1900-01-01T00:00:00.000Z")}}});
mongo> mongoTuning.executionStats(exp);

1   IXSCAN ( dateOfBirth_1 ms:16 keys:411121)
2   FETCH ( ms:53 docs:411121)

Totals:  ms: 805  keys: 411121  Docs: 411121
```

The execution plan shows that the IXSCAN step retrieves all 411,121 rows of the collection: the use of an index was not ideal in this case.

We can change force this query to use a collection scan by adding a *hint*. If we append `.hint({$natural:1})`, we instruct MongoDB to perform a collection scan to resolve the query:

```
mongo> var exp=db.customers.explain('executionStats').
...     find({dateOfBirth:{
               $gt:new Date("1900-01-01T00:00:00.000Z")}}).
...     hint({$natural:1});
mongo> mongoTuning.executionStats(exp);

1  COLLSCAN ( ms:16 docs:411121)

Totals:  ms: 383  keys: 0  Docs: 411121
```

We can also use a hint to specify the index that we want MongoDB to use. For instance, in this query we see that MongoDB has chosen an index on Country:

```
mongo> var exp=db.customers.explain('executionStats').
...     find({Country:'India',
           dateOfBirth:{$gt:new Date("1990-01-01T00:00:00.000Z") }});

mongo> mongoTuning.executionStats(exp);

1    IXSCAN ( Country_1 ms:0 keys:41180)
2    FETCH ( ms:7 docs:41180)

Totals:  ms: 78  keys: 41180  Docs: 41180
```

If we think that MongoDB has chosen the wrong index, then we can specify the index key in the hint that we want MongoDB to use. Here, we force the use of an index on `dateOfBirth`:

```
mongo> var exp=db.customers.explain('executionStats').
...     find({Country:'India',
           dateOfBirth:{$gt:new Date("1990-01-01T00:00:00.000Z")
}}).hint({dateOfBirth:1});

mongo>
```

```
mongo> mongoTuning.executionStats(exp);

1   IXSCAN ( dateOfBirth_1 ms:6 keys:63921)
2   FETCH ( ms:13 docs:63921)

Totals:  ms: 143  keys: 63921  Docs: 63921
```

Using hints in application code is not best practice. A hint might prevent a query from taking advantage of new indexes when they are added to the database and might prevent optimizations introduced by MongoDB as new versions of the server are introduced. However, if all else fails, a hint might be the only way to coerce MongoDB into using the correct index or forcing MongoDB to use a collection scan.

Warning   Consider the use of hints in queries as a last resort. A hint may prevent MongoDB from taking advantage of new indexes or responding to changes in data distribution.

Optimizing Sort Operations

If a query includes a sort directive and there is no index on the sorted attributes, MongoDB must fetch all of the data and then sort the resulting data in memory. Until all of the rows are sorted, the first row from the query cannot be returned – because we can't identify the first document in the sorted result until we've sorted all of the documents. For this reason, a non-index sort is often referred to as a *blocking sort*.

A blocking sort might actually be faster than an index sort if you want the entire sorted set of data. However, using the index gets you the first few documents almost immediately, and in many applications, the user wants to see the first "page" of sorted data quickly and may never page through the entire set. In these cases, an index sort is very desirable.

Furthermore, a blocking sort will fail if it runs out of memory. You might get an error like this with a blocking sort[1]:

---

[1]You can allocate more memory for the sort using `internalQueryExecMaxBlockingSortBytes` – we'll discuss this parameter in Chapter 7. From MongoDB 4.4 onward, you can also perform a "disk sort" by adding the `allowDiskUse()` modifier to your query.

Executor error during find command: OperationFailed: Sort operation used more than the maximum 33554432 bytes of RAM. Add an index, or specify a smaller limit.

A find() operation that specifies a sort() option and which performs a blocking sort will show a SORT_KEY_GENERATOR step followed by a SORT step in the execution plan:

```
mongo> var plan=db.customers.explain()
                  .find().sort({dateOfBirth:1});
mongo> mongoTuning.quickExplain(plan);
```

```
1    COLLSCAN
2    SORT_KEY_GENERATOR
3    SORT
```

If we create an index on the sort criteria, then we'll just see an IXSCAN and FETCH:

```
mongo> var plan=db.customers.explain()
              .find().sort({dateOfBirth:1});
mongo> mongoTuning.quickExplain(plan);
```

```
1    IXSCAN dateOfBirth_1
2    FETCH
```

If we have a query that performs a filter and then a sort, then we will need to have an index on both the filter condition and the sort condition – in that order.

For instance, if we have a query like this:

```
Mongo> db.customers.find({Country:'Japan'})
            .sort({dateOfBirth:1});
```

we might initially be happy to see that the plan is resolved using the index:

```
mongo> var plan=db.customers.explain()
      .find({Country:'Japan'}).sort({dateOfBirth:1});

mongo> mongoTuning.quickExplain(plan);
```

```
1    IXSCAN dateOfBirth_1
2    FETCH
```

However, that index only supported the sort. If we want the index to support the sort and the query filter, then we need to create an index like this:

```
db.customers.createIndex({Country:1,dateOfBirth:1});
```

Tip   To create an index that supports both a filter and a sort, create the index with the filter conditions first, followed by the sort attributes.

Using an index to return documents in a specific order is not always the best option. If you are looking for the *first* few documents, then the indexed will work better than the blocking sort. However, if you need *all* the documents returned in sorted order, then the blocking sort may be superior.

Figure 6-6 shows how an index radically reduces the response time to retrieve the first sorted document, but actually degrades the time required to get the last sorted document in the collection.

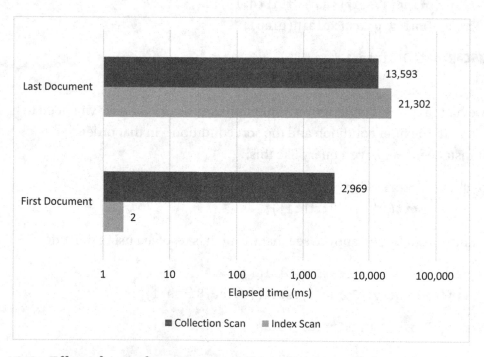

Figure 6-6. *Effect of an index on sorting when retrieving all documents or only the first document (note the logarithmic scale)*

Tip   Using an index to optimize a sort is a good strategy if you are only interested in the first few documents from the sort. When you need all the documents returned in sorted order, then a blocking (non-indexed) sort will usually be faster.

If you are going to to do a blocking sort on a large amount of data, you may need to allocate more memory for the sort. You can do this by adjusting the internal parameter internalQueryExecMaxBlockingSortBytes. For instance, to set the sort memory size to 100MB, you could issue the following command:

```
db.getSiblingDB("admin").
    runCommand({ setParameter: 1, internalQueryExecMaxBlockingSortBytes:
    1001048576 });
```

Be aware, however, that increasing this limit will allow MongoDB to load that much extra data into memory, utilizing more overall system resources. The query itself may also take longer to execute if the server does not have sufficient free memory. This is discussed in further depth in Chapter 11.

Picking or Creating the Right Index

As we saw in the last chapter and earlier in this chapter, probably the most effective tool for query optimization is indexing. When looking at a query – at least one that doesn't fetch all or most of the collection – our first question is usually "do I have the right index to support this query?"

As we've seen, indexes can perform three levels of optimization for a query:

1. An index can quickly locate the matching documents for a filter condition.

2. An index can avoid a blocking sort.

3. A *covering* index can resolve a query without involving any collection access at all.

Therefore, the ideal index for any query would be one that

1. Includes all the attributes of the filter condition

2. Then includes the attributes of the sort() criteria

3. And then – optionally – all the attributes in the projection clause

Of course, adding all the attributes in a projection is only practical if only a few attributes are projected.

Tip A perfect index for a query will contain all the attributes from the filter condition, all the attributes from any sort conditions, and – only if practical – the attributes included in the queries projection.

If you have such a perfect index, you'll see an IXSCAN followed by PROJECTION_ COVERED in the execution plan. Here's an example of a perfectly covered query that includes an index-supported sort:

```
mongo>db.customers.createIndex(
      {Country:1,'views.title':1,LastName:1,Phone:1},
      {name:'CntTitleLastPhone_ix'});

mongo> var exp = db.customers.
...    explain('executionStats').
...    find(
...      { Country: 'Japan', 'views.title': 'MUSKETEERS WAIT' },
...      { Phone: 1, _id: 0 }
...    ).
...    sort({ LastName: 1 });

mongo> mongoTuning.executionStats(exp);

1   IXSCAN ( CntTitleLastPhone_ix ms:0 keys:770)
2   PROJECTION_COVERED ( ms:0)
```

In the following example, there is no projection specified in the query, so we can't expect to see PROJECTION_COVERED. Instead, we have a FETCH operation – but note that the number of rows handled in the FETCH is exactly the same as the number of documents in the IXSCAN – this indicates that the index retrieved **all** the documents we needed.

```
mongo> var exp = db.customers.
...    explain('executionStats').
...    find(
```

```
...       { Country: 'Japan', 'views.title': 'MUSKETEERS WAIT' }
...     ).
...     sort({ LastName: 1 });
mongo>
mongo> mongoTuning.executionStats(exp);

1    IXSCAN ( CntTitleLastPhone_ix ms:0 keys:770)
2    FETCH ( ms:0 docs:770)

Totals:   ms: 3   keys: 770   Docs: 770
```

Tip   If the number of documents processed in the FETCH step is the same as the number of documents processed in the IXSCAN, then the index successfully retrieved all the documents required.

Filter Strategies

In this section, we'll discuss strategies for some specific filter scenarios, such as those involving "not equals" and range queries.

Not Equals Conditions

From time to time, you'll be issuing filter conditions based on a $ne (not equals) condition. You might initially be pleased to find that MongoDB will use an index to resolve this sort of query. For instance, in the following query, we retrieve all emails except those originating from "Eric Bass":

```
mongo> var exp = db.enron_messages.
...     explain('executionStats').
...     find({ 'headers.From': { $ne: 'eric.bass@enron.com' } });

mongo> mongoTuning.executionStats(exp);

1    IXSCAN ( headers.From_1 ms:251 keys:481269)
2    FETCH ( ms:4863 docs:481268)
```

Totals: ms: 6432   keys: 481269   Docs: 481268

MongoDB can use an index to satisfy a not equals condition. If we look at the raw execution plan, we can see how MongoDB uses the index. The indexBounds section shows that we scan the index from the lowest key value through to the required value and then scan again from that value to the maximum key value in the index.

```
mongo> exp.queryPlanner.winningPlan;
{
  "stage": "FETCH",
  "inputStage": {
    "stage": "IXSCAN",
    "keyPattern": {
      "headers.From": 1
    },
    "indexName": "headers.From_1",
    . . .
    "direction": "forward",
    "indexBounds": {
      "headers.From": [
        "[MinKey, \"eric.bass@enron.com\")",
        "(\"eric.bass@enron.com\", MaxKey]"
      ]
    }
  }
}
```

This sort of "not equals" index scan can be effective if the not equals condition matches a small proportion of the collection, but if not, then we might be using the index to retrieve the bulk of the collection. And as we saw earlier, this can be very ineffective. Indeed, for the query we just examine, we would have been better off doing a collection scan:

```
mongo> var exp = db.enron_messages.
...    explain('executionStats').
...    find({'headers.From': {$ne:'eric.bass@enron.com'}}).
...    hint({ $natural: 1 });
```

```
mongo> var exp = exp.next();

mongo> mongoTuning.executionStats(exp);
```

1 **COLLSCAN** (ms:9 docs:481908)

```
Totals:  ms: 377   keys: 0  Docs: 481908
```

Figure 6-7 compares the performance for the not exists index scan and collection scan. Remember, your results will depend on how frequently the not equals value occurs in your collection. However, you may often find that MongoDB chooses an index when a collection scan would have been preferred.

Hint   Beware of index-supported $ne queries. They resolve to multiple index range scans which might be less effective than a collection scan.

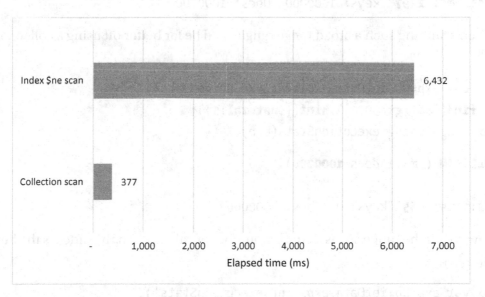

Figure 6-7. *Sometimes a $ne index scan can be much worse than a collection scan*

Range Queries

We saw earlier how a $ne condition is resolved by index range scans. The B-tree index is designed to support such scans, and MongoDB will gladly use such an index scan whenever possible. But again, it might not be the best solution if the range covers the majority of the data in the index.

In the following example, the iotData collection has 1,000,000 documents and the attribute "a" takes a value between 0 and 1000. Even if we construct a range query that will find every document, MongoDB will by default use an index:

```
mongo> var exp=db.iotData.explain('executionStats').
    find({a:{$gt:0}});
mongo> mongoTuning.executionStats(exp);

1   IXSCAN ( a_1 ms:83 keys:1000000)
2   FETCH ( ms:193 docs:1000000)
```

Totals: ms: **2197** keys: 1000000 Docs: 1000000

When scanning such a broad range range, we'd be far better off using a collection scan:

```
mongo> var exp=db.iotData.explain('executionStats').
    find({a:{$gt:990}}).hint({$natural:1});
mongo> mongoTuning.executionStats(exp);

1 COLLSCAN ( ms:1 docs:1000000)
```

Totals: ms: **465** keys: 0 Docs: 1000000

However, if the range spans a smaller number of values, then the index is the best option:

```
mongo> var exp=db.iotData.explain('executionStats').
    find({a:{$gt:990}});
mongo> mongoTuning.executionStats(exp);

1   IXSCAN ( a_1 ms:0 keys:10434)
2   FETCH ( ms:1 docs:10434)
```

Totals: ms: 23 keys: **10434** Docs: 10434

Figure 6-8 illustrates these results. When a range scan covers all or most of the data, then a collection scan will be faster than an index scan. However, for a narrow range of data, the index scan is superior.

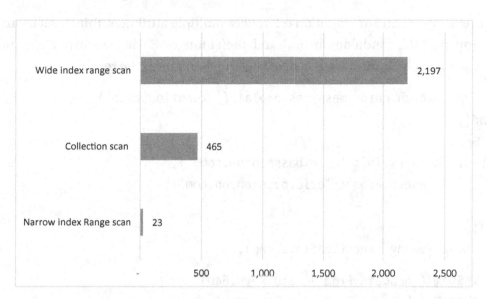

Figure 6-8. *Index range scan performance*

Tip   Only use indexes for relatively narrow range scans of collection data. If the majority of the collection is being accessed, use a collection scan.

$OR or $IN Operations

An $or query against a single indexed attribute will be resolved in the same way as an $in query. So, for instance, these two queries are effectively equivalent:

```
db.enron_messages.
  find({ 'headers.To': { $in: ['ebass@enron.com',
                               'eric.bass@enron.com']
  } });

db.enron_messages.find({
  $or: [
    { 'headers.To': 'ebass@enron.com' },
```

```
          { 'headers.To': 'eric.bass@enron.com' }
    ]
});
```

However, when an $or condition references multiple attributes, things get more interesting. If all the conditions are indexed, then MongoDB will usually perform an index scan on each of the indexes concerned and then merge the results:

```
mongo> var exp=db.enron_messages.explain('executionStats').
    find({
...    $or: [
...        { 'headers.To': 'eric.bass@enron.com' },
...        { 'headers.From': 'eric.bass@enron.com' }
...    ]
... });
mongo> mongoTuning.executionStats(exp);

1      IXSCAN ( headers.From_1 ms:0 keys:640)
2      IXSCAN ( headers.To_1 ms:0 keys:832)
3      OR ( ms:0)
4    FETCH ( ms:0 docs:1472)
5    SUBPLAN ( ms:0)

Totals:  ms: 3  keys: 1472  Docs: 1472
```

MongoDB retrieves data from both of the index scans and then combines them (eliminating duplicates) in the OR stage of the execution plan.

However, this only works if all the attributes are indexed. If we add an unindexed condition to the $or, MongoDB reverts to a collection scan:

```
mongo> var exp=db.enron_messages.explain('executionStats').
    find({
...    $or: [
...        { 'headers.To': 'eric.bass@enron.com' },
...        { 'headers.From': 'eric.bass@enron.com' },
...        {"X-To": "EBASS@ENRON.COM"}
...    ]
... });
```

```
mongo> mongoTuning.executionStats(exp);

1   COLLSCAN ( ms:69 docs:481908)
2   SUBPLAN ( ms:69)

Totals:  ms: 873  keys: 0  Docs: 481908
```

Tip   To fully optimize an $or query, index all the attributes in the $or array.

The $nor operator, which returns documents that satisfy neither of the conditions, will generally not take advantage of indexes.

Array Queries

MongoDB provides rich query operations against array elements, and these are capable of being resolved efficiently through indexes. For instance, the following query looks for emails addressed to Jim Schwieger and Thomas Martin[2]:

```
mongo> var exp = db.enron_messages.explain('executionStats').find({
...     'headers.To': {
...        $eq: ['jim.schwieger@enron.com',
                'thomas.martin@enron.com']
...     }
... });
mongo> mongoTuning.executionStats(exp);

1   IXSCAN ( headers.To_1 ms:0 keys:2130)
2   FETCH ( ms:1 docs:2128)
Totals:  ms: 10  keys: 2130  Docs: 2128
```

The same index can support this query, which finds all emails where Thomas and Jim are recipients, including those with additional recipients:

```
mongo> var exp = db.enron_messages.
...     find({
```

---

[2]This is arguably not a very clever query, since the email addresses would have to occur in exactly the order specified.

```
...        'headers.To': {
...          $all: ['jim.schwieger@enron.com',
             'thomas.martin@enron.com']
...        }
...    }).
...    explain('executionStats');
mongo> mongoTuning.executionStats(exp);

1   IXSCAN ( headers.To_1 ms:0 keys:2128)
2   FETCH ( ms:1 docs:2128)

Totals:   ms: 11   keys: 2128   Docs: 2128
```

The same index can support **$elemMatch** queries. However, the **$size** operator, which finds arrays with a specific number of elements, does not benefit from an index on the array:

```
mongo> var exp = db.enron_messages.
...    explain('executionStats').
...    find({
...        'headers.To': { $size: 1 }});
mongo> mongoTuning.executionStats(exp);

1   COLLSCAN ( ms:788 docs:481908)
```

Note   MongoDB indexes can be used to search for elements of an array.

Regular Expressions

Regular expressions allow us to perform advanced matches on strings. So, for instance, the following query uses a regular expression to find customers with the string "HARRIS" in their LastName:

```
mongo> var exp=db.customers.explain('executionStats').
       find({LastName:/HARRIS/});
mongo>
```

```
mongo> mongoTuning.executionStats(exp);
```

```
1   IXSCAN ( LastName_1 ms:9 keys:410071)
2   FETCH ( ms:12 docs:1365)
```

```
Totals:  ms: 273  keys: 410071  Docs: 1365
```

Although this query is functional, it's not efficient. We actually scanned all 410,000 index entries because the regular expression could theoretically include last names such as "MACHARRISON". If what we are actually trying to do is match only names beginning with HARRIS (such as HARRIS and HARRISON), then we should use the "^" regular expression to indicate that the string is to match the first characters of the target. If we do this, then the index scan is efficient – only 1366 index entries are scanned:

```
mongo> var exp=db.customers.explain('executionStats').
      find({LastName:/^HARRIS/});
mongo>
mongo> mongoTuning.executionStats(exp);
```

```
1   IXSCAN ( LastName_1 ms:0 keys:1366)
2   FETCH ( ms:0 docs:1365)
```

```
Totals:  ms: 3  keys: 1366  Docs: 1365
```

Tip   To perform efficient index-supported regular expression searches, make sure that the regular expression is anchored to the start of the target string with the "^" operator.

Regular expressions are often used to perform case-insensitive searches. For instance, this query searches for the surname "Harris" no matter how it is spelled. The trailing "i" in the regular expression specifies a case-insensitive search:

```
mongo> var e = db.customers.
...    explain('executionStats').
...    find({ LastName: /^Harris$/i }, {});
```

```
mongo> mongoTuning.executionStats(e);
```

```
1   IXSCAN ( LastName_1 ms:4 keys:410071)
2   FETCH ( ms:6 docs:635)

Totals:  ms: 282  keys: 410071  Docs: 635
```

As we explained in Chapter 5, this sort of case-insensitive query can only be efficient if the index involved is case-insensitive – see the section in Chapter 5 on case-insensitive indexes for more details.

Tip   To perform efficient case-insensitive index searches, you must create a case-insensitive index as outlined in Chapter 5.

$exists Queries

Queries that use an $exists operation can take advantage of an index:

```
mongo> var exp=db.customers.explain('executionStats').
      find({updateFlag: {$exists:true}});

mongo> mongoTuning.executionStats(exp);

1   IXSCAN ( updateFlag_1 ms:11 keys:411121)
2   FETCH ( ms:32 docs:411121)

Totals:  ms: 525  keys: 411121  Docs: 411121
```

However, note that this can be a particularly expensive operation since MongoDB will scan through the index to find all entries that contain the key:

```
"indexBounds": {
    "updateFlag": [
      "[MinKey, MaxKey]"
    ]
  }
```

You might be better off seeking a particular value for the column:

```
mongo> var exp=db.customers.explain('executionStats').
```

```
      find({updateFlag:true});
```

```
mongo> mongoTuning.executionStats(exp);
```

```
1   IXSCAN ( updateFlag_1 ms:0 keys:1)
2   FETCH ( ms:0 docs:1)
```

```
Totals:  ms: 0  keys: 1  Docs: 1
```

Alternatively, you could consider creating a sparse index that only indexes documents where the value exists:

```
mongo> db.customers.createIndex({updateFlag:1},{sparse:true});
{
  "createdCollectionAutomatically": false,
  "numIndexesBefore": 1,
  "numIndexesAfter": 2,
  "ok": 1
}
mongo> var exp=db.customers.explain('executionStats').find({
...    updateFlag: {$exists:true}});
mongo>
mongo> mongoTuning.executionStats(exp);
```

```
1   IXSCAN ( updateFlag_1 ms:0 keys:1)
2   FETCH ( ms:0 docs:1)
```

```
Totals:  ms: 0  keys: 1  Docs: 1
```

The disadvantage of the sparse index is that it cannot be used to find documents where the attribute is not present:

```
mongo> var exp=db.customers.explain('executionStats').
      find({updateFlag: {$exists:false}});
mongo> mongoTuning.executionStats(exp);
```

```
1  COLLSCAN ( ms:10 docs:411121)
```

```
Totals:  ms: 295  keys: 0  Docs: 411121
```

> **Tip** An $exists:true lookup can be optimized by a sparse index on the attribute concerned. However, such an index cannot optimize an $exists:false query.

Optimizing Collection Scans

Our emphasis on indexing in MongoDB query tuning tends to skew our thinking – we are at risk of falling into the trap of thinking that the only good way to execute a query is via an index lookup.

Yet, we've seen many examples in this chapter of queries where the index access was less efficient than a collection scan. So if a collection scan is unavoidable, are there options for optimizing these scans?

The answer is yes! If you find that you have an unavoidable collection scan and you need to improve the performance of the scan, then the primary technique is to make the collection smaller.

One way to reduce the collection size is to move large, infrequently accessed elements to another collection. We looked at this *vertical partitioning* technique in Chapter 4.

Sharding a collection can improve the performance of collection scans by allowing multiple clusters to collaborate on the scan. We discuss aspects of sharding performance in Chapter 14.

It's also possible that a collection that is subjected to a lot of updates and deletes has become bloated over time. MongoDB will try to reuse empty space created when documents are deleted or shrink in size, but it won't release space allocated back to disk, and it's possible that your collection is bigger than it needs to be. Generally, WiredTiger reuses space effectively, but in some extreme circumstances, you might consider running the compact command to recover wasted space.

Be aware that the compact command blocks operations on the database containing the collection concerned, so you can only issue a compact command during a downtime window.

Summary

In this chapter, we've looked at how to optimize MongoDB queries involving the `find()` command, which is the workhorse of MongoDB data access.

The best way to avoid data access overhead is to avoid unnecessary data accesses – we discussed how to cache data on the client side to achieve this.

Network overhead can be reduced by using projections, exploiting batch processing, and avoiding unnecessary network round trips in code.

Indexes can be incredibly effective in query optimization but mostly when a subset of collection data is being retrieved. We looked at how hints can be used to force MongoDB to use the index you choose or to perform a collection scan.

Indexes can be used to optimize sort operations, particularly when you are trying to optimize for the first documents in the sort. If you are trying to optimize for the entire set of sorted results, a collection scan might be indicated.

Collection scan performance is ultimately determined by the size of the collection, and we looked at a few strategies for shrinking a collection if a collection scan is unavoidable.

CHAPTER 7

Tuning Aggregation Pipelines

When getting started with MongoDB, most developers will begin with the basic
CRUD operations (Create-Read-Update-Delete) that they are familiar with from other
databases. `insert`, `find`, `update`, and `delete` operations will indeed form the backbone
of most applications. However, in almost all applications, complex data retrieval
and manipulation requirements will exist that exceed what is possible with the basic
MongoDB commands.

The MongoDB `find()` command is versatile and easy to use, but the aggregation
framework allows you to take it to the next level. Aggregation pipelines can do anything
a `find()` operation can do and much more. As MongoDB themselves like to say in blogs,
marketing materials, and even on T-shirts: *aggregate is the new find.*

Aggregation pipelines allow you to simplify your application code by reducing logic
that might otherwise require multiple find operations and complex data manipulation.
When leveraged correctly, a single aggregation can replace many queries and their
associated network round trip times.

As you may recall from earlier chapters, an essential part of tuning your application
is to ensure that as much work as possible takes place on the database. Aggregation
allows you to take data transformation logic that would usually sit on the application
and move it to the database. A properly tuned aggregation pipeline can consequently
massively outperform alternative solutions.

However, with all the added benefits that using aggregations brings, it also creates
a new set of tuning challenges. In this chapter, we will make sure you have all the
knowledge required to leverage and tune aggregation pipelines.

© Guy Harrison, Michael Harrison 2021
G. Harrison and M. Harrison, *MongoDB Performance Tuning*, https://doi.org/10.1007/978-1-4842-6879-7_7

Tuning Aggregation Pipelines

In order to effectively tune aggregation pipelines, we must first be able to effectively identify which aggregations are in need of tuning and what aspects can be improved. As with find() queries, the explain() command is our best friend here. As you may recall from earlier chapters, to examine the execution plan of a query, we add the .explain() method after the collection name. For example, to explain a find(), we might use the following command:

```
db.customers.
  explain().
  find(
    { Country: 'Japan', LastName: 'Smith' },
    { _id: 0, FirstName: 1, LastName: 1 }
  ).
  sort({ FirstName: -1 }).
  limit(3);
```

We can explain an aggregation pipeline in the same way:

```
db.customers.explain().aggregate([
  { $match: {
      Country: 'Japan',
      LastName: 'Smith',
  } },
  { $project: {
      _id: 0,
      FirstName: 1,
      LastName: 1,
  } },
  { $sort: {
      FirstName: -1,
  } },
  { $limit: 3 } ] );
```

However, there are significant differences between the execution plan from a find() command and one from an aggregate().

When running the explain() against a standard find command, we can see information about the execution by looking at the queryPlanner.winningPlan object.

The explain() output for an aggregation pipeline is similar but also critically different. Firstly, the queryPlanner object we are previously used to now resides within a new object, which resides within an array called stages. The stages array contains each of the aggregation stages as individual objects. For example, the aggregation we looked at earlier would have the following simplified explain output:

```
{
  "stages": [
    {"$cursor": {
        "queryPlanner": {
          // . . .
          "winningPlan": {
            "stage": "PROJECTION_SIMPLE",
            //        . . .
            "inputStage": {
              "stage": "FETCH",
              //     . . .
              "inputStage": {
                "stage": "IXSCAN",
                . . .
              } } },
          "rejectedPlans": []
        } } },
    { "$sort": {
        "sortKey": {
          "FirstName": -1
        },
        "limit": 3
      } } ],
  . . .
}
```

Inside the execution plan for an aggregation pipeline, the queryPlanner stage reveals the initial data access operations required to bring data into the pipeline. This will usually represent the operation that supports an initial $match operation or – if there is no $match condition specified – a collection scan to retrieve all data from the collection.

The stages array shows information about each subsequent step in the aggregation pipeline. Note that MongoDB can merge and reorder aggregation stages during execution so these stages might not match the stages you have in your raw pipeline definition – more on this in the next section.

We've written a helper script to simplify the interpretation of aggregation execution plans within our tuning script package.[1] The method mongoTuning. aggregationExecutionStats() will provide a top-level summary of the time taken by each step. Here's an example of using aggregationExecutionSteps:

```
mongo> var exp = db.customers.explain('executionStats').aggregate([
...    { $match:{
...          "Country":{ $eq:"Japan" }}
...    },
...    { $group:{ _id:{ "City":"$City"  },
...               "count":{$sum:1} }
...    },
...    { $sort:{  "_id.City":-1 }},
...    { $limit:  10 },
... ] );

mongo>  mongoTuning.aggregationExecutionStats(exp);

1  IXSCAN ( Country_1_LastName_1 ms:0 keys:21368 nReturned:21368)
2  FETCH ( ms:13 docsExamined:21368 nReturned:21368)
3  PROJECTION_SIMPLE ( ms:15 nReturned:21368)
4  $GROUP ( ms:70 returned:31)
5  $SORT ( ms:70 returned:10)

Totals:  ms: 72  keys: 21368  Docs: 21368
```

---

[1]See the introduction for information on how to use the tuning package.

Optimizing Aggregation Ordering

An aggregation is constructed from a series of stages, represented by an array of documents which are executed in order from first to last. The output from each stage is passed to the next stage for processing, with the initial input being an entire collection.

The sequential nature of these stages is the reason aggregations are referred to as pipelines: data flows through the pipes, being filtered and transformed at each stage until finally exiting the pipeline as a result. The easiest way to optimize these pipelines is to reduce the amount of data as early as possible; this will reduce the amount of work done by each successive step. It logically follows that the stages in your aggregation that will perform the most work should operate on as little data as possible, with as much filtering as possible being performed in earlier stages.

Tip   When constructed aggregation pipelines, filter early and filter often! The earlier data is removed from a pipeline, the lower the overall data processing load for MongoDB.

MongoDB will automatically resequence the order of operations in a pipeline to optimize performance – we'll see an example of some optimizations in the next section. However, for complex pipelines, you may need to set the order yourself.

One such case where automatic reordering is not possible is aggregations using $lookup. The $lookup stage allows you to join two collections. If you're joining two collections, you may have a choice between filtering before or after the join, and in this case, it is very important to try and reduce the size of the data *before* the join operation, because for each document that is passed into a lookup operation, MongoDB must attempt to find a matching document in a separate collection. Every document we can filter out before the lookout will reduce the number of lookups that need to occur. It's an obvious but critical optimization.

Let's look at an example aggregation which generates a "top 5" list of product purchases:

```
db.lineitems.aggregate([
  { $group:{ _id:{ "orderId":"$orderId" ,"prodId":"$prodId"  },
             "itemCount-sum":{$sum:"$itemCount"} } },
  { $lookup:
```

```
      { from:           "orders",  localField:"_id.orderId",
        foreignField: "_id",                 as:"orders"
      } },
  { $lookup:
      { from:           "customers", localField:"orders.customerId",
        foreignField: "_id",                   as:"customers"
      } },
  { $lookup:
      { from:           "products",  localField:"_id.prodId",
        foreignField: "_id",                 as:"products"
      } },
  { $sort:{  "count":-1 }},
  { $limit:  5 },
],{allowDiskUse: true});
```

This is quite a big aggregation pipeline. In fact, without the `allowDiskUse:true` flag, it will generate an out of memory error; we will cover why this error occurs later in the chapter.

Note that we join `orders`, `customers`, and `products` *before* we sort the results and limit the output. As a result, we have to perform all three join lookups for each lineItem. We could – and should – position the $sort and $limit directly after the $group operation:

```
db.lineitems.aggregate([
  { $group:{ _id:{ "orderId":"$orderId" ,"prodId":"$prodId"  },
           "itemCount-sum":{$sum:"$itemCount"} } },
  { $sort:{  "count":-1 }},
  { $limit:  5 },
  { $lookup:
      { from:           "orders",  localField:"_id.orderId",
        foreignField: "_id",                 as:"orders"
      } },
  { $lookup:
      { from:           "customers", localField:"orders.customerId",
        foreignField: "_id",                   as:"customers"
      } },
  { $lookup:
```

```
    { from:          "products",  localField:"_id.prodId",
      foreignField: "_id",                    as:"products"
    } }
],{allowDiskUse: true});
```

The difference in performance is striking. By moving the $sort and $limit a few lines earlier, we have created a much more efficient and scalable solution. Figure 7-1 illustrates the performance improvement obtained by moving $limit earlier in the pipeline.

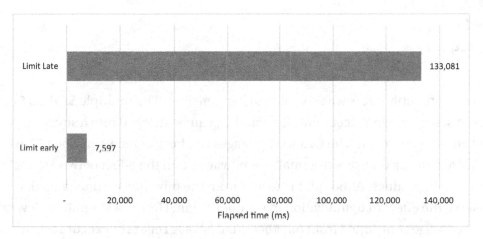

Figure 7-1. *Effect of moving limit clause earlier in a $lookup pipeline*

Tip   Take care to sequence aggregation pipelines to eliminate documents earlier rather than later. The earlier data is eliminated from a pipeline, the less work will be required in later pipelines.

Automatic Pipeline Optimizations

MongoDB will perform some optimizations on aggregation pipelines to improve performance. The exact optimizations change from release to release, and when running an aggregation through a driver or the MongoDB shell, there is no obvious sign that optimization has occurred. In fact, the only way for you to be certain is to check the query plan using explain(). If you are surprised to see that your aggregation explain does not match what you just sent to MongoDB, do not be alarmed. That's the optimizer doing its job.

Let's run a few aggregations and observe how MongoDB decides to improve the pipeline using explain(). Here is a very badly constructed aggregation pipeline:

```
> var explain = db.listingsAndReviews.explain("executionStats").
  aggregate([
    {$match: {"property_type" : "House"}},
    {$match: {"bedrooms" : 3}},
    {$limit: 100},
    {$limit: 5},
    {$skip: 3},
    {$skip: 2}
]);
```

You can probably guess what is going to happen here. The multiple $match, $limit, and $skip stages, when placed one after another, can be merged into a single stage without altering the result. The two $match stages can be merged using $and. The result of two $limit stages is always the smaller limit value, and the effect of two $skips is the sum of $skip values. Although the results from the pipeline are unchanged, we can observe the effect of optimization in the query plan. Here is a simplified view of our merged stages outputted from our mongoTuning.aggregationExecutionStats command:

```
1  COLLSCAN ( ms:0 docsExamined:525 nReturned:5)
2  LIMIT ( ms:0 nReturned:5)
3  $SKIP ( ms:0 returned:0)

Totals:  ms: 1  keys: 0  Docs: 525
```

As you can see, MongoDB has merged the six steps from our pipeline into just three operations.

There are a few other smart merges that MongoDB can perform on your behalf. If you have a $lookup stage where you immediately $unwind the joined documents, MongoDB will merge the $unwind into the $lookup. For example, this aggregation joins a user with their blog comments:

```
> var explain = db.users.explain("executionStats").aggregate([
  { $lookup: {
      from: "comments",
```

```
    as: "comments",
    localField: "email",
    foreignField: "email"
}},
{ $unwind: "$comments"}
]);
```

The $lookup and $unwind will become a single stage in the execution, which will eliminate the creation of large joined documents that will immediately be unwound into smaller documents. The execution plan will look like the following snippet:

```
> mongoTuning.aggregationExecutionStats(explain);


1  COLLSCAN ( ms:9 docsExamined:183 nReturned:183)
2  $LOOKUP ( ms:4470 returned:50146)

Totals:  ms: 4479  keys: 0  Docs: 183
```

Similarly, $sort and $limit stages will be merged, allowing the $sort to only maintain the limited number of documents instead of its entire input. Here is an example of such an optimization. The query

```
> var explain = db.users.explain("executionStats").
 aggregate([
   { $sort: {year: -1}},
   { $limit: 1}
 ]);
> mongoTuning.aggregationExecutionStats(explain);
```

will result in a single stage in the explain output:

```
1  COLLSCAN ( ms:0 docsExamined:183 nReturned:183)
2  SORT ( ms:0 nReturned:1)

Totals:  ms: 0  keys: 0  Docs: 183
```

There is another important optimization that does not involve merging or moving stages in your pipeline. If your aggregation only requires a subset of document attributes, MongoDB may add a projection to remove all unused fields. This reduces the size of the datasets passing through the pipeline. For example, the following aggregation only actually uses two fields – Country and City:

```
mongo> var exp = db.customers.
...    explain('executionStats').
...    aggregate([
...       { $match: { Country: 'Japan' } },
...       { $group: { _id: { City: '$City' } } }
...    ]);
```

MongoDB inserts a projection into the execution plan to eliminate all unneeded attributes:

```
mongo> mongoTuning.aggregationExecutionStats(exp);

1  IXSCAN ( Country_1_LastName_1 ms:4 keys:21368 nReturned:21368)
2  FETCH ( ms:12 docsExamined:21368 nReturned:21368)
3  PROJECTION_SIMPLE ( ms:12 nReturned:21368)
4  $GROUP ( ms:61 returned:31)

Totals:   ms: 68   keys: 21368   Docs: 21368
```

So, we now know MongoDB will effectively add and merge stages to improve your pipeline. There are also some cases where the optimizer will reorder your stages. The most important of these is reordering of $match operations.

If a pipeline contains a $match after a stage that will project new fields into the document (such as $group, $project, $unset, $addFields, or $set) and if the $match stage does not require the projected fields, MongoDB will move that $match stage earlier in the pipeline. This reduces the number of documents that must be processed in later stages.

For instance, consider this aggregation:

```
var exp=db.customers.explain("executionStats").aggregate([
  { '$group': {
      '_id': '$Country',
```

```
      'numCustomers': {
        '$sum': 1
     } } },
  { '$match': {
     '$or': [
        { '_id': 'Netherlands' },
        { '_id': 'Sudan' },
        { '_id': 'Argentina' } ] } }
]);
```

Prior to MongoDB 4.0, MongoDB would perform the exact steps specified in the pipeline – perform a `$group` operation, and then use `$match` to eliminate countries other than those specified. This is wasteful, especially since we have an index on Country which could be used to rapidly find the documents required.

However, in modern versions of MongoDB, the `$match` operation will be relocated prior to the `$group` operation, reducing the number of documents that need to be grouped and allowing the index to be used. Here is the resulting execution plan:

```
mongo> mongoTuning.aggregationExecutionStats(exp);

1   IXSCAN ( Country_1_LastName_1 ms:1 keys:13720 nReturned:13717)
2   PROJECTION_COVERED ( ms:1 nReturned:13717)
3   SUBPLAN ( ms:1 nReturned:13717)
4   $GROUP ( ms:20 returned:3)
```

The MongoDB automatic optimizations are one of the unsung heroes of recent MongoDB releases, improving performance without requiring any work on your part. Understanding how these optimizations work should empower you to make good decisions when creating your aggregations as well as understand anomalies in the execution plans

For more information on exactly what will occur in the optimization for any given MongoDB release, refer to the official documentation at http://bit.ly/ MongoAggregatePerf.

Optimizing Multi-collection Joins

One of the really significant capabilities provided only by the aggregation framework is the ability to merge data from multiple collections. The most significant and mature capability is found in the $lookup operator, which allows a join between two collections.

In Chapter 4, we experimented with some alternative schema designs, some of which would frequently require joins to assemble information. For instance, we created a schema in which customers and orders were held in separate collections. In this case, we'd use $lookup to join the customer data and order data like this:

```
db.customers.aggregate([
  { $lookup:
    { from:          "orders",
      localField:    "_id",
      foreignField:  "customerId",
      as:            "orders"
    }
  },
]);
```

This statement embeds an array of orders within each customer document. The _id attribute in the customer document is matched to the customerId attribute in the orders collection.

It's not too challenging to construct a join using $lookup, but there are some definite potential issues concerning join performance. Because the $lookup function is executed once for each document in the source data, it's essential that the $lookup be quick. In practice, this means that the $lookup should be supported by an index. In the preceding case, we would need to be sure that there is an index on the customerId attribute within the orders collection.

Unfortunately, the explain() command doesn't help us to determine if the join is efficient or that an index has been used. For instance, here is the explain output (using mongoTuning.aggregationExecutionStats) from the preceding operation:

```
1  COLLSCAN ( ms:10 docsExamined:411121 nReturned:411121)
2  $LOOKUP ( ms:5475 returned:411121)
```

The explain output tells us that we used a collection scan to perform the initial retrieval of customers, but doesn't show us if we used an index within the $lookup stage.

However, if you don't have a supporting index, you will almost certainly notice the performance degradation that results. Figure 7-2 shows how performance degrades as more and more documents are involved in a join. With an index, join performance is efficient and predictable. Without an index, join performance degrades steeply as more documents are added to the join.

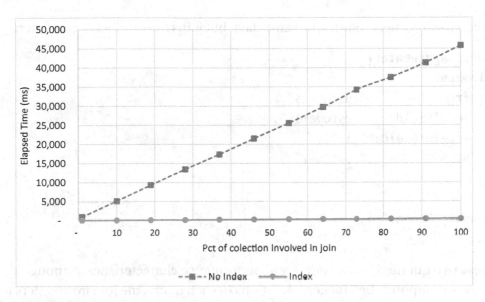

Figure 7-2. $lookup performance – indexed vs. non-indexed

Tip   Always create an index on the `foreignField` attributes in a `$lookup`, unless the collections are of trivial size.

Join Order

When joining collections, we sometimes have a choice of the order in which we join. For instance, this query joins *from* customers *to* orders:

```
db.customers.aggregate([
  { $lookup:
    { from:         "orders",
      localField:   "_id",
      foreignField: "customerId",
```

```
            as:                "orders"
        }
    },
    { $unwind:   "$orders" },
    { $count: "count" },
]);
```

The following query returns the same data, but joins *from* orders *to* customers:

```
db.orders.aggregate([
    { $lookup:
        { from:            "customers",
          localField:    "customerId",
          foreignField: "_id",
          as:             "customer"
        }
    },
    { $count: "count" },
] );
```

These two queries have very different performance characteristics. Although there are indexes to support the $lookup operations in each query, the join from orders to customers results in far more $lookup calls – simply because there are more orders than customers. Consequently, joining from orders to customers takes much longer than the reverse. Figure 7-3 shows the relative performance.

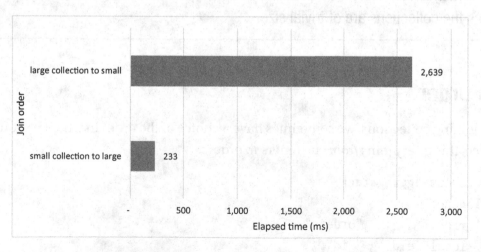

Figure 7-3. *Join order and $lookup performance*

When deciding upon the join order, follow these guidelines:

1. You should try to reduce the amount of data to be joined as much as possible before the join. So if one of the collections is to be filtered, that collection should come first in the join order.

2. If you only have an index to support one of the two join orders, then you should use the join order that has the supporting index.

3. If the preceding two criteria are met for both join orders, then you should try to join from the smallest collection to the largest collection.

Tip   When all else is equal, join from a small collection to a large collection, rather than from a large collection to a smaller one.

Optimizing Graph Lookups

Graph databases such as Neo4J specialize in traversing graphs of relationships – such as those you might find in a social network. Many non-graph databases have been incorporating Graph Compute Engines to perform similar tasks. Using older versions of MongoDB, you may have been forced to fetch large amounts of graph data across the network and run some computation on the application level. The process would have been slow and cumbersome. Luckily for us, since MongoDB 3.4, we can perform simple graph traversal using the $graphLookup aggregation framework stage.

Imagine you have data stored in MongoDB that represents a social network. In this network, a single user is connected to a large number of other users as friends. These sorts of networks are a common use of graph database. Let's run through an example using the following sample data:

```
db.getSiblingDB("GraphTest").socialGraph.findOne();
{
    "_id" : ObjectId("5a739cda0c31c5f5afcff87f"),
    "person" : 561596,
    "name" : "User# 561596",
    "friends" : [
```

```
            94230,
            224410,
            387968,
            406744,
            707890,
            965522,
            1189677,
            1208173
        ]
}
```

Using an aggregation pipeline with the $graphLookup stage, we can expand our social network for an individual user. Here's an example pipeline:

```
db.socialGraph.aggregate([
  {$match:{person:1476767}},
  {$graphLookup: {
      from: "socialGraph",
      startWith: [1476767],
      connectFromField: "friends",
      connectToField: "person",
      maxDepth: 2,
      depthField: "Depth",
      as: "GraphOutput"
  }
  },{$unwind:"$GraphOutput"}
], {allowDiskUse: true});
```

What we are doing here is starting with person 1476767 and then following the elements of the friends array out to two levels, essentially finding "friends of friends."

Increasing the value of the maxDepth field exponentially increases the amount of data we must cope with. You can think of each level of depth as requiring a sort of self-join into the collection. For each document in the initial dataset, we read the collection to find a friend; then for each document in that dataset, read the collection to find those friends; and so on. We stop once we have hit maxDepth connections.

It's clear that if each self-join requires a collection scan, the performance is going to degrade rapidly as we increase the depth of the network. Consequently, it is important to ensure there is an index available for MongoDB to use while traversing the connections. That index should be on the `connectToField` attribute.

Figure 7-4 illustrates the performance of a `$graphLookup` operation with and without an index. Without an index, performance degrades rapidly as we increase the depth of the operation. With an index, the graph lookup is far more scalable and efficient.

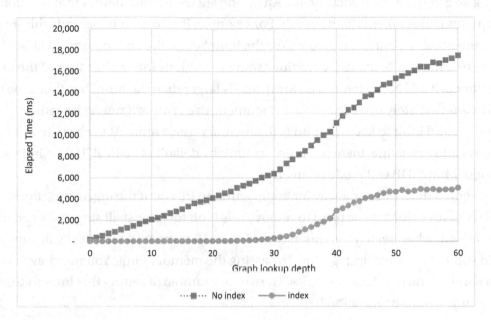

Figure 7-4. *$graphLookup performance with or without indexing*

Tip   When performing `$graphLookup` operations, ensure you have an index on the `connectToField` attribute.

Aggregation Memory Utilization

When performing aggregations in MongoDB, there are two important limits to remember that apply to all aggregations regardless of what stages the pipeline is constructed from. Alongside these are some specific limitations that will need to be considered when tuning your application. The two limits that you will always have to keep in mind are the document size limit and the memory usage limit.

In MongoDB, the size limit for a single document is 16MB. This is true for aggregations as well. When performing aggregations, if any of the output documents can exceed this limit, then an error will be thrown. This may not be a problem when performing simple aggregations. However, when grouping, manipulating, unwinding, and joining documents across multiple collections, you will have to consider the growing size of the output documents. An important distinction here is that this limit only applies to documents in the result. For example, if a document exceeds this limit during the pipeline, but is reduced below the limit before the end, no error will be thrown. In addition, MongoDB combines some operations internally to avoid the limit. For instance, if a $lookup returns an array that is larger than the limit, but that $lookup is followed immediately by an $unwind, a document size error will not be issued.

The second limit to keep in mind is the memory usage limit. At each stage in the aggregation pipeline, there is a memory limit by default of 100MB. If this limit is exceeded, MongoDB will produce an error.

MongoDB does provide a way for getting around this limit during aggregations. The allowDiskUse option can be used to remove this limit for almost all stages. As you may have guessed, when set to true, this allows MongoDB to create a temporary file on disk to hold some data while aggregating, bypassing the memory limit. You may have noticed this in some of the previous examples. Here is an example of setting this limit to true in one of our previous aggregations:

```
db.customers.aggregate([
  { '$group': {
      '_id': '$Country',
      'numCustomers': {
        '$sum': 1
      } } },
  { '$match': {
      '$or': [
        { '_id': 'Netherlands' },
        { '_id': 'Sudan' },
        { '_id': 'Argentina' } ] } }
],{allowDiskUse:true});
```

As we said, the `allowDiskUse` option will bypass the limit for *almost* all stages. Unfortunately, there are still a few stages that are limited to 100MB even with `allowDiskUse` set to true. The two accumulators `$addToSet` and `$push` will not spill to disk, because these accumulators could add huge amounts of data into the next stage if not properly optimized.

There is currently no obvious work around for these three limited stages, meaning you will have to optimize the query and pipeline itself to ensure you do not run into this limit and receive an error from MongoDB.

To avoid hitting these memory limits, you should think about how much data you actually need to fetch. Ask yourself if you're using all the fields being returned from the query, and could the data be represented more succinctly? Removing unnecessary attributes from intermediary documents is an easy and powerful way to reduce memory use.

If all else fails or if you want to avoid the performance drag when data spills to disk, you could try increasing the internal memory limits for these operations. These memory limits are controlled by undocumented parameters of the form "`internal*Bytes`". The three most important of these are

- `internalQueryMaxBlockingSortMemoryUsageBytes`: The maximum memory available to a `$sort` (see the next section for more details)

- `internalLookupStageIntermediateDocumentMaxSizeBytes`: The maximum memory available to a `$lookup` operation

- `internalDocumentSourceGroupMaxMemoryBytes`: The maximum memory available to a `$group` operation

You can adjust these parameters using the `setParameter` command. For instance, to increase sort memory, you could issue this command:

```
db.getSiblingDB("admin").
  runCommand({ setParameter: 1,
  internalQueryMaxBlockingSortMemoryUsageBytes: 1048576000 });
```

We'll discuss this further in the next section in the context of sort optimization. Be very careful when adjusting memory limits, however, since you might hurt the overall performance of your MongoDB cluster if you exceed the memory capacity of its server.

Sorting in Aggregation Pipelines

We looked at optimizing sorting within find() operations in Chapter 6. Sorts in aggregation pipelines differ from sorts in a couple of significant ways:

1.   An aggregation can exceed the memory limit for a blocking sort by performing a "disk sort." In a disk sort, excess data is written to and from disk during the sort operation.

2.   Aggregations might not be able to take advantage of indexed sorting options unless the sort is very early in the pipeline.

Indexed Aggregation Sorts

Similarly to find(), aggregations are able to use an index to resolve a sort and thus avoid high memory utilization or a disk sort. However, this usually can only occur if the $sort occurs early enough the pipeline to be rolled into the initial data access operation.

For instance, consider this operation in which we sort some data and add a field:

```
mongo> var exp=db.baseCollection.explain('executionStats').
...      aggregate([
...          { $sort:{  d:1 }},
...          {$addFields:{x:0}}
...      ],{allowDiskUse: true});
mongo> mongoTuning.aggregationExecutionStats(exp);

1  IXSCAN ( d_1 ms:97 keys:1000000 nReturned:1000000)
2  FETCH ( ms:500 docsExamined:1000000 nReturned:1000000)
3  $ADDFIELDS ( ms:3316 returned:1000000)

Totals:  ms: 3358  keys: 1000000  Docs: 1000000
```

There is an index on the sorted attribute, and we are able to use that index to optimize the sort. However, if we move the $addFields operation before the sort, then the aggregation is unable to utilize the index, and a costly "disk sort" occurs:

```
mongo> var exp=db.baseCollection.explain('executionStats').
...      aggregate([
...          {$addFields:{x:0}},
```

```
...          { $sort:{   d:1 }},
... ],{allowDiskUse: true});

mongo> mongoTuning.aggregationExecutionStats(exp);

1  COLLSCAN ( ms:16 docsExamined:1000000 nReturned:1000000)
2  $ADDFIELDS ( ms:1164 returned:1000000)
3  $SORT ( ms:12125 returned:1000000)

Totals:  ms: 12498  keys: 0  Docs: 1000000
```

Figure 7-5 compares the performance of the two aggregations. By moving the sort to the start of the aggregation pipeline, a costly disk sort was avoided and elapsed time was significantly reduced.

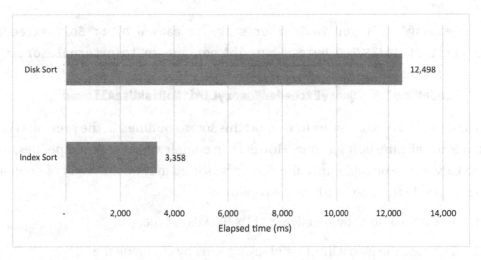

Figure 7-5. *Disk sort vs. indexed sort in an aggregation pipeline*

Tip   Move sorts that have a supporting index as early in the aggregation pipeline as possible to avoid an expensive disk sort.

Disk Sorts

If there is no index supporting a sort and the sort exceeds the 100MB limit, then you will receive a QueryExceededMemoryLimitNoDiskUseAllowed error:

```
mongo>var exp=db.baseCollection.
...       aggregate([
...          { $sort:{  d:1 }},
...          {$addFields:{x:0}}
...       ],{allowDiskUse: false});

2020-08-22T15:36:01.890+1000 E  QUERY    [js] uncaught exception: Error:
command failed: {
        "operationTime" : Timestamp(1598074560, 3),
        "ok" : 0,
        "errmsg" : "Error in $cursor stage :: caused by :: Sort exceeded
memory limit of 104857600 bytes, but did not opt in to external sorting.",
        "code" : 292,
        "codeName" : "QueryExceededMemoryLimitNoDiskUseAllowed",
```

If it's possible to use an index to support this sort as outlined in the previous section, then that is usually the best solution. However, in complex aggregation pipelines, this won't always be possible since the data to be sorted may be the result of previous pipeline stages. In this case, we have two options:

1. Use a "disk sort" by specifying allowDiskUse:true.

2. Increase the global limit for blocking sorts by changing the internalQueryMaxBlockingSortMemoryUsageBytes parameter.

Changing MongoDB default memory parameters should only be undertaken with extreme care, since there is a risk of causing memory starvation on the server, which could make global performance worse. However, 100MB is not a lot of memory in today's world, and so increasing the parameter may be the best option. Here, we increase the maximum sort memory to 1GB:

```
mongo>db.getSiblingDB("admin").
...       runCommand({ setParameter: 1,
internalQueryMaxBlockingSortMemoryUsageBytes: 1048576000 });
```

```
{
        "was" : 104857600,
        "ok" : 1,
...
```

Figure 7-6 shows how performance is improved for the example query when we increased `internalQueryMaxBlockingSortMemoryUsageBytes` to avoid a disk sort.

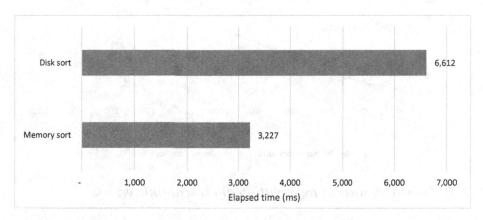

Figure 7-6. *Disk sort vs. memory sort in aggregation*

Another thing to think about with disk sorts is scalability. If you set `diskUsage:true`, then you can rest assured that your query will run even if there is not enough memory to complete the sort. However, when the query switches from memory sort to disk sort, performance will suddenly degrade. In a production context, it might seem like your application suddenly "hits a wall."

Figure 7-7 shows how the switch to a disk sort results in a sudden jump in execution time, compared with the relatively linear trend when there is sufficient memory to support the sort.

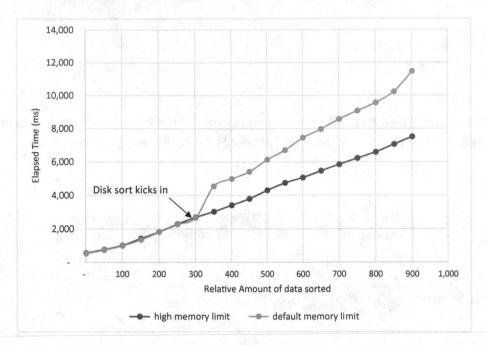

Figure 7-7. *How disk sorts in aggregation affect scalability*

Tip   Disk sorts in aggregation pipelines are expensive and slow. You may wish to increase the default memory limit for aggregation sorting if you want to improve the performance of large aggregation sorts.

Optimizing Views

If you have worked with SQL databases before, you are probably familiar with the concept of *views*. In MongoDB, a view is a sort of synthetic collection that contains the results of an aggregation pipeline. From a query perspective, views look and feel just like a normal collection, except that they are read-only.

The main advantage of creating a view is to simplify and unify application logic by storing complex pipeline definitions in the database.

When it comes to performance, it is important to understand that when a view is created, the result is not stored in memory or copied into a new collection. When you query a view, you are still querying the original collection. MongoDB will take the aggregation pipeline defined for the view and then append your additional query parameters, creating a new pipeline. This gives the appearance of querying the view, but under the hood, a complex aggregation pipeline is still being issued.

Consequently creating a view will not give you a performance advantage when compared to executing the pipeline that defines the view.

Because a view is essentially just an aggregation against a collection, our methods for optimizing a view are the same as for any aggregation. If your view is performing poorly, optimize the pipeline that defines the view using the techniques described earlier in this chapter.

When writing queries against a view, bear in mind that indexes on the underlying collection cannot generally be exploited when executing queries against the view. For instance, consider this view which aggregates product codes by order count:

```
db.createView('productTotals', 'lineitems', [
  { $group: {
      _id: { prodId: '$prodId' },
      'itemCount-sum': { $sum: '$itemCount' }
    }
  },
  { $project: {
      ProdId: '$_id.prodId',
      OrderCount: '$itemCount-sum',
      _id: 0
    }
  }]);
```

We can use this view to find totals for a particular product code:

```
mongo> db.productTotals.find({ ProdId: 83 });
{
  "ProdId": 83,
  "OrderCount": 460051
}
```

However, even if there were an index on `prodId` within the `lineItems` collection, the index will not be used when querying from the view. Even though we are only asking for a single product code, MongoDB will aggregate data from all products before returning results.

Although it's far more tedious, this aggregation pipeline will use an index on `ProdId` and consequently will return data much faster:

```
db.lineitems.aggregate(
  [ {  $match: { prodId: 83 }},
    {  $group: {
        _id: { prodId: '$prodId' },
        'itemCount-sum': { $sum: '$itemCount' }  }
    },
    { $project: {
        ProdId: '$_id.prodId',
        OrderCount: '$itemCount-sum',
        _id: 0
      }
    }
  ] );
```

Tip   Views can't always take advantage of indexes on the underlying collection when resolving queries. If you are querying from a view for attributes that are indexed in the underlying collection, you might get better performance from bypassing the view and querying the underlying collection directly.

Materialized Views

As we have discussed, MongoDB views do not improve query performance and, in some cases, might actually hurt performance by suppressing indexes. Even if the view only contains a few documents, it can still take a long time to query because the data needs to be reconstructed every time the view is queried.

Materialized views offer a solution here – especially when a view returns small amounts of aggregated information from large source collections. A materialized view is a collection that contains the documents that would be returned by a view definition, but stores the view results in the database so that the view doesn't have to be executed every time you read the data.

In MongoDB, we can use the $merge or $out aggregation operator to create a materialized view. $out completely replaces a target collection with the results of an aggregation. $merge provides a sort of "upsert" into an existing collection, allowing for incremental changes to the target. We'll look a bit more at $merge in Chapter 8.

To create a materialized view, we simply run an aggregation pipeline that might usually be used to define a view, but, as the final step of that aggregation, we use $merge to output the resulting documents into a collection. By running this aggregation pipeline, we can create a new collection that reflects an aggregation of the data in another collection at the time of execution. Unlike a view, however, this collection may be much smaller, allowing for improved performance.

Let's look at an example of this. Here's a complex pipeline that creates a summary of sales by product and city:

```
db.customers.aggregate([
  { $lookup:
    { from:         "orders",
      localField:   "_id",
      foreignField: "customerId",
      as:           "orders"  } },
  { $unwind:  "$orders" },
  { $lookup:
    { from:         "lineitems",
      localField:   "orders._id",
      foreignField: "orderId",
      as:           "lineItems"  } },
  { $unwind:  "$lineItems" },
  { $group:{ _id:{ "City":"$City" ,
                   "lineItems_prodId":"$lineItems.prodId"  },
            "count":{$sum:1},
            "lineItems_itemCount-sum":{$sum:"$lineItems.itemCount"} } },
  { $project: {
        "CityName": "$_id.City"  ,
```

```
        "ProductId": "$_id.lineItems_prodId"  ,
        "OrderCount": "$lineItems_itemCount-sum"  ,
        "_id": 0
    } } ] );
```

If we add the following $merge operation to that pipeline, then we'll create a collection salesByCityMV that contains the outputs of the aggregation:[2]

{$merge:
```
    {        into:"salesByCityMV"}}
```

Figure 7-8 shows the execution time for querying from the materialized view as compared to querying from a normal view. As you can see, the performance of the materialized view is far superior. This is because the bulk of the work has already been completed by the time the final find query was sent.

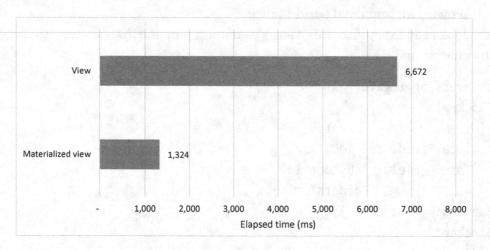

Figure 7-8. *Materialized view vs. direct view*

There is one obvious weakness to this method: the materialized view becomes out of date the second data changes in the original collection. It becomes the responsibility of the application or database administrator to ensure the materialized view is refreshed at intervals that make sense. For example, a materialized view might contain access sales records for the previous day. The aggregation could be run at midnight each night, ensuring that the data was correct for each new day.

---

[2]Merge has a lot of extra options for dealing with existing data that we'll discuss in Chapter 8.

Tip   For complex aggregations where speed of the query is more important that absolute point in time accuracy, a materialized view offers a powerful way to provide quick access to aggregation output.

When creating materialized views, ensure that the refresh of the view is not going to be run more often than the queries on that view. The database still has to use resources to create the view, so there is little reason to refresh a materialized view each hour that may only be queried once a day.

If the source table is updated infrequently, you could arrange for the refresh of the materialized view to occur automatically whenever an update is detected. The MongoDB *Change Stream* facility allows you to listen for changes in a collection. When the change notification is received, you could trigger the rebuild of the materialized view.

We'll look at some more uses of the $merge operator in Chapter 8.

Summary

MongoDB created an incredibly powerful method to construct complex queries with the aggregation framework. Over the years, they have expanded this framework to support a wider range of use cases and even to take responsibility for some data transformation that may have previously occurred on the application level. If the past is any indication, the aggregate command will grow over time to accommodate more and more complex functionality. With all this in mind, if you wish to create an advanced and performant MongoDB application, you should be leveraging everything that aggregate has to offer.

But with the great power of aggregation pipelines comes the great responsibility to ensure that the pipelines are optimized. In this chapter, we have outlined some of the key performance concerns you will want to keep in mind as you create your aggregations.

Filtering and stage order will allow you to minimize data flowing through your pipeline. Indexing relevant fields for $lookup and $graphLookup will ensure quick retrieval of the relevant documents. You will also need to ensure you use the allowDiskUse option when fetching large results to avoid hitting memory limits or alter those memory limits to avoid expensive "disk sorts."

In the next chapter, we will cover the C, U, and D of CRUD – Create, Update, and Delete – and consider the optimization of data manipulation statements such as insert, update, and delete.

CHAPTER 8

Inserts, Updates, and Deletes

In this chapter, we look at issues relating to the performance of *data manipulation*
statements. These statements (insert, update, and delete) alter the information
contained within your MongoDB database.

Even in transaction processing environments, most database activity is related
to data retrieval. You have to find data in order to change or delete it, and even insert
operations often involve queries to obtain lookup keys or to embed data held in other
collections. For this reason, the majority of your tuning efforts typically involve query
optimization.

Nevertheless, there are some data manipulation–specific optimizations available in
MongoDB, and we will cover them in this chapter.

Fundamentals

The overhead of all data manipulation statements is directly affected by the following
factors:

- The efficiency of any filter conditions clause included in the
  statement

- The amount of index maintenance that has to be performed as a
  result of the statement

© Guy Harrison, Michael Harrison 2021
G. Harrison and M. Harrison, *MongoDB Performance Tuning*, https://doi.org/10.1007/978-1-4842-6879-7_8

Filter Optimizations

A lot of the overhead involved in modifying and removing documents is incurred locating the documents to be processed. Delete and update statements usually contain a filter clause which identifies the documents to be deleted or updated. The obvious first step in optimizing the performance of these statements is to optimize these filter clauses, using the principles discussed in previous chapters. In particular, consider creating indexes on attributes contained in the filter condition.

Tip   If an update or delete statement contains a filter condition, ensure that the filter condition is optimized using the principles outlined in Chapter 6.

Explaining a Data Manipulation Statement

It's perfectly possible and definitely desirable to use explain() on data manipulation statements. For delete and update commands, explain() will reveal how MongoDB will find the documents to be processed. For instance, here we see an update that will use a collection scan to find the rows to process:

```
mongo> var exp=db.customers.explain().
            update({viewCount:{$gt:50}},
                    {$set:{discount:10}},{multi:true});
mongo> mongoTuning.quickExplain(exp);
```

```
1   COLLSCAN
2   UPDATE
```

You can also safely use the executionStats mode of explain(). Although executionStats does execute the statement concerned and will report on the number of documents that would be modified, it does not actually modify any documents.

In the following example, explain() reports that 45 documents would match the filter condition and be updated:

```
mongo> var exp=db.customers.explain('executionStats').
...            update({viewCount:{$gt:50}},
...                    {$set:{discount:10}},{multi:true});
```

```
mongo> mongoTuning.executionStats(exp);

1   COLLSCAN ( ms:29 docs:411121)
2   UPDATE ( ms:31 upd:45)

Totals:  ms: 385  keys: 0  Docs: 411121
```

Index Overhead

Although indexes can dramatically improve query performance, they do reduce the
performance of updates, inserts, and deletes. All of a collection's indexes will normally
be updated when a document is inserted or deleted, and an index must also be amended
when an update changes any attribute which appears in the index.

It is therefore important that all our indexes contribute to query performance since
these indexes will otherwise needlessly degrade update, insert, and delete execution.
In particular, you should be especially careful when creating indexes on frequently
updated attributes. A document can only be inserted or deleted once but may be
updated many times. Indexes on heavily updated attributes or on collections that have a
very high insert/delete rate will, therefore, exact a particularly high cost.

Figure 8-1 illustrates the effect on indexes on insert and delete performance. It shows
how the amount of time taken to insert and then delete 100,000 documents changed as
more indexes were added to a collection.

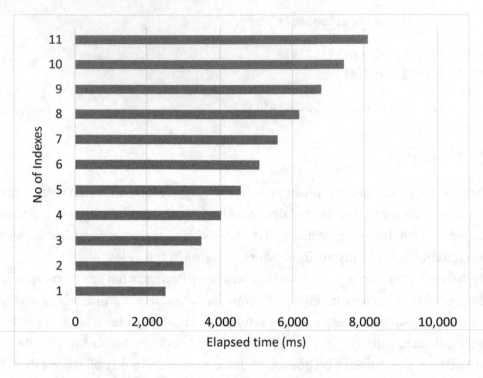

Figure 8-1. *Effect of indexes on insert/delete performance*

Tip   Indexes always add to the overhead of `insert` and `delete` statements and may add to the overhead of `update` statements. Avoid over-indexing, especially on columns which are frequently updated.

Finding Unused Indexes

It's common for the query tuning process to result in a lot of index creation, and sometimes there may be indexes that become redundant and unused. You can take a look at index utilization by using the $indexStats aggregation command:

```
mongo>db.customers.aggregate([
...    { $indexStats: {} },
...    { $project: { name: 1,
                    'accesses.ops': 1 } }]);
```

```
{ "name" : "LastName_1_FirstName_1",
        "accesses" : { "ops" : NumberLong(2068) } }
{ "name" : "_id_", "accesses" : { "ops" : NumberLong(1442414) } }
{ "name" : "updateFlag_1", "accesses" : { "ops" : NumberLong(0) } }
```

From this output, we can see that the updateFlag_1 index has not contributed to any operations since the last time the MongoDB server was started. We might want to consider removing that index. However, keep in mind if the server was restarted recently or this index supports a periodic query which last occurred before the restart, this operation counter may be misleading.

Tip   Periodically use $indexStats to identify any unused or underutilized indexes. These indexes might be slowing down data manipulation without accelerating queries.

There are some exceptions to this guideline:

- A unique index might exist purely to prevent duplicate values being created and therefore serves a purpose even if it does not contribute to query performance.

- A *Time To Live* (TTL) index might similarly be in place to purge old data, rather than to accelerate queries.

Write Concern

When manipulating data in a cluster, *write concern* controls how many members in the cluster must acknowledge the operation before returning control to the application. Specifying a level of write concern greater than 1 will usually increase latency and reduce throughput, but will result in more reliable writes since it eliminates the possibility of a lost write if a single replica set node fails. We'll discuss write concern in detail in Chapter 13.

You should generally not sacrifice data integrity in order to obtain a performance improvement. Nevertheless, it is worth remembering that writeConcern has a direct effect on the performance of data manipulation statements. Figure 8-2 shows the effect of different writeConcern settings when inserting 100,000 documents. We'll discuss this in greater detail in Chapter 13.

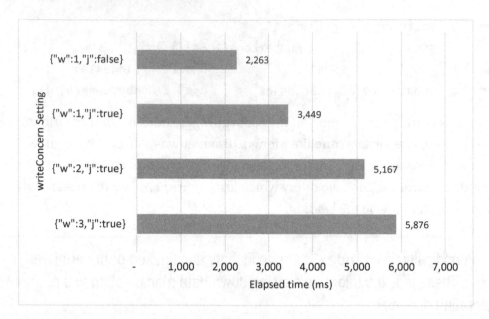

Figure 8-2. *Effect of writeConcern on insert performance*

Warning   Adjusting writeConcern can improve performance, but it may come at the expense of data integrity or safety. Don't adjust writeConcern to improve performance unless you are fully aware of these trade-offs.

Inserts

Getting data into a MongoDB database is a necessary prerequisite to getting the data out, and inserting data is susceptible to a variety of bottlenecks and tuning opportunities.

Batch Processing

In Chapter 6, we looked at how we can use batch processing to optimize fetching data from a MongoDB server. We use batch processing to ensure that we don't perform unnecessary network round trips, by making sure that each network transmission has a "full" load. If we use a batch size of 1000, we do 100 times fewer network transmissions than if we use a batch size of 10.

The same principle applies to inserting data. We want to make sure that we push data to MongoDB in batches so that we don't perform unnecessary network round trips. Unfortunately, while MongoDB can automatically send us batches of information when we issue a find(), it's up to us to construct the batches for an insert.

For instance, consider the following code:

```
myDocuments.forEach((document)=>{
  db.batchInsert.insert(document);
});
```

For each document in myDocuments, we issue a MongoDB insert statement. If there are 10,000 documents, we will issue 10,000 MongoDB calls and therefore 10,000 network round trips. This will perform very badly.

It would be much better to insert all of the documents in a single database call. This could be simply done by issuing an insertMany command:

```
db.batchInsert.insertMany(db.myDocuments.find().toArray());
```

This performs much better. In a simple test case, it returns in under 10% of the time taken for the "one-at-a-time" method.

However, we can't always insert data all at once. If we have a streaming application or if the amount of data to be inserted is massive, we might not be able to accumulate the data all in memory before inserting. In this case, we can use a MongoDB *bulk* operation.

A bulk object is created by a collection method. You can insert into the bulk object incrementally and then issue the execute method of the bulk object to push the batch into the database. The following code performs this task for the array of data used in the previous examples. Data is inserted in batches of 1000:

```
var bulk = db.batchInsert.initializeUnorderedBulkOp();
var i=0;
myDocuments.forEach((document)=>{
  bulk.insert(document);
  i++;
  if (i%1000===0) {
    bulk.execute();
    bulk = db.batchInsert.initializeUnorderedBulkOp();
  }
});
bulk.execute;
```

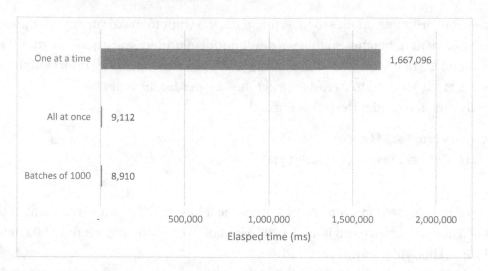

Figure 8-3. *Performance improvements gained by batch insert (10,000 documents)*

Figure 8-3 shows the relative performance of "one-at-a-time" inserts, "all-at-once" inserts, and batch inserts.

Tip   Never insert non-trivial data volumes one document at a time. Always use batch inserts when possible to reduce network overhead.

Cloning Data

From time to time, you may wish to copy – or clone – data from one set of documents in a collection into the same collection or another collection.

For instance, in an ecommerce application, you might implement a "repeat order" button – which would copy all the line items from one order into a new order.

We might implement such a facility using logic like this:

```
function repeatOrder(orderId) {
  let newOrder = db.orders.findOne({ _id: orderId },
                 { _id: 0 });
  let orderInsertRC = db.orders.insertOne(newOrder);
  let newOrderId = orderInsertRC.insertedId;
  let newLineItems = db.lineitems.
```

```
    find({ orderId: orderId },
        { _id: 0 }).toArray();
  for (let li = 0; li < newLineItems.length; li++) {
    newLineItems[li].orderId = newOrderId;
  }
  db.lineItems.insertMany(newLineItems);
  return newOrderId;
}
```

This function retrieves the existing line items, modifies then with the new order Id, and then inserts the items back into the collection.

If there are a lot of line items, then the biggest bottleneck involved will be the network latency involved in pulling the line items out of the database and then pushing those line items into the new order.

From MongoDB 4.4 onward, we can employ an alternative technique involving an aggregation framework pipeline to clone the data. This approach has the advantage of not needing to move the data outside of the database – the cloning takes place within the database server without any network overhead. The $merge operator allows us to perform inserts based on the output of an aggregation pipeline.

Here's an example of the aggregation alternative:

```
function repeatOrder(orderId) {
  let newOrder = db.orders.findOne({ _id: orderId }, { _id: 0 });
  let orderInsertRC = db.orders.insertOne(newOrder);
  let newOrderId = orderInsertRC.insertedId;
  db.lineitems.aggregate([
    {
      $match: {
        orderId: { $eq: orderId }
      }
    },
    {
      $project: {
        _id: 0,
        orderId: 0
      }
```

```
    },
    { $addFields: { orderId: newOrderId } },
    {
      $merge: {
        into: 'lineitems'
      }
    }
  ]);
  return newOrderId;
}
```

This function uses the $merge pipeline operator to push the output of the pipeline back into the collection. Figure 8-4 compares the performance of the two approaches – over 500 data cloning operations, the elapsed time was roughly halved by using the aggregation $merge approach.

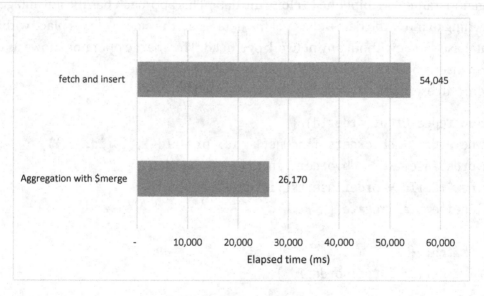

Figure 8-4. *Accelerating data cloning using an aggregation $merge pipeline (500 documents)*

The MongoDB $out aggregation operator offers similar functionality to $merge, although it cannot insert back into the source collection and – as we'll see later in this chapter – has fewer options for performing upsert-type merges.

Tip   When inserting bulk data which is derived from data in a collection, use the aggregation framework $out and $merge operators to avoid moving data across the network.

Loading from Files

MongoDB provides the mongoimport and mongorestore commands to load data from JSON or CSV files or from the output of mongodump.

Regardless of the method you are using, the most significant factor in this sort of data load is generally network latency. It is almost always faster to compress a file, move it across the network to the MongoDB server host, decompress, and then run the import than to import directly from another server.

In the case of MongoDB Atlas, you are unable to move files directly onto the Atlas servers. However, you might find that creating a virtual machine in the same region and staging the load from that machine provides a significant performance boost.

Updates

A document can only be inserted or deleted once but can be updated many times. Therefore, update optimization is an essential aspect of MongoDB performance tuning.

Dynamic Value Bulk Updates

From time to time, you may need to update multiple rows in a collection in which the value to be set is dependent on other attributes in the document or on values inside another collection.

For instance, let's imagine we wanted to insert a "view count" into our video streaming customers collection. The value to be set is different for each customer, so we might retrieve each customer document and then update the same customer document using the number of elements in the views array. The logic might look something like this:

```
db.customers.find({}, { _id: 1, views: 1 }).
  forEach(customer => {
```

```
  let updRC=db.customers.update(
    { _id: customer['_id'] },
    { $set: { viewCount: customer.views.length } }
  );
});
```

This solution is easy to code but performs poorly: we have to pull a lot of data across the network, and we must issue as many update statements as we have customers. However, before MongoDB 4.2, this was probably the best solution available.

However, starting with MongoDB 4.2, we have the ability to embed aggregation framework pipelines within an update statement. These pipelines allow us to set a value that is derived from, or dependent on, other values in the document. For instance, we could populate the viewCount attribute with this single statement:

```
db.customers.update(
           {},
           [{ $set: { viewCount: { $size: '$views' } } }],
           {multi: true});
```

Figure 8-5 compares performance for the two approaches. The aggregation pipeline reduced execution time by about 95%.

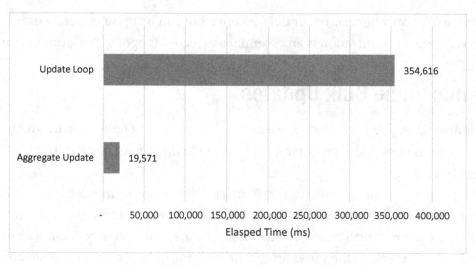

Figure 8-5. *Using an aggregation pipeline vs. multiple updates (about 411,000 documents)*

Tip   Consider using embedded aggregation pipelines in update statements when you need to dynamically update data based on existing values.

The multi:true Flag

The MongoDB update command accepts a `multi` parameter, which determines whether multiple documents will be updated within the operation. When `multi:false` is set, then MongoDB will stop processing as soon as a single document is updated.

The following example shows an update statement that is issued without the `multi` flag:

```
mongo> var exp = db.customers.
...    explain('executionStats').
...    update({ flag: true }, { $set: { flag: false } });
mongo> mongoTuning.executionStats(exp);

1   COLLSCAN ( ms:1 docs:9999)
2  UPDATE ( ms:1 upd:1)

Totals:  ms: 10  keys: 0  Docs: 9999
```

MongoDB scans through the collection until it finds a matching value and then performs the update. Once that single document is found, the scan ends.

If we know that there is only one value to be updated, but include the `multi:true` anyway, we'll see this execution plan:

```
mongo> var exp = db.customers.
...    explain('executionStats').
...    update({ flag: true }, { $set: { flag: false } },
...            {multi:true});
mongo> mongoTuning.executionStats(exp);

1   COLLSCAN ( ms:35 docs:411119)
2  UPDATE ( ms:35 upd:1)

Totals:  ms: 368  keys: 0  Docs: 411119
```

The number of documents updated is the same, but the number of document processed is much higher (411,000 vs. 999). As a result, the statement takes a lot longer to run. The update continues to scan the collection after the initial update, looking for more eligible documents.

Tip   Don't set `multi:true` if you know you are only going to update a single document. If there is an index or collection scan involved, MongoDB may perform unnecessary work looking for additional documents to update.

Upserts

Upserts allow you to issue a single statement that will perform an update if a matching document exists or an insert otherwise. Upserts can improve performance when you are trying to merge documents into a collection, and you don't want to have to explicitly check for the document's existence.

For instance, if we are loading data into a collection but don't know if we need to insert or replace, we might implement logic something like this:

```
db.source.find().forEach(doc => {
  let matchingDocs = db.target.count({ _id: doc['_id'] });

  if (matchingDocs === 0) {
    db.target.insert(doc);
    inserts++;
  } else {
    db.target.update({ _id: doc['_id'] }, doc,
                     { multi: false });
    updates++;
  }
});
```

We look for a matching value, and if found, perform an update; otherwise, perform an insert.

Upsert allows us to combine the insert and update operations into a single operation and removes the need to check for a matching value first. Here's the upsert logic:

```
db.source.find().forEach(doc => {
  let returnCodes = db.target.update({ _id: doc['_id'] }, doc,
        {upsert: true});
  inserts += returnCodes.nUpserted;
  updates += returnCodes.nModified;
});
```

The new logic is simpler and also reduces the number of database commands that need to be processed. Over a remote network connection, the upsert solution is much faster. Figure 8-6 compares the performance of the two results.

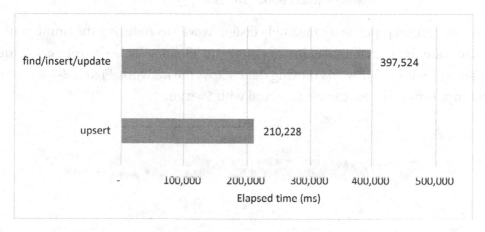

Figure 8-6. *Upsert performance compared to find/insert/update (10,000 documents)*

Tip   Use upsert instead of conditional insert/update statement if you are unsure whether to insert or update a document.

Bulk Upsert with $merge

The solutions compared in Figure 8-6 insert or update a single document at a time. As we've seen, single document processing takes longer than bulk processing, so it would be better if we are able to insert or update multiple documents in a single operation.

Starting with MongoDB 4.2, we can use the $merge aggregation operator to do this, providing that our input data is already in a MongoDB collection. $merge operates a lot like upsert, allowing us to update documents if there is a match or insert a document otherwise. The logic from the previous section could be implemented in a single $merge operation with the following statement:

```
db.source.aggregate([{$merge:
                     {          into:"target",
                          on:  "_id",
                    whenMatched:"replace",
                 whenNotMatched:"insert"}}]);
```

The aggregation pipeline is amazingly faster. As well as reducing the number of MongoDB statements that have to be executed and allowing for bulk processing, the aggregation pipeline also avoids moving data across the network. Figure 8-7 shows the performance improvement can be achieved with $merge.

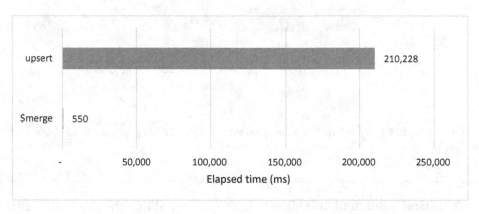

Figure 8-7. *Multiple upserts vs. a single $merge statement (10,000 documents)*

Delete Optimizations

Like inserts, deletes must amend all the indexes that exist for a collection. For that reason, deletes from heavily indexed collections can often become a serious issue for systems that deal with large amounts of transitory streaming data.

In this scenario, it might be useful to "logically" delete the documents concerned by setting a delete flag. The delete flag can be used to indicate to the application that the documents should be ignored. These documents could be physically removed periodically in a maintenance window.

If you pursue this "logical delete" strategy, then you need to make the delete flag an attribute within all indexes and include the delete flag in all queries against that collection.

Summary

In this chapter, we've looked at how to optimize data manipulation statements – `insert`, `update`, and `delete`.

Data manipulation throughput is heavily dependent on the number of indexes on a collection. The indexes you used to speed up your queries slow down your data manipulation statements, so make sure every index pays its way.

`Update` and `delete` statements accept filter conditions, and the principles for optimizing these filter conditions are identical to those for `find()` and aggregation `$match` operations.

When inserting, make sure you are inserting in batches, and – wherever possible – using aggregation pipelines if inserting data from another collection. Aggregation pipelines can also massively improve bulk update operations that are dependent on data already inside MongoDB.

CHAPTER 9

Transactions

Transactions are new in MongoDB but have existed in SQL databases for more than 30 years. Transactions are used to maintain consistency and correctness in database systems that are subjected to concurrent changes issued by multiple users.

Transactions generally result in improved *consistency* at the cost of reduced *concurrency*. Therefore, transactions have a large bearing on database performance.

This chapter is not intended as a tutorial on transactions. To learn how to program transactions, see the MongoDB manual section on transactions.[1] In this chapter, we will concentrate on maximizing transaction throughput and minimizing transaction wait times.

Transaction Theory

Databases generally meet requirements of consistency using two major architectural patterns: *ACID transactions* and *Multi-Version Concurrency Control* (*MVCC*).

The ACID transaction model was developed in the 1980s. ACID transactions should be

- **Atomic**: The transaction is indivisible – either all the statements in the transaction are applied to the database, or none are applied.

- **Consistent**: The database remains in a consistent state before and after transaction execution.

- **Isolated**: While multiple transactions can be executed by one or more users simultaneously, one transaction should not see the effects of other in-progress transactions.

- **Durable**: Once a transaction is saved to the database (typically by the COMMIT command), its changes are expected to persist even if there is a failure of operating system or hardware.

---

[1]https://docs.mongodb.com/manual/core/transactions/

© Guy Harrison, Michael Harrison 2021
G. Harrison and M. Harrison, *MongoDB Performance Tuning*, https://doi.org/10.1007/978-1-4842-6879-7_9

The easiest way to implement ACID consistency is with *locks*. Using lock-based consistency, if a session is reading an item, no other session can modify it, and if a session is modifying an item, no other session can read it. However, lock-based consistency can lead to unacceptably high contention and low concurrency.

To provide ACID consistency without excessive locking, modern database systems almost universally adopted the *Multi-Version Concurrency Control* (*MVCC*) model. In the MVCC model, multiple copies of data are tagged with timestamps or change identifiers that allow the database to construct a *snapshot* of the database at a given point in time. In this way, MVCC provides for transaction isolation and consistency while maximizing concurrency.

For example in MVCC, if a database table is subjected to modifications between the time a session starts reading the table and the time the session finishes, the database will use previous versions of table data to ensure that the session sees a consistent version. MVCC also means that until a transaction commits other sessions do not see the transaction's modifications – other sessions look at older versions of the data. These older copies of data are also used to roll back transactions that do not complete successfully.

Figure 9-1 illustrates the MVCC model. A database session initiates a transaction at time t1 (1). At time t2, the session updates a document (2): this results in a new version of that document being created (3). At about the same time a second database session queries the document, but because the transaction from the first session has not yet been committed, they see the previous version of the document (4). After the first session commits the transaction (5), the second database session will read from the modified version of the document (6).

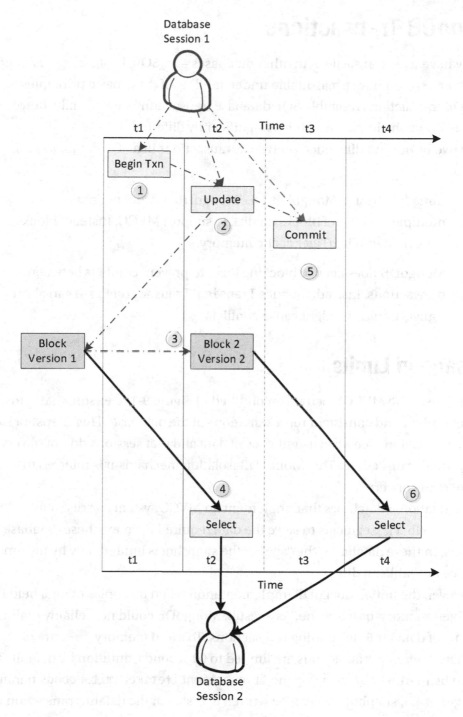

Figure 9-1. *Multi-Version Consistency Control*

MongoDB Transactions

You may have used transactions in other databases – MySQL, PostgreSQL, or another SQL database – and have a reasonable understanding of these basic principles. MongoDB transactions resemble SQL database transactions superficially; however, under the hood, the implementation is significantly different.

The two important differences between transactions in a SQL database and MongoDB are

- Initially - prior to MongoDB 4.4 - MongoDB did not maintain multiple versions of blocks on disk to support MVCC. Instead, blocks were held in WiredTiger cache memory.

- MongoDB does not use blocking locks to prevent conflicts between transactions. Instead, it issues `TransientTransactionErrors` to abort transactions that might cause conflicts.

Transaction Limits

MongoDB uses the MVCC mechanism outlined in Figure 9-1 to ensure that transactions see independent and consistent representations of the database. This snapshot isolation ensures transactions see a consistent view of data and that sessions do not observe uncommitted transactions. This MongoDB isolation mechanism is referred to as the *snapshot* read concern.

Most relational databases that implement an MVCC system use disk-based "before image" or "rollback" segments to store the data required to create these database snapshots. In these databases, the "age" of the snapshot is limited only by the amount of disk space available on disk.

However, the initial MongoDB implementation relied on copies of data held in the WiredTiger memory-based cache. As a result, MongoDB could not reliably maintain snapshots of data for long-running transactions. To avoid memory pressure on WiredTiger memory, transactions are limited to 60 seconds' duration by default. This limit can be modified by changing the `transactionLifetimeLimitSeconds` parameter. In MongoDB 4.4, snaphot data can be written to disk, but the default transaction time limit remains 60 seconds.

TransientTransactionErrors

Almost without exception, relational databases like PostgreSQL or MySQL use locks to implement transactional consistency. Figure 9-2 illustrates how this works. When a session modifies a row in a table, it places a lock on that row to prevent concurrent modifications. If a second session tries to modify the same row, it has to wait until the lock is released when the original transaction commits.

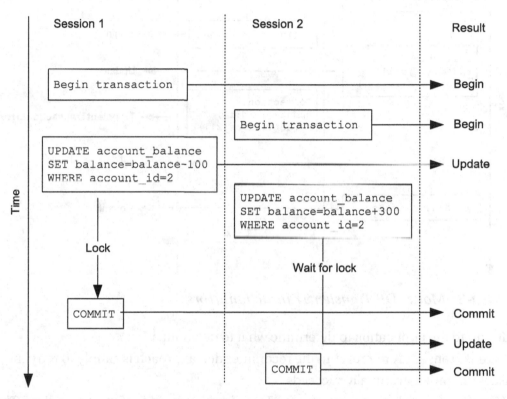

Figure 9-2. *Locks in relational database transactions*

Many developers are familiar with the blocking locks of relational databases and may assume that MongoDB does the same thing. However, MongoDB's approach is completely different. In MongoDB, when the second session attempts to modify a document modified in another transaction, it does not wait for a lock to be released. Instead, it receives a TransientTransactionError event. The second session must then retry the transaction (ideally after the first transaction completes).

Figure 9-3 illustrates the MongoDB paradigm. When a session updates a document, it does not lock it. However, if a second session tries to modify the document in a transaction, a TransientTransactionError is issued.

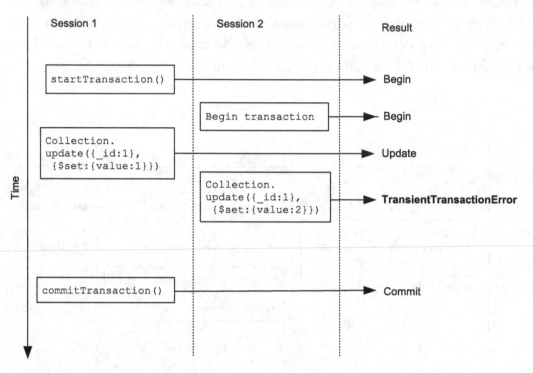

Figure 9-3. *MongoDB TransientTransactionErrors*

It's up to the application to determine what to do about a TransientTransactionError, but the recommended approach is simply to retry the transaction until it eventually succeeds.

Here is some code that illustrates the TransientTransactionError paradigm. The code snippet creates two sessions, each within its own transaction. We then attempt to update the same document within each transaction.

```
var session1=db.getMongo().startSession();
var session2=db.getMongo().startSession();
var session1Collection=session1.getDatabase(db.getName())
          .transTest;
var session2Collection=session2.getDatabase(db.getName())
          .transTest;
session1.startTransaction();
```

```
session2.startTransaction();

session1Collection.update({_id:1},{$set:{value:1}});
session2Collection.update({_id:1},{$set:{value:2}});

session1.commitTransaction();
session2.commitTransaction();
```

When the second update statement is encountered, MongoDB issues an error:

```
mongo>session1Collection.update({_id:1},{$set:{value:1}});
WriteCommandError({
        "errorLabels" : [
                "TransientTransactionError"
        ],
        "operationTime" : Timestamp(1596785629, 1),
        "ok" : 0,
        "errmsg" : "WriteConflict error: this operation conflicted
with another operation. Please retry your operation or multi-document
transaction.",
        "code" : 112,
        "codeName" : "WriteConflict",
```

Transactions in the MongoDB Drivers

From MongoDB 4.2 onward, the MongoDB drivers hide transientTransationErrors
from you, by automatically retrying the transaction. For instance, you can run
multiple copies of this NodeJS code simultaneously, without encountering any
TransientTransactionErrors:

```
async function myTransaction(session, db, fromAcc,
                             toAcc, dollars) {
    try {
        await session.withTransaction(async () => {

            await db.collection('accounts').
              updateOne({ _id: fromAcc },
                { $inc: {  balance: -1*dollars }  },
```

```
            { session });

        await db.collection('accounts').
          updateOne({ _id: toAcc },
            { $inc: {  balance: dollars }  },
            { session });

    }, transactionOptions);
  } catch (error) {
    console.log(error.message);
  }
}
```

The NodeJS driver – and drivers for other languages such as Java, Python, Go, and so on – automatically handles any `TransientTransactionErrors` and resubmits any aborted transactions. However, the errors are still being issued by the MongoDB server, and you can see them recorded in the MongoDB log:

```
~$ grep -i 'assertion.*writeconflict' \
        /usr/local/var/log/mongodb/mongo.log \
        |tail -1|jq
{
  "t": {
    "$date": "2020-08-08T14:04:47.643+10:00"
  },
  …
  "msg": "Assertion while executing command",
  "attr": {
    "command": "update",
    "db": "MongoDBTuningBook",
    "commandArgs": {
      "update": "transTest",
      "updates": [
        {
          "q": {
            "_id": 1
          },
```

```
      "u": {
        "$inc": {
          "value": 2
        }
      },
      "upsert": false,
      "multi": false
    }
  ],
  /* Other transaction information */
},
"error": "WriteConflict: WriteConflict error: this operation conflicted
```
with another operation. Please retry your operation or multi-document
transaction."
```
  }
}
```

In the NodeJS driver, you can also log server-level debug messages[2] to see the aborted transactions that are going on under the hood. When a transaction aborts under the hood, you'll see the following message in the output stream:

```
[DEBUG-Server:20690] 1596872732041 executing command [{"ns":"admin.$cmd","
cmd":{"abortTransaction":1,"writeConcern":{"w":"majority"}},"options":{}}]
against localhost:27017 {
  type: 'debug',
  message: 'executing command [{"ns":"admin.$cmd","cmd":{"abortTran
saction":1,"writeConcern":{"w":"majority"}},"options":{}}] against
localhost:27017',
  className: 'Server',
  pid: 20690,
  date: 1596872732041
}
```

Other drivers may provide similar methods for viewing transaction retries.

---

[2]See https://docs.mongodb.com/drivers/node/fundamentals/logging

At a global level, the retries are visible in the db.serverStatus counter transactions.totalAborted. We can use the following function to examine the number of transactions started, aborted, and committed:

```
function txnCounts() {
  var ssTxns = db.serverStatus().transactions;
  print(ssTxns.totalStarted + 0, 'transactions started');
  print(ssTxns.totalAborted + 0, 'transactions aborted');
  print(ssTxns.totalCommitted + 0, 'transactions committed');
  print(Math.round(ssTxns.totalAborted * 100 /
          ssTxns.totalStarted) + '% txns aborted');
}

mongo> txnCounts();
203628 transactions started
167989 transactions aborted
35639 transactions committed
82% txns aborted
```

The Performance Implications of TransientTransactionErrors

The retries that result from TransientTransactionErrors are expensive – they involve not just discarding any work done in the transaction so far but also reverting database state back to the start of the transaction. It is the impact of transaction retries more than anything else that makes MongoDB transactions expensive. Figure 9-4 shows that as the percentage of transaction aborts increases, the elapsed time for transactions degrades rapidly.

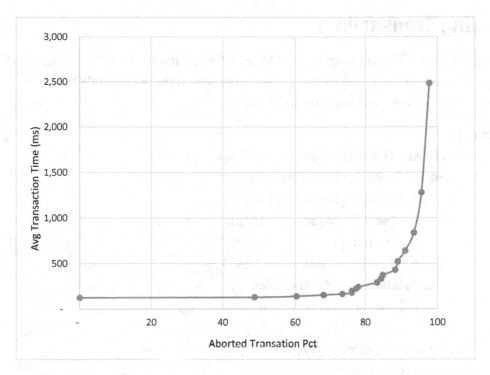

Figure 9-4. *Performance impact of aborted transactions*

Note   The MongoDB transactional model involves aborting transactions that are in conflict with other transactions. These aborts are expensive operations that are the primary bottleneck on MongoDB transactional performance.

Transaction Optimization

Given that `TransientTransactionError` retries have such a severe effect on transaction performance, it follows that we need to do whatever is possible to minimize these retries. There are a couple of strategies that we can employ:

- Avoid a transaction altogether.

- Order operations to minimize the number of conflicting operations.

- Partition "hot" documents that are subject to high levels of write conflict.

213

Avoiding Transactions

It's possible that you don't need to use MongoDB transactions to achieve a transactional outcome. For instance, consider this transaction, which transfers funds between branches in a hypothetical banking application:

```
try {
    await session.withTransaction(async () => {
        await db.collection('branches').
          updateOne({ _id: fromBranch },
            { $inc: {  balance: -1*dollars }  },
            { session });
        await db.collection('branches').
          updateOne({ _id: toBranch },
            { $inc: {  balance: dollars }  },
            { session });
    }, transactionOptions);
} catch (error) {
    console.log(error.message);
}
```

It certainly seems like a candidate for transactions – the two update statements should both succeed or fail as a unit. However, if the number of branches is relatively small – small enough to fit into a single document – then we could store all the balances in an embedded array within a single document, something like this:

```
mongo> db.embeddedBranches.findOne();
{
  "_id": 1,
  "branchTotals": [
    {
      "branchId": 0,
      "balance": 101208675
    },
    {
      "branchId": 1,
      "balance": 98409758
```

```
  },
  {
    "branchId": 2,
    "balance": 99407654
  },
  {
    "branchId": 3,
    "balance": 98807890
  }
 ]
}
```

We could then atomically move data between branches using a relatively simple update statement. Our new "transaction" would look like this:

```
try {
  let updateString =
      `{"$inc":{
      "branchTotals.`+fromBranch+`.balance":`+dollars+`,
      "branchTotals.`+toBranch +`.balance":`+dollars+`}}`;
  let updateClause = JSON.parse(updateString);

  await db.collection('embeddedBranches').updateOne(
    {_id: 1 }, updateClause);
} catch (error) {
  console.log(error.message);
}
```

We've reduced four statements down to just one, and we've completely eliminated any chance of TransientTransactionErrors. Figure 9-5 compares the performance – the non-transactional method was more than 100 times faster than the transactional approach.

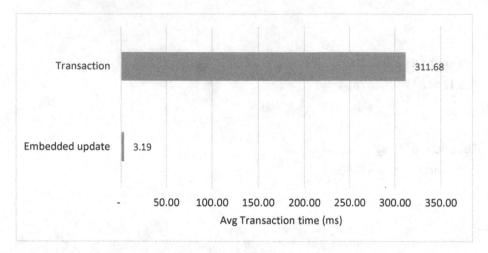

Figure 9-5. *MongoDB transaction vs. embedded array*

Tip   There may be alternative application strategies to MongoDB transactions, and these may perform better than a formal transaction, especially if there is a high chance of write conflicts.

Ordering of Operations

Transactions by their very nature will issue more than one operation to the MongoDB database. It may be that some of these operations are more likely to create write conflicts than other operations. In these scenarios, it is possible that changing the order of operations might give you a performance advantage.

For example, consider the following transaction:

```
await session.withTransaction(async () => {
  await db.collection('txnTotals').
    updateOne({ _id: 1 },
      { $inc: {  counter: 1 }  },
      { session });
  await db.collection('accounts').
    updateOne({ _id: fromAcc },
      { $inc: {  balance: -1*dollars }  },
      { session });
```

```
    await db.collection('accounts').
      updateOne({ _id: toAcc },
        { $inc: {  balance: dollars }  },
        { session });

  }, transactionOptions);
```

This transaction transfers funds between two accounts, but first, it updates a global "transaction counter." Every transaction that tries to issue this transaction will attempt to update this counter, and many will encounter `TransientTransactionError` retries as a result.

If we move the contentious statement to the end of the transaction, then the chance of a `TransientTransactionError` will be reduced, since the window for conflict will be reduced to the final few moments in the execution of the transaction. The modified code looks like this – we simply moved the `txnTotals` update to the end of the transaction:

```
    await session.withTransaction(async () => {
      await db.collection('accounts').
        updateOne({ _id: fromAcc },
          { $inc: {  balance: -1*dollars }  },
          { session });
      await db.collection('accounts').
        updateOne({ _id: toAcc },
          { $inc: {  balance: dollars }  },
          { session });
      await db.collection('txnTotals').
        updateOne({ _id: 1 },
          { $inc: {  counter: 1 }  },
          { session });

    }, transactionOptions);
```

Figure 9-6 provides an example of the effect of changing the transaction order for the example transaction. Placing the "hot" operation last reduced contention and improved transaction execution time significantly.

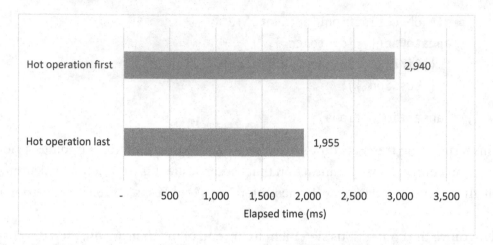

Figure 9-6. *Effect of reordering operations in a transaction*

Tip   Consider placing "hot" operations – those likely to encounter `TransientTransactionErrors` – last in your transactions to reduce the conflict time window.

Partitioning Hot Documents

`TransientTransactionErrors` occur when multiple transactions try to modify a particular document. These "hot" documents become transaction bottlenecks. In some cases, we might be able to relieve the bottleneck by partitioning the data in the document into multiple distinct documents.

For instance, consider the transaction we looked at in the previous section. This transaction updated a transaction counter document:

```
await db.collection('txnTotals').
  updateOne({ _id: 1 },
    { $inc: { counter: 1 } },
    { session });
```

This is a perfect example of a "hot" document – a document that every single transaction wants to update. If we really need to keep some sort of running total like this within a transaction, we could split the totals up across multiple documents. For instance, this alternative syntax splits the totals across ten documents:

```
let id=Math.floor(Math.random()*10);

await db.collection('txnTotals').
  updateOne({ _id: id },
    { $inc: { counter: 1 } },
    { session });
```

Of course, if we want to get a grand total, we'll need to aggregate the data from the ten sub-totals, but that's a small price to pay to improve our transactional performance.

Figure 9-7 shows the performance improvements gained from this partitioning. We reduced average transaction time by almost 90% by partitioning the hot document.

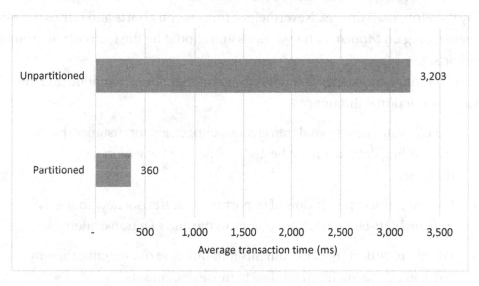

Figure 9-7. *Partitioning a "hot" document to improve transaction time*

Tip   Consider partitioning "hot" documents – those updated simultaneously by multiple transactions – into multiple documents.

Conclusion

Transactions are an essential requirement for many applications, and the introduction of transaction support in MongoDB 4.0 was a big step forward for MongoDB.

Unfortunately, unlike many other MongoDB new features, transactions do not inherently improve performance. By introducing contention between sessions, transactions by their very nature reduce concurrency and therefore reduce throughput and increase response time.

The MongoDB transactional architecture does not make use of the blocking locks employed by most SQL databases. Rather, it aborts transactions that attempt to simultaneously modify a document. These aborts and retries are handled "under the hood" by the MongoDB drivers. Nevertheless, transaction aborts and retries are a critical performance drag on MongoDB transactions and should be the focus of your transaction tuning efforts.

In this chapter, we looked at a couple of ways of reducing contention and therefore improving transactional throughput:

- We can sometimes avoid transactions altogether, for instance, by embedding data that must be updated atomically within a single document.

- We can reduce the window of opportunity for transaction aborts by moving high-contention operations to the end of a transaction.

- We can partition "hot" documents into multiple documents, thereby reducing the contention for data in those documents.

CHAPTER 10

Server Monitoring

So far, we've been concentrating on managing performance by optimizing application code and database design. In an ideal world, this is where we start our tuning efforts, by optimizing the application we make MongoDB work smarter, not harder. We reduce the amount of effort MongoDB has to do to achieve a task by optimizing our schema, application code, and indexes.

However, there may come a time when you've done all the practical application tuning possible. Furthermore, there are occasions where you don't have the luxury of being able to rework application code at all – when you are working with a third-party application, for instance.

Now is the time to look at your server configuration and ensure that the server is optimized for the application workload. This server-side tuning ideally occurs in four phases:

- Ensuring that there is sufficient memory and CPU on the server host to support the workload

- Ensuring that there is sufficient and correctly configured memory to reduce IO demand

- Optimizing disk IO to ensure that disk requests return without excessive latency

- Ensuring that the cluster configuration is optimized to avoid delays in cluster coordination and to maximize cluster resources

These topics are the subject of the next four chapters of this book. In this chapter, we'll look at the basics of monitoring server performance and some useful tools for assisting in this process.

© Guy Harrison, Michael Harrison 2021
G. Harrison and M. Harrison, *MongoDB Performance Tuning*, https://doi.org/10.1007/978-1-4842-6879-7_10

Host-Level Monitoring

All MongoDB servers run within an operating system which is in turn hosted within some hardware platform. In today's world of virtual machines, containers, and cloud infrastructure, the hardware topology might be obscured. But even when you cannot directly observe the underlying hardware, you can observe the operating system container that provides the raw resources which support your MongoDB servers.

At the most fundamental level, the operating system provides four essential resources:

- **Network** bandwidth, which allows data to be transferred in and out of the machine

- **CPU**, which allows for the execution of program code

- **Memory**, which allows for fast access to impermanent data

- **Disk IO**, which allows massive amounts of data to be stored permanently

There are a wide variety of tools to help you monitor host utilization, both commercial and free. In our experience, it is best to understand how to use the built-in performance utilities, since these will always be available.

On Linux, you should be familiar with the following commands:

- `top`

- `uptime`

- `vmstat`

- `iostat`

- `netstat`

- `bwm-ng`

On Windows, you can use the *resource monitor* application for a graphical view and get raw statistics from the PowerShell `Get-Counter` command.

Network

The network is responsible for transmitting data from your server to your application and between the servers that comprise your cluster.

We've looked at the role of network round trips in Chapter 6, and we'll talk more about network traffic in the context of cluster optimization in Chapter 13.

It's unusual for the network interfaces within a MongoDB server to be a bottleneck – the network bottleneck is more commonly found in the many network hops between the server and various clients. That is to say, the amount of data that can be processed by the MongoDB server is usually less than the amount of data that can be transferred through a typical network interface. You can monitor the amount of traffic transferring through the network interface with the bwm-ng command:

```
bwm-ng v0.6.2 (probing every 5.200s), press 'h' for help
  input: /proc/net/dev type: rate
iface                   Rx                    Tx               Total
  =================================================================
     lo:       0.00  B/s        0.00  B/s        0.00  B/s
   eth0:     173.52 KB/s        8.84 MB/s        9.01 MB/s
 virbr0:       0.00  B/s        0.00  B/s        0.00  B/s
  -----------------------------------------------------------------
  total:     173.52 KB/s        8.84 MB/s        9.01 MB/s
```

The network interfaces in modern servers are generally 10 or 100 Gigabit Ethernet cards, and the chance that these cards are limiting the amount of data that can be transferred between client and server is small. However, if you have an older server using something less than a 10GbE card, then upgrading your network card is a cheap optimization.

However, while the network interface on the server is unlikely to be a problem, the network between client and server is likely to contain a variety of routers and switches with disparate performance characteristics. Furthermore, the distance between client and server creates latency that cannot be avoided. The network round trip time between an application and MongoDB server is very often a limiting factor on overall performance.

You can measure the round trip time between two servers by using a command like ping or traceroute. Here, we measure the network latency to three widely dispersed replica set members:

```
$ traceroute mongors01.eastasia.cloudapp.azure.com --port=27017 -T

traceroute to mongors01.eastasia.cloudapp.azure.com (23.100.91.199), 30
hops max, 60 byte packets
 1  * * *
 . . .
18  * * 23.100.91.199 (23.100.91.199)  118.392 ms
$ traceroute mongors02.japaneast.cloudapp.azure.com --port=27017 -T
traceroute to mongors02.japaneast.cloudapp.azure.com (20.46.164.146), 30
hops max, 60 byte packets
 1  * * *
      . . .
19  * 20.46.164.146 (20.46.164.146)  128.611 ms
$ traceroute mongors03.koreacentral.cloudapp.azure.com --port=27017 -T
traceroute to mongors03.koreacentral.cloudapp.azure.com (20.194.1.136), 30
hops max, 60 byte packets
 1  * * *
 . . .
26  * * *
27  20.194.1.136 (20.194.1.136)  152.857 ms
```

It can also be useful to measure the time taken to respond to a very simple MongoDB
command such as rs.isMaster(). When we run rs.isMaster() from a shell on the
server host, we see a minimal delay:

```
mongo> var start=new Date();
mongo> var isMaster=rs.isMaster();
mongo> print ('Elapsed time', (new Date())-start);
Elapsed time 14
```

When we run rs.isMaster() from a remote host, the elapsed time is several
hundred milliseconds longer as a result of network latency:

```
mongo> var start=new Date();
mongo> var isMaster=rs.isMaster();
mongo> print ('Elapsed time', (new Date())-start);
Elapsed time 316
```

If your network latency is unreasonably high – more than a couple of 100ms – then you might check your network configuration. Your network administrator or ISP might need to be involved in tracking down the cause of the delay.

However, in a complex network topology, the cause of the network latency might be outside of your control. In general, the best ways to deal with network latency are

- Move your application workload "closer" to your database server. Application servers should ideally be in the same region, data center, or even in the same rack as your MongoDB servers.

- Reduce the number of network round trips in your application. We discussed ways of optimizing network round trips in Chapters 6 and 8.

Tip Network latencies of more than a few 100ms are a cause of concern. Investigate your network hardware and topology, and consider moving your application code "closer" to your MongoDB server. In either case, make sure you are minimizing network round trips using the techniques discussed earlier in this book.

CPU

CPU bottlenecks often cause poor performance. The MongoDB server process consumes CPU when parsing requests, accessing data in the cache, and for a myriad of other purposes.

When investigating CPU utilization, it's understandable that most people start with the *CPU percent busy* metric. However, this metric is only useful when the CPU utilization is under 100%. Once the CPU utilization hits 100%, the much more important metric is the *run queue*.

The run queue – sometimes called *load average* – reflects the average number of processes that want to use a CPU, but must wait while some other process is currently monopolizing the CPU. The run queue is a better measure of CPU load than CPU percent busy because even when the CPUs are fully utilized, the demand for CPU can still increase and hence the run queue can still grow. Large run queues are almost always associated with poor response time.

We like to think of CPUs and run queues as analogous to a supermarket checkout. Even when all the checkouts are busy, you'll still get out of the supermarket quickly, providing that there are not large queues in front of the checkouts. It's when the queues start to grow that you start to worry.

Figure 10-1 illustrates the relationship between run queue, CPU percent busy, and response time. As the workload increases, all three measures increase. However, CPU percent busy maxes out at 100%, while the run queue and response time continue to increase in a highly correlated fashion. The run queue is, therefore, your best measure of CPU utilization.

Ideally, the run queue should not exceed about two times the number of CPUs on your system. For instance, in Figure 10-1, the host system had four CPUs; therefore, run queues of about 8–10 represented maximum CPU utilization.

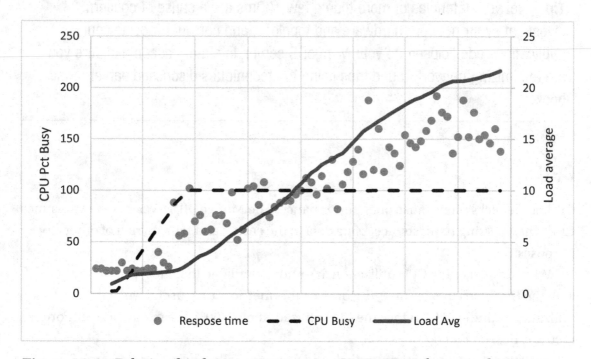

Figure 10-1. *Relationship between run queue, CPU percent busy, and response time*

Tip   "CPU run queue" or "load average" is the best single metric of CPU load. The run queue should stay below about two times the number of CPUs available on the system.

To get run queue values on Linux, you can issue the uptime command:

```
$ uptime
 06:38:39 up 42 days …  load average: 12.77, 3.66, 1.37
```

The command reports the average run queue length (load average) over the last 1, 5, and 15 minutes.

On Windows, you can issue the following Get-Counter command from a PowerShell prompt:

```
PS C:\Users\guy> Get-Counter '\System\Processor Queue Length' -MaxSamples 5

Timestamp                   CounterSamples
---------                   --------------
29/08/2020 1:32:20 PM       \\win10\system\processor queue length :
                            4

29/08/2020 1:32:21 PM       \\win10\system\processor queue length :
                            1
```

Memory

All computer applications use memory to store data being processed. Databases are particularly heavy users of memory because they typically cache data in memory to avoid performing excessive disk IO.

We've dedicated the next chapter to MongoDB memory management. Please check out Chapter 11 to learn more about memory monitoring in general and MongoDB memory management specifically.

Disk IO

Disk IO is so central to database performance that we have allocated Chapters 12 and 13 to this topic. We'll cover all aspects of disk IO performance management in those chapters.

MongoDB Server Monitoring

The db.serverStatus() command is the ultimate source for most of the raw metrics you need to understand MongoDB server performance. We introduced db.serverStatus() in Chapter 3. However, raw numbers can be challenging to interpret, and so there are a variety of tuning tools that present the information in a more readily consumable format.

Compass

MongoDB Compass (Figure 10-2) is the official GUI for working with MongoDB and is available for free at mongodb.com. Although the Compass performance dashboard is relatively simple, it can be a useful getting started point. If you've downloaded MongoDB community edition, you probably already have Compass.

Figure 10-2. *MongoDB Compass monitoring*

Free Monitoring

MongoDB also provides a simple way to access a cloud-based performance dashboard for any MongoDB server. Similar to the Compass dashboard, the Free Monitoring dashboard (Figure 10-3) provides a minimal view on performance but serves as a free and straightforward way to get a summary of MongoDB performance.

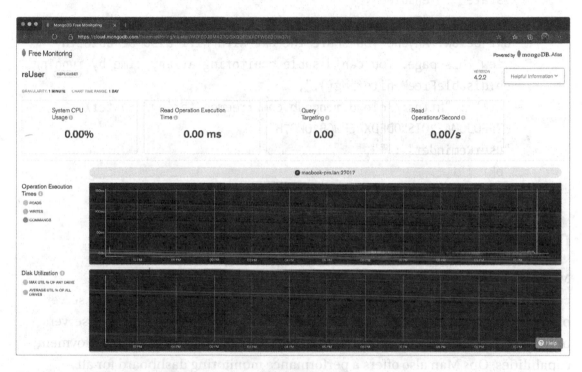

Figure 10-3. *MongoDB Free Monitoring*

Free Monitoring is available for community edition servers from version 4.0 onward. The server host firewall must allow access to `http://cloud.mongodb.com/freemonitoring`.

To enable Free Monitoring, simply log in to your MongoDB server and run db. enableFreeMonitoring(). If all goes well, you'll be provided with an URL that points to your monitoring dashboard:

```
rsUser:PRIMARY> db.enableFreeMonitoring()
{
        "state" : "enabled",
        "message": "To see your monitoring data, navigate to the unique
        URL below. Anyone you share the URL with will also be able to
        view this page. You can disable monitoring at any time by running
        db.disableFreeMonitoring().",
        "url" : "https://cloud.mongodb.com/freemonitoring/cluster/
        WZFEDJBMA23QISXQDEDXACFWGB2OWQ7H",
        "userReminder" : "",
        "ok" : 1,
        "operationTime" : Timestamp(1599995708,
```

Ops Manager

MongoDB Ops Manager (often referred to just as "Ops Man") is MongoDB's commercial platform for managing, monitoring, and automating MongoDB server operations (Figure 10-4). Ops Man can be deployed alongside your existing servers or be used to create new infrastructure. Along with the automation and deployment capabilities, Ops Man also offers a performance monitoring dashboard for all registered deployments.

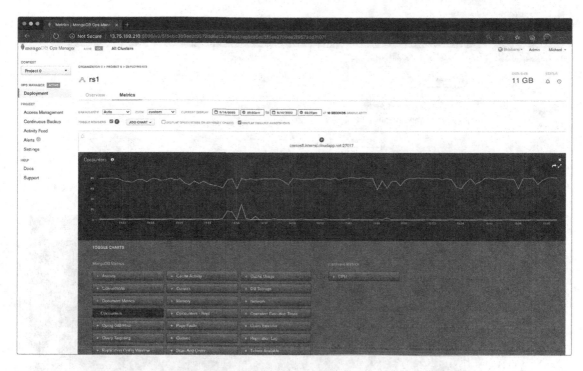

Figure 10-4. MongoDB Ops Manager

MongoDB Atlas

If you've created a cluster on MongoDB's Atlas database-as-a-service platform, you'll have access to a graphical monitoring interface which is very similar to MongoDB Ops Manager. The Atlas dashboard (Figure 10-5) provides the ability to configure metrics and select time windows for generating activity graphs. Premium clusters (M10 and above) will also have access to real-time monitoring.

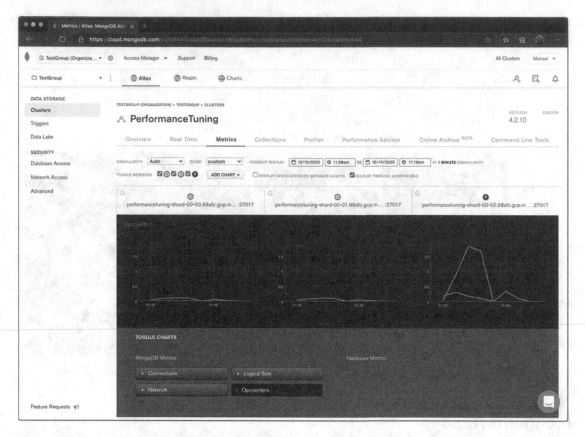

Figure 10-5. *MongoDB Atlas monitoring*

Third-Party Monitoring Tools

There are also a wide variety of free and commercial monitoring tools that offer strong support for MongoDB. Some of the most popular are

- **Percona** specializes in open source database software and services. As well as offering their own distribution of MongoDB, they offer the Percona Monitoring and Management platform, which provides real-time and historical performance monitoring of MongoDB servers.

- **Datadog** is a popular monitoring platform that offers diagnostics for all elements of an application stack. They offer a dedicated module for MongoDB.

- **SolarWinds** acquired **VividCortex** in 2019. The VividCortex product for MongoDB offered a somewhat unique monitoring solution for MongoDB that used low-level instrumentation to enable high-granularity tracing of MongoDB performance.

Summary

We've argued throughout this book that you should optimize your workload and database design before changing hardware or server configuration. However, once you have a well-tuned application, it's time to monitor and tune your server.

The operating system provides four critical resources to the MongoDB server – network, CPU, memory, and disk IO. In this chapter, we looked at monitoring and understanding CPU and memory. In the next two chapters, we'll dig deep into memory and disk IO.

In Chapter 3, we reviewed the essential tools for MongoDB tuning. Graphical monitoring can supplement these tools by providing better visualization and historical trending. MongoDB provides free graphical monitoring in the Compass desktop GUI and the cloud-based Free Monitoring dashboard. More extensive monitoring can be found in MongoDB's commercial offerings: MongoDB Atlas and MongoDB Ops Manager. Many commercial monitoring tools also offer insight into MongoDB performance.

PART IV

Server Tuning

CHAPTER 11

Memory Tuning

In the earlier chapters of this book, we looked at techniques for reducing the workload demands on the MongoDB server. We considered options for structuring and indexing our datasets and tuning our MongoDB requests to minimize the amount of data that has to be processed in response to a work request. Maybe 80% of the performance gains from performance tuning come from these application-level optimizations.

However, at some point, our application schema and code is as optimized as it is ever going to be, and the demands we are placing on the MongoDB server are reasonable. Our priority now is to ensure that MongoDB can respond quickly to our requests. When we send a data request to MongoDB, the most critical factor becomes *is the data in memory or does it have to be fetched from disk?*

Like all databases, MongoDB uses memory to avoid disk IO. A read from memory typically takes about 20 nanoseconds. A read from a very fast Solid State Disk takes about 25 microseconds – 1000 times as long. A read from a magnetic disk might take 4–10 milliseconds – that's another 2000 times slower! So MongoDB – like all databases – is architected to avoid disk IO whenever possible.

MongoDB Memory Architecture

MongoDB supports a variety of pluggable storage engines, each of which utilizes memory differently. Indeed, there is even an *in-memory* storage engine which stores active data only in memory. However, in this chapter, we are going to focus solely on the default WiredTiger storage engine.

When using the WiredTiger storage engine, the bulk of the memory consumed by MongoDB is usually the WiredTiger cache.

© Guy Harrison, Michael Harrison 2021
G. Harrison and M. Harrison, *MongoDB Performance Tuning*, https://doi.org/10.1007/978-1-4842-6879-7_11

MongoDB allocates additional memory based on workload demand. You can't directly control the amount of additional memory allocated, although workload and some server configuration parameters do influence the total amount of memory allocated. The most significant memory allocations are associated with sorting and aggregation operations – we looked at these in Chapter 7. Every connection to MongoDB also requires memory.

Within the WiredTiger cache, memory is allocated to caching collection and index data, for snapshots supporting transaction Multi-Version Consistency Control (see Chapter 9), and to buffer the WiredTiger write-ahead log.

Figure 11-1 illustrates the significant components of MongoDB memory.

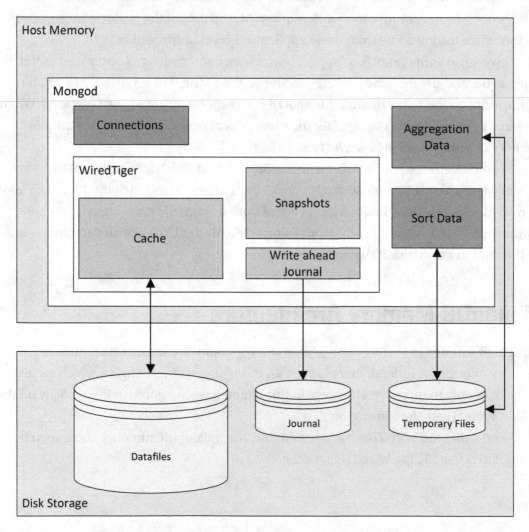

Figure 11-1. *MongoDB memory architecture*

Host Memory

Although configuring MongoDB memory is a big topic, from an operating system perspective, memory management is very simple. Either there is some free memory available, and everything is fine, or there is not enough free memory and things are awful.

When physical free memory is exhausted, then attempts to allocate memory will result in existing memory allocations "swapping out" to disk. Since the disk is many hundreds of times slower than memory, memory allocations suddenly take many orders of magnitude longer to satisfy.

Figure 11-2 shows how response time suddenly declines when memory runs out. Response time remains stable as free memory decreases, but as soon as memory is exhausted and disk-based swap is involved, response time degrades suddenly and significantly.

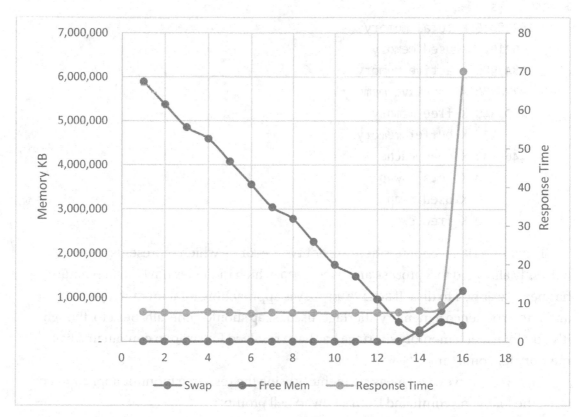

Figure 11-2. *Memory, swap, and response time*

> **Tip**   When server memory is over-utilized, then memory may be swapped to disk. On a MongoDB server, this almost always indicates that there is insufficient memory for the MongoDB memory configuration.

While we don't want to see memory over-allocation and swapping, we also don't want to see massive amounts of unallocated memory. Unused memory serves no useful purpose – it's probably better to allocate that memory to the WiredTiger cache than to allow it to be unused.

Measuring Memory

On Linux systems, you can use the `vmstat` command to show available memory:

```
$ vmstat -s
    16398036 K total memory
    10921928 K used memory
    10847980 K active memory
     3778780 K inactive memory
     1002340 K free memory
        4236 K buffer memory
     4469532 K swap cache
           0 K total swap
           0 K used swap
           0 K free swap
```

The most critical counters here are `active memory` – which represents memory currently allocated to a process and `used swap`, which indicates how much memory has been swapped to disk. If `active memory` is approaching total memory, you may be about to experience a memory shortage. `Used swap` should generally be zero, though it's possible after a memory shortage has been resolved for swap to contain inactive memory for some time.

On Windows, you can measure memory using the resource monitor application or issue the following command from a PowerShell prompt:

```
PS C:\Users\guy> systeminfo |Select-string Memory
```

```
Total Physical Memory:      16,305 MB
Available Physical Memory:  3,363 MB
Virtual Memory: Max Size:   27,569 MB
Virtual Memory: Available:  6,664 MB
Virtual Memory: In Use:     20,905 MB
```

The db.serverStatus() command provides details of how much memory MongoDB is using. The following script prints out a top-level summary of memory utilization:[1]

```
mongo>function memory() {
...     let serverStats = db.serverStatus();
...     print('Mongod virtual memory ', serverStats.mem.virtual);
...     print('Mongod resident memory', serverStats.mem.resident);
...     print(
...         'WiredTiger cache size',
...         Math.round(
...             serverStats.wiredTiger.cache
...                 ['bytes currently in the cache'] / 1048576
...         )
...     );
... }
mongo>memory();
Mongod virtual memory  9854
Mongod resident memory 8101
WiredTiger cache size 6195
```

The report tells us that MongoDB had allocated 9.8GB of virtual memory, 8.1GB of which was currently actively allocated to physical memory. The difference between virtual and resident memory often represents memory that has been allocated, but not yet used.

Of the 9.8GB of memory allocated, 6.1GB is assigned to the WiredTiger cache.

---

[1]This script in included within our tuning scripts as mongoTuning.memoryReport().

WiredTiger Memory

The vast majority of MongoDB production deployments use the WiredTiger storage engine. And for those deployments, the largest chunk of memory will be the WiredTiger cache. In this chapter, we'll discuss only the WiredTiger storage engine, since while other storage engines exist, they are nowhere near as widely deployed as WiredTiger.

The WiredTiger cache has a massive effect on server performance. Without the cache, every data read would be a disk read. The cache typically reduces the number of disk reads by more than 90% and consequently allows for orders of magnitude improvements in throughput.

Cache Size

By default, the WiredTiger cache will be set to either 50% of total memory minus 1GB or to 256MB, whichever is largest. So, for instance, on a 16GB server, you would expect a default size of 7GB ((16/2) – 1). The remaining memory is left available for sort and aggregation areas, connection memory, and operating system memory.

The default WiredTiger cache size is a useful starting point, but rarely the optimal value. If other workloads are running on the same host, it may be too high. Conversely, on a large memory system dedicated to MongoDB, it may be too low. Given the importance of the WiredTiger cache to performance, you should be ready to adjust the cache size to meet your needs.

Tip   The default WiredTiger cache size is a useful starting point, but rarely the optimum value. Determining and setting the optimal value will usually be worthwhile.

The mongod configuration parameter wiredTigerCacheSizeGB controls the maximum size of the cache. In the MongoDB configuration file, this is represented by the storage/WiredTiger/engineConfig/cacheSizeGB path. For instance, to set the cache size to 12GB, you would specify the following in your mongod.conf file:

```
storage:
  wiredTiger:
    engineConfig:
      cacheSizeGB: 12
```

You can adjust the size of the WiredTiger cache on a running server. The following command adjusts the cache size to 8GB:

```
db.getSiblingDB('admin').runCommand({setParameter: 1,
      wiredTigerEngineRuntimeConfig: 'cache_size=8G'});
```

Determining the Optimum Cache Size

A cache that is too small can result in an increase in IO, which can degrade performance. On the other hand, increasing the cache size beyond the available operating system memory can lead to swapping and even more disastrous performance degradation. Increasingly, MongoDB is deployed in cloud containers where the amount of available memory can be adjusted dynamically. Even so, memory is often the most expensive resource in a cloud environment, and so "throwing more memory" at the server without evidence is undesirable.

So, how do we determine the correct amount of cache memory? There is no definitive method of determining if more cache memory will lead to better performance, but we do have a few indicators that might guide us. The two most important are

- The cache "hit" ratio

- The eviction rate

The Database Cache "Hit" Ratio

The database *cache hit ratio* is a somewhat notorious metric with a long history. Simplistically, the cache hit ratio describes how often you find a block of data you want in memory:

$$CacheHitRatio = \frac{Number\ of\ IO\ requests\ that\ were\ satisfied\ in\ the\ cache}{Total\ IO\ requests}$$

The cache hit ratio represents the proportion of block requests that are satisfied by the database cache without requiring a disk read. Each "hit" – when the block is found in memory – is a good thing, since it avoids a time-consuming disk IO. Therefore, it seems intuitively obvious that a high buffer cache hit ratio is also a good thing.

Unfortunately, while the cache hit ratio clearly measures *something*, it's not always or even usually true that a high cache hit ratio is indicative of a well-tuned database. In particular, poorly tuned workloads often read the same data blocks over and over again; these blocks are almost certainly in memory, so the most grossly inefficient operations ironically tend to generate very high Cache Hit Ratios. An Oracle DBA Connor McDonald famously created a script that could generate any desired hit ratio, essentially by reading the same blocks over and over again. Connor's script performs no useful work but can achieve an almost perfect hit ratio.

Tip   There is no "correct" value for the cache hit ratio – high values are just as likely to be the result of poorly tuned workloads as the result of well-tuned memory configuration.

That having all been said, for a well-tuned workload (one with a sound schema design, appropriate indexes, and optimized aggregation pipelines), observing the WiredTiger hit ratio can give you an idea of how well your WiredTiger cache is sustaining your MongoDB workload demand.

Here's a script to calculate the hit rate:

```
mongo> var cache=db.serverStatus().wiredTiger.cache;
mongo> var missRatio=cache['pages read into cache']*100/cache['pages
requested from the cache'];
mongo> var hitRatio=100-missRatio;
mongo> print(hitRatio);
99.93843137484377
```

This calculation returns the cache hit rate since the server was last started. To calculate the rate over a shorter period of time, you can use the following command from our tuning scripts:

```
mongo> mongoTuning.monitorServerDerived(5000,/cacheHitRate/)
{
    "cacheHitRate": "58.9262"
}
```

This shows that the cache hit ratio over the preceding 5 seconds was 58%.

Providing our workload is well tuned, a low cache hit ratio suggests that increasing the WiredTiger cache might improve performance.

Figure 11-3 shows how various cache sizes affected the miss rate and throughput. As we increase the size of the cache, our hit rate increases and throughput also increases. The low initial hit rate, therefore, was an indication that increasing the cache size might increase throughput.

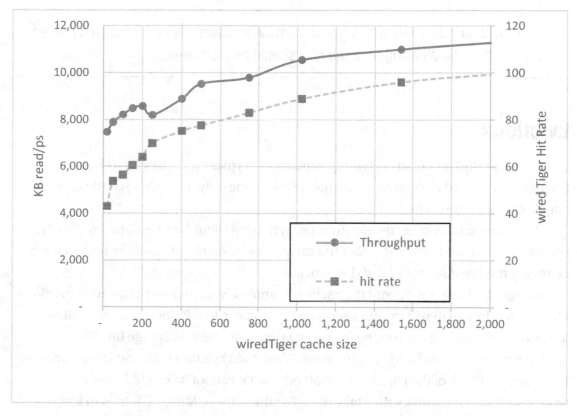

Figure 11-3. *WiredTiger cache size (MB), miss rates, and throughput*

As we increase the size of the cache, we *might* see an increase in the hit rate and an increase in throughput. The key word in the last sentence is *might*: some workloads will see little or no benefit from an increased cache size, either because all the data needed is already in memory or because some of the data is never re-read and therefore can't benefit from caching.

As imperfect as it is, the WiredTiger miss rate is a crucial health metric for many MongoDB databases.

To quote the Mongodb manual:

Performance issues may indicate that the database is operating at capacity and that it is time to add additional capacity to the database. In particular, the application's working set should fit in the available physical memory.

A high cache hit ratio is the best indicator we have that the working set does fit into memory.

Tip   Providing your workload is tuned, a low WiredTiger cache hit rate may be an indication that the WiredTiger cache size should be increased.

Evictions

Caches generally can't hold *everything* in memory. Typically, caches try to keep the most frequently accessed documents in memory by keeping only the most recently accessed pages of data in the cache.

Once the cache reaches its maximum size, making room for new data requires that old data be removed – *evicted* – from the cache. The pages of data that are removed are generally the *Least Recently Used* (LRU) pages.

MongoDB doesn't wait until the cache is completely full before performing evictions. By default, MongoDB will try and keep 20% of the cache free for new data and will start to restrict new pages from coming into cache when the free percentage hits 5%.

If a data item in cache has not been modified, then eviction is almost instantaneous. However, if a block of data has been modified, then it cannot be evicted until it is written to disk. These disk writes take time. For this reason, MongoDB tries to keep the percentage of modified – "dirty" – blocks under 5%. If the percentage of modified blocks hits 20%, then operations will be blocked until the target value is achieved.

The MongoDB server allocates dedicated threads to eviction processing – by default, four eviction threads are allocated.

Blocking Evictions

When the number of clean blocks or dirty blocks hits the higher threshold values, then sessions that try to bring new blocks into the cache will be required to perform an eviction before the read operation can complete.

Because "urgent" evictions can block operations, you want to make sure that the eviction configuration is avoiding this scenario. These "blocking" evictions are recorded in the WiredTiger parameter "page acquire eviction blocked":

```
db.serverStatus().wiredTiger["thread-yield"]["page acquire eviction blocked"]
```

These blocking evictions should be kept relatively rare. You can calculate the overall ratio of blocking evictions to overall evictions as follows:

```
mongo> var wt=db.serverStatus().wiredTiger;
mongo> var blockingEvictRate=wt['thread-yield']['page acquire eviction
blocked'] *100 / wt['cache']['eviction server evicting pages'];
mongo>
mongo> print(blockingEvictRate);
0.10212131891589296
```

You can calculate the ratio over a smaller time period using our tuning script:

```
mongo> mongoTuning.monitorServerDerived(5000,/evictionBlock/)
{
  "evictionBlockedPs": 0,
  "evictionBlockRate": 0
}
```

If the blocking eviction rate is significant, it might indicate a more aggressive eviction policy is warranted. Either start evictions earlier or apply more threads to the eviction process. It is possible to change WiredTiger eviction configuration values, but it's a risky procedure, partially because although you can set the values, you cannot directly retrieve the existing values.

For instance, the following command set the eviction thread counts and targets to their published default values:

```
mongo>db.adminCommand({
...    setParameter: 1,
...    wiredTigerEngineRuntimeConfig:
...       `eviction=(threads_min=4,threads_max=4),
...       eviction_dirty_trigger=5,eviction_dirty_target=1,
...       eviction_trigger=95,eviction_target=80`
... });
```

If evictions appeared to be problematic, we could try increasing the number of threads or changing the threshold values to promote a more or less aggressive eviction processing regime.

Tip   If there is a high rate of "blocking" evictions, then a more aggressive eviction policy might be warranted. But be very cautious when adjusting WiredTiger internal parameters.

Checkpoints

When an update or other data manipulation statement changes data in the cache, it is not immediately reflected in the datafiles that represent the durable representation of the document. A representation of the data change is written to a sequential write-ahead *journal*. These sequential journal writes can be used to recover the data in the case of a server crash, and the sequential writes involved are much faster than the random writes that would be required to keep the datafiles in absolute sync with the cache.

However, we don't want the cache to move too far in advance of the datafiles – partially because it will increase the time to recover the database in the case of a server crash. For this reason, MongoDB periodically ensures that the datafiles are synchronized with the changes in the cache. These *checkpoints* involve writing out the modified "dirty" blocks to disk. By default, checkpoints occur every 60 seconds.

Checkpoints are IO-intensive – depending on the size of the cache and the amount of dirty data in the cache, many gigabytes of information might have to be flushed to disk. As a result, checkpoints generally cause noticeable slowdowns in throughput – especially for data manipulation statements.

Figure 11-4 illustrates the impact of checkpoints – every 60 seconds; there is a sudden drop in throughput when checkpoints occur. The result is a "sawtooth" performance pattern.

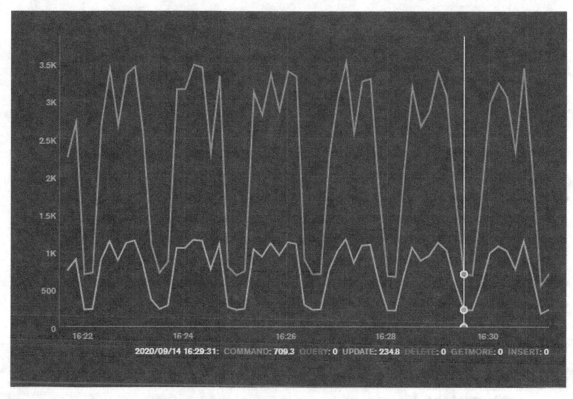

Figure 11-4. *Checkpoints can create uneven performance*

This sawtooth performance profile may or may not be of concern. However, there are a few options for changing the impacts of checkpoints. The following settings are relevant:

- The `eviction_dirty_trigger` and `eviction_dirty_target` settings – discussed in the previous section – control how many modified blocks are allowed in the cache before eviction processing kicks in. These can be adjusted to reduce the number of modified blocks in the cache, reducing the amount of data that must be written to disk during a checkpoint.

- The `eviction.threads_min` and `eviction.threads_max` settings specify how many threads will be dedicated to eviction processing. Allocating more threads to evictions will accelerate the rate of eviction processing, which could, in turn, leave fewer blocks in the cache to flush during a checkpoint.

- The checkpoint.wait setting can be adjusted to increase or reduce the time between checkpoints. If a high value is set, then the probability is that eviction processing will end up writing most of the blocks to disk before the checkpoint occurs, and the overall impact of the checkpoints might be reduced. However, it's also possible that the overhead of these delayed checkpoints will be massive.

There is no one correct setting for checkpointing, and sometimes the impact of checkpointing can be counter-intuitive. For instance, the overhead of checkpointing can be greater when you have a large WiredTiger cache. This is because the default eviction policies for modified blocks are set to a percentage of the WiredTiger cache – the greater the cache size, the more "lazy" the eviction processor will become.

However, if you are willing to experiment, you might be able to establish a lower checkpoint overhead by adjusting the time between checkpoints and the aggressiveness of eviction processing. For instance, here we adjust checkpoints to occur every 5 minutes, increase the eviction thread count, and lower the target threshold for dirty block evictions:

```
db.adminCommand({
    setParameter: 1,
        wiredTigerEngineRuntimeConfig:
            `eviction=(threads_min=10,threads_max=10),
            checkpoint=(wait=500),
            eviction_dirty_trigger=5,
            eviction_dirty_target=1`
        });
```

We want to make it absolutely clear that we are not recommending the preceding settings, nor are we recommending you modify these parameters at all. However, if you are concerned that checkpoints are creating unpredictable response times, these settings might be helpful.

Tip   Checkpoints write out modified pages to disk every one minute by default. If you are experiencing a dip in performance on a one-minute cycle, you might consider adjusting – carefully – the WiredTiger checkpoint and dirty eviction policies.

WiredTiger Concurrency

Reading and writing data in the WiredTiger cache requires that a thread obtain a read or write "ticket." By default, there are 128 of these tickets available. db.serverStatus() reports on the number of tickets available in the wiredTiger.concurrentTransactions section:

```
mongo> db.serverStatus().wiredTiger.concurrentTransactions
{
  "write": {
    "out": 7,
    "available": 121,
    "totalTickets": 128
  },
  "read": {
    "out": 28,
    "available": 100,
    "totalTickets": 128
  }
}
```

In the preceding example, 28 of 128 read tickets are in use, and 7 of 128 write tickets.

Given the short duration of most MongoDB operations, 128 tickets are usually adequate – if there are more than 128 concurrent operations, a bottleneck elsewhere in the server or operating system is likely – either queuing for CPU or queuing for MongoDB internal locks. However, these ticket counts can be increased by adjusting the parameters wiredTigerConcurrentReadTransactions and wiredTigerConcurrentWriteTransactions. For instance, to increase the number of concurrent readers to 256, we could issue the following command:

```
db.getSiblingDB("admin").
   runCommand({ setParameter: 1, wiredTigerConcurrentReadTransactions: 256
   });
```

However, be careful when increasing the number of concurrent readers, as higher values may overwhelm available hardware resources.

Reducing Application Memory Demand

As we emphasized earlier, the best tuning outcomes occur when you tune your application design and workload before tuning your hardware and server configuration. You can often get a performance improvement by adding memory to a server that is experiencing a high IO overhead. However, memory is not free, whereas creating an index or adjusting some code costs you nothing – at least in dollar terms.

We covered the key application tuning principles in the first ten chapters of this book. However, it's worth recapping on a few here, with respect to how they affect memory consumption.

Document Design

The WiredTiger cache stored complete document copies, not just the parts of the document you are interested in. So, for instance, if you have a document which looks like this:

```
{
  _id: 23,
  Ssn: 605-21-9090,
  Name: 'Guy Harrison',
  Address: '89 InfiniteLoop Drive, Cupertino, CA 9000',
  HiResScanOfDriversLicense : BinData(0,"eJy0kb201UAMhV ……… ==")
}
```

the document is fairly small, except for a massive binary representation of the users' driver's licenses. The WiredTiger cache will need to store all the high-resolution scans of driver's license in the cache, whether you ask for them or not. Therefore, to maximize memory, you may wish to adopt the *vertical partitioning* design pattern introduced in Chapter 4. We could put the driver's license scans in a separate collection which would only be loaded into the cache when needed, rather than whenever an SSN record is accessed.

Tip   Remember, the larger the document size, the fewer documents can be stored in the cache. Keeping documents small improves cache efficiency.

Indexing

Indexes offer a fast path to selected data, but also help with memory as well. When we search for data using a full collection scan, all documents are loaded into the cache regardless of whether the document matches the filter criteria. Therefore, indexed lookups help keep the cache relevant and effective.

Indexes also reduce the memory required by sorts. We saw in Chapters 6 and 7 how to avoid disk sorts using indexes. However, if we perform lots of memory sorts, then we are going to require operating system memory (outside of the WiredTiger cache) to perform these sorts. Indexed sorts don't have the same sort of memory overhead.

Tip   Indexes help reduce memory demand by introducing only required documents into the cache and by reducing the memory overhead of sorts.

Transactions

We saw in Chapter 9 how MongoDB transactions use snapshots of data to ensure that sessions do not read from uncommitted versions of documents. Prior to MongoDB 4.4, these snapshots are held in the WiredTiger cache and reduce the amount of memory available for other purposes.

Consequently, prior to MongoDB 4.4, adding transactions to your application will increase the amount of memory required in your WiredTiger cache. Furthermore, if you adjust the `transactionLifetimeLimitSeconds` parameter to allow for longer transactions, you will increase the memory pressure even more. From MongoDB 4.4 onwards, snapshots are stored to disk as "durable history" and the memory impact of long transactions is less significant.

Summary

Like all databases, MongoDB uses memory primarily to avoid disk IO. If possible, you should tune your application workload before tuning memory, since changes to schema design, indexing, and queries will all change the memory demands of your application.

In a WiredTiger implementation, MongoDB memory consists of the WiredTiger cache – primarily used to cache frequently accessed documents – and operating system memory which is used for a variety of purposes, including connection data and sort areas. Whatever your memory footprint, make sure it never exceeds the operating system memory limit; otherwise, some of this memory may be swapped out to disk.

The most significant tuning knob you have available is the WiredTiger cache size. It defaults to a little under one-half of operating system memory and can be increased in many cases, especially if there is abundant free memory on your server. The "hit rate" in the cache is one indicator that might suggest a need to increase memory.

The cache and other areas of memory serve to avoid disk IO, but eventually, some disk IO has to occur for the database to do its work. In the next chapter, we will consider how to measure and optimize necessary disk IO.

CHAPTER 12

Disk IO

In the preceding chapters, we've done everything we possibly could to avoid disk IO. By optimizing our database design and tuning queries, we minimized the workload demand and consequently reduced the logical IO demand on MongoDB. Optimizing memory reduced the amount of that workload that translated into disk activity. If you've applied the practices in the previous chapters, then your physical disk demand has been minimized: now it's time to optimize the disk subsystem to meet that demand.

Reducing IO demand should almost always come before disk IO tuning. Disk tuning is often expensive in terms of time, money, and database availability. It may involve buying expensive new disk devices and performing time-consuming data reorganizations that result in reduced availability and performance. If you attempt these things before tuning workload and memory, then you may be unnecessarily optimizing the disks for an unrealistic demand.

IO Fundamentals

Before we look at how MongoDB performs disk IO operations and at the various types of IO systems that you might deploy, it's worthwhile reviewing some of the fundamental concepts that apply to any disk IO system and any database system.

Latency and Throughput

Disk devices have two fundamental characteristics that concern us from a performance point of view: *latency* and *throughput*.

© Guy Harrison, Michael Harrison 2021
G. Harrison and M. Harrison, *MongoDB Performance Tuning*, https://doi.org/10.1007/978-1-4842-6879-7_12

Latency describes the time it takes to retrieve a single item of information from the disk. For a spinning disk drive, this is the time it takes to rotate the disk platter into the correct position (*rotational latency*), plus the time it takes to move the read/write head into position (*seek time*) plus the time taken to transfer the data from the disk to the server. For Solid State Disks, there is no mechanical seek time or rotational latency, just the transfer time.

IO *throughput* describes the number of IOs that can be performed by the disk devices in a given unit of time. Throughput is generally expressed in terms of IO operations per second, often abbreviated as *IOPS*.

For a single disk device – and especially for an SSD – throughput and latency are intimately related. The throughput is directly determined by the latency – if each IO takes one-thousandth of a second, then the throughput should be 1000 IOPS. However, when multiple devices are combined into a logical volume, the latency and throughput have a less direct relationship. Furthermore, in magnetic disks, the throughput for sequential reads is much higher than for random reads.

For most database servers, data is stored on multiple disk devices and "striped" across the disks concerned. In this case, IO bandwidth is a function of the types of IO operations (random vs. sequential), service time, and the number of disks. For instance, a perfectly striped disk array containing ten disks with 10ms service times would have a random IO bandwidth of approximately 1000 IOPS (100 IOPS for each disk times ten disks).

Queuing

The service time for disk devices remains fairly predictable when the disk is idle and awaiting requests. The service time will vary somewhat depending on the disk's internal cache and – for a magnetic disk – the distance that the read/write head needs to move to acquire the relevant data. But in general, the response time will be within the range quoted by the disk manufacturer.

However, as the number of requests increases, some requests will have to wait while other requests are serviced. As the request rate increases, eventually a queue forms. Just as in a busy supermarket, you soon find you are spending more time in the queue than actually being serviced.

Because of queuing, disk latency increases sharply as a disk system approaches full capacity. When the disk becomes 100% busy, any additional requests simply increase the length of the queue and service time increases without any consequent increase in throughput.

The lesson here is that latency increases as we increase the throughput of a disk. Figure 12-1 illustrates the typical relationship between throughput and latency: increasing throughput is usually associated with increasing latency. Eventually, no more throughput can be achieved; at this point, any increase in the request rate increases latency without increasing throughput.

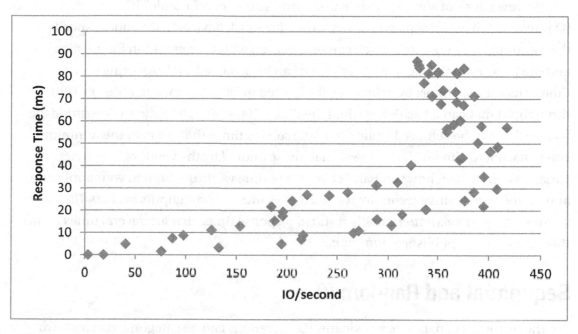

Figure 12-1. *Latency vs. throughput*

Note   Latency and throughput are correlated: increasing the throughput or demand on disk devices will usually result in an increase in latency. To minimize latency, it may be necessary to run disks at less than maximum throughput.

If an individual disk has a limit on its maximum IOPS, then achieving a higher IO throughput rate will require deploying more physical disks. Unlike latency calculations – which are governed by the relatively complex queuing theory calculations – the calculation for the number of disk devices required is simple. If an individual disk can perform 100 IOPS while delivering acceptable latency and we believe we need to deliver 500 IOPS, then we are likely to need at least five disk devices.

Tip   The throughput of an IO system is primarily determined by the number of physical disk devices it contains. To increase IO throughput, increase the number of physical disks in disk volumes.

However, it's not always possible to determine the "comfortable" IO rate – the IO rate that delivers acceptable service time – for a disk device. Disk vendors specify the minimum latency – that which can be achieved with no contention for the disk – and the maximum throughput – that which can be achieved while ignoring service time constraints. Almost by definition, the quoted throughput for a disk device is the throughput that can be achieved when the disk is 100% busy. In order to determine the IO rate that can be achieved while obtaining service times that are near the minimum, you will want to aim for IO rate lower than those quoted by the vendors. The exact variance depends on how you balance response time vs. throughput in your application and on the type of drive technologies you use. However, throughputs over 50–70% of the vendor's quoted *maximum* usually result in response times that are several times *higher* than the vendor's published *minimums*.

Sequential and Random IO

For the purposes of database workloads, IO operations can be categorized across two dimensions: *read* vs. *write* IO and *sequential* vs. *random* IO.

Sequential IO occurs when blocks of data are read in sequence. For instance, when we read all the documents in a collection using a collection scan, we are performing sequential IO. Random IO accesses pages of data in an arbitrary order. For instance, when we retrieve a single document from a collection following an index lookup, we are performing a random IO.

Table 12-1 shows how database IO maps to these two dimensions.

Table 12-1. *Categories of database IO*

	Read	**Write**
Random	Reading individual documents using an index	Writing data from the cache to disk following an eviction (see Chapter 11)
Sequential	Reading all the documents in a collection using a full collection scan Scanning index entries in order to avoid a disk sort	Writing to the WiredTiger Journal or Oplog Bulk loading data into the database

Disk Hardware

In this section, we'll review the various hardware components that comprise a storage subsystem from individual magnetic or SSD disks through to hardware and cloud-based storage arrays.

Magnetic Disks (HDD)

Magnetic disk or *hard disk drive* (*HDD*) has been a ubiquitous component of mainstream computer equipment for generations of IT professionals. First introduced in the 1950s, the fundamental technology has remained remarkably constant: one or more platters contain magnetic charges that represent bits of information. These magnetic charges are read and written by an actuator arm, which moves across the disk to a specific position on the radius of the platter and then waits for the platter to rotate to the appropriate location. The time taken to read an item of information is the sum of the time taken to move the head into position (seek time), the time taken to rotate the item into place (rotational latency), and the time taken to transmit the item through the disk controller (transfer time). Figure 12-2[1] illustrates the core architecture of a magnetic disk device.

---

[1]Wikipedia: `http://en.wikipedia.org/wiki/Hard_disk_drive`

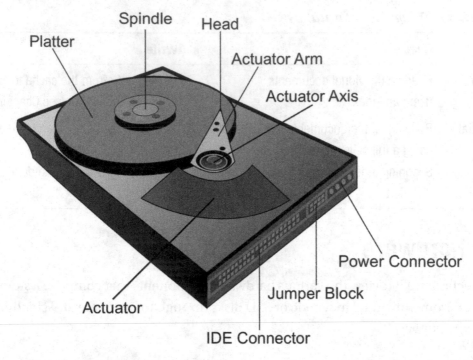

Figure 12-2. *Hard disk drive architecture*

This architecture has a few implications that we should be aware of with respect to database workloads. Although random accesses are very slow – since we must wait for the disk head to move into position – sequential reads and writes can be quite fast, since the read head can remain in position while the sequential data rotates beneath it. This has some implications when we compare HDD and SSD write performance a bit later.

Moore's Law – first articulated by Intel founder Gordon Moore – observes that transistor density doubles every 18–24 months. In its broadest interpretation, Moore's Law reflects the exponential growth that is commonly observed in almost all electronic components – influencing CPU speed, RAM, and disk storage capacity.

While this exponential growth is observed in almost all electronic aspects of computing – including hard disk densities – it does not apply to mechanical technologies such as those underlying magnetic disk IO. For instance, had Moore's Law been in effect for the rotation speed of disk devices, magnetic disks today should be rotating 20 million times faster than in the early 1960s – in fact, they are rotating only eight times faster.

Solid State Drives

Solid State Drives (SSDs) store data in semiconductor cells and have no moving parts. They offer far lower latencies for data transfer since there is no wait for the mechanical movement of the disk or actuator arm that is required in magnetic disk devices.

Note It's common to refer to Solid State Devices as "disks" even though they have no spinning disk component.

However, it was only in the past 10–15 years that Solid State Disks became cheap enough to become an economical choice for database systems. Even now, magnetic disks offer far cheaper storage per GB than SSDs, and for some systems, magnetic disk or a combination of SSD and magnetic disk will offer the best price/performance mix.

The performance differences between SSDs and magnetic disks are more complex than simply fast reads. Just as the fundamental architecture of magnetic disk favors certain IO operations, the architecture of SSDs favors different types of IO. Understanding how an SSD handles the different types of operations helps us make the best decision for SSD deployment.

Note In the following discussion, we'll concentrate on flash-based SSD technologies, since this technology is almost universally used in database systems. However, there are also DRAM-based SSD devices that have a higher cost and superior performance.

SSD Storage Hierarchy

SSDs have a three-level hierarchy of storage. Individual bits of information are stored in *cells*. In a single-level cell (*SLC*) SSD, each cell stores only a single bit. In a multi-level cell (*MLC*), each cell may store two or more bits of information. MLC SSD devices consequently have greater storage densities, but lower performance and reliability.

Cells are arranged in pages – typically 4K in size – and pages into blocks of between 128K and 1M.

Write Performance

The page and block structure is particularly significant for SSD performance because of the special characteristics of write IO in flash technology. Read operations, and an initial write, require only a single page IO. However, changing the contents of a page requires an erase and over-write of a complete block. Even the initial write is significantly slower than a read, but the block erase operation is particularly slow – around two milliseconds.

Figure 12-3 shows the approximate times for a page seek, initial page write, and block erase.

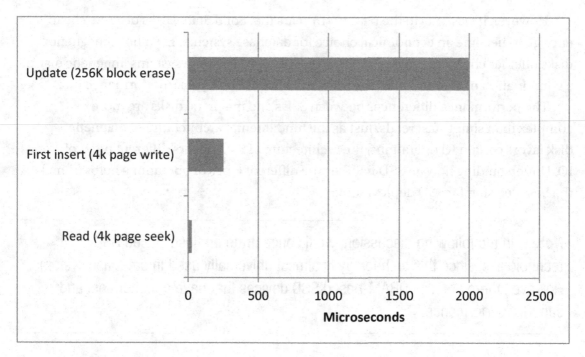

Figure 12-3. *SSD performance characteristics*

Write Endurance

Write IO has another consequence in SSDs: after a certain number of writes, a cell may become unusable. This *write endurance limit* differs between drives but is typically between 10,000 cycles for a low-end MLC device and up to 1,000,000 cycles for a high-end SLC device.

Garbage Collection and Wear Levelling

Enterprise SSD manufacturers go to great efforts to avoid the performance penalty of the erase operation and the reliability concerns raised by write endurance. Sophisticated algorithms are used to ensure that erase operations are minimized and that writes are evenly distributed across the device.

In an Enterprise SSD, erase operations are avoided through the use of *free lists* and *garbage collection*. During an update, the SSD will mark the block to be modified as invalid and copy the updated contents to an empty block, retrieved from a "free list." Later, garbage collection routines will recover the invalid block, placing it on a free list for subsequent operations. Some SSDs will maintain storage above the advertised capacity of the drive to ensure that the free list does not run out of empty blocks for this purpose.

Wear levelling is the algorithm that ensures that no particular block is subjected to a disproportionate number of writes. It may involve moving the contents of "hot" blocks to blocks from the free list and eventually marking overused blocks as unusable.

SATA vs. PCI

SSDs are typically deployed in one of three form factors:

- *SATA-* or *SAS*-based flash drives are packaged in the same form factor as other magnetic HDDs that attach using the traditional SAS or SATA connectors. An example of this can be seen in Figure 12-4.

- *PCI*-based SSDs such as the one in Figure 12-5 connect directly to the *PCIe* interface on the computer motherboard. The *NVMe*, or non-volatile memory express, specification describes how SSDs should attach to the PCIe and so these types of disks are often referred to as *NVMe SSDs*.

- Flash storage servers present multiple SSDs within a rack-mounted server with multiple high-speed network interface cards.

Figure 12-4. *SSD drives in SATA and mSATA format*[2]

---

[2]Wikipedia: https://tinyurl.com/y4tfn3n7

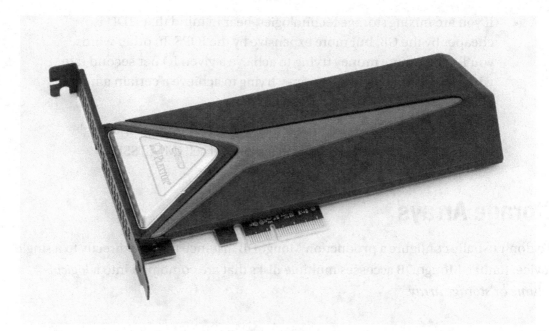

Figure 12-5. *SSD with PCIe/NVMe connector[3]*

SATA or SAS flash drives are substantially cheaper than PCI. However, the SATA interface was designed for slower devices with millisecond latencies and, therefore, imposes significant overhead on Solid State Drive service times. PCI-based devices can interface directly with the server and provide the most optimal performance.

Recommendations for SSDs

We've covered a lot of hardware internals in the last few pages, and you might be wondering how to apply these to your MongoDB deployment. We can summarize the implications of magnetic disk and SSD architectures as follows:

- Wherever possible, you should use SSD-based storage for MongoDB databases. Only if you have massive amounts of "cold" – rarely accessed – data would magnetic disk be suitable.

---

[3]Wikipedia: `https://tinyurl.com/y6dr2tm5`

- If you are mixing storage technologies, bear in mind that HDD is cheaper by the GB, but more expensive by the IOPS. In other words, you'll spend more money trying to achieve a given IO per second rate with HDD and spend more money trying to achieve a certain amount of GB storage with SSD.

- PCI-based SSDs (NVMe) are faster than SATA-based SSDs, and single-level cell (SLC) SSDs are faster than multi-level cell (MLC) SSDs.

Storage Arrays

We don't usually configure a production MongoDB instance to write directly to a single device. Rather, MongoDB accesses multiple disks that are combined into a *logical volume* or *storage array*.

RAID Levels

RAID – originally an acronym for *Redundant Array of Inexpensive Disks*[4] – defines a variety of striping and redundancy schemes. The term "RAID array" typically refers to a storage device comprising a number of physical disk devices which can be attached to a server and accessed as one or more logical devices.

There are three levels of RAID commonly provided by storage vendors:

- **RAID 0** is referred to as "striping" disks. In this configuration, a logical disk is constructed from multiple physical disks. The data contained on the logical disk is spread evenly across the physical disk, and hence random IOs are also likely to be spread evenly. There is no redundancy built into this configuration, so if a disk fails, the data on it will have to be recovered from a backup.

- **RAID 1** is referred to as disk "mirroring." In this configuration, a logical disk is comprised of two physical disks. In the event that one physical disk fails, processing can continue using the other physical

---

[4]Changed later on by disk vendors to *Redundant Array of Independent Disks*; RAID systems are usually anything but inexpensive.

disk. Each disk contains identical data and writes are processed in parallel, so there should be little or no negative effects on write performance. Reads can occur from either of the disk pairs, so read throughput should be increased.

- In **RAID 5**, a logical disk is comprised of multiple physical disks. Data is arranged across the physical devices in a similar way to disk striping (RAID 0). However, a certain proportion of the data on the physical devices is *parity* data. This parity data contains enough information to derive data on other disks should a single physical device fail.

Lower RAID levels (2–4) have similar characteristics to RAID 5, but are rarely encountered in practice. *RAID 6* is similar to RAID 5 but has more redundancy: two disks can fail simultaneously without data loss.

It's common to combine RAID 0 and RAID 1 (usually called *RAID 10* or *RAID 0+1*). Such striped and mirrored configurations offer protection against hardware failure, together with the benefits of IO striping. RAID 10 is sometimes referred to as the *SAME* (Stripe And Mirror Everything) strategy.

Figure 12-6 illustrates the various raid levels.

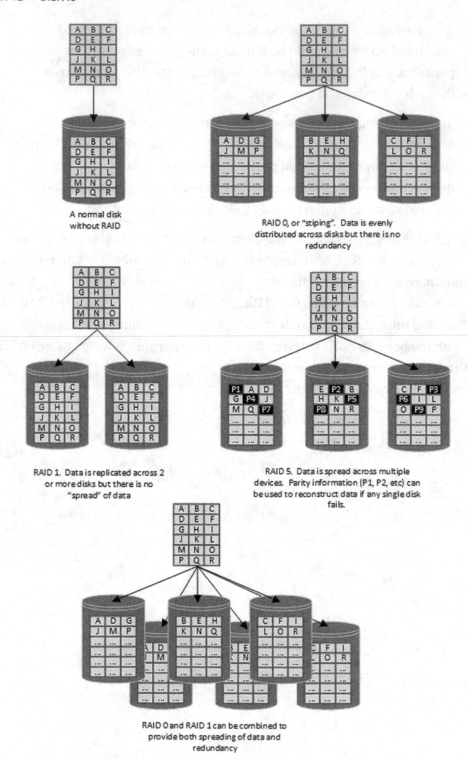

Figure 12-6. *RAID levels*

You can implement RAID using directly attached disk devices using *Logical Volume Management* (*LVM*) software provided with Linux and Windows. More commonly, RAID is configured within hardware storage arrays. We'll look at both of these shortly.

The RAID 5 Write Penalty

RAID 5 provides the most economical architecture for delivering fault-tolerant storage with IO distributed across multiple physical disks. Consequently, it's popular both among storage vendors and MIS departments. However, it's a very dubious configuration for database servers.

Both RAID 0 and RAID 5 improve the performance of concurrent random reads by spreading the load across multiple devices. However, RAID 5 degrades write IO, since, during a write, both the source block and the parity block must be read and then updated – four IOs in total. This degradation becomes even more extreme if a disk fails since all disks must be accessed in order to rebuild a logical view of the failed disk.

From a performance point of view, RAID 5 offers few advantages and very significant drawbacks. The write penalty incurred by RAID 5 will generally degrade the performance of checkpoints, evictions, and journal IO. RAID 5 should only ever be considered for databases that are predominantly read-only. Even for a read intensive database such as a data warehouse, RAID 5 can still result in disastrous performance when large aggregations are performed: the temporary file IO will be severely degraded and even apparently read-only performance significantly affected.

Caution   The write penalty of RAID 5 renders it unsuitable for most databases. Even apparently read-only databases can be degraded by RAID 5 when temporary file IO occurs.

Non-volatile Caches in RAID 5 Devices

The write penalty associated with RAID 5 devices can be reduced by the use of a *non-volatile cache*. The non-volatile cache is a memory store with a battery backup, which ensures that the data in the cache is not lost in the event of a power failure. Because the data in the cache is protected against loss, it is permissible for the disk device to report that the data has been written to disk as soon as it is stored into the cache. The data can be written down to the physical disk at a later point in time.

Battery-backed caches can improve the performance of writes immensely, especially when the application requests confirmation that the data written has actually been committed to disk – which MongoDB almost always does. Such caches are very common in RAID devices, partially because they help to alleviate the overhead of disk writes in a RAID 5 configuration. With a large enough cache, the RAID 5 writes overhead can be practically eliminated for bursts of write activity. However, if the write activity is sustained over time, then the cache will fill up with modified data, array performance will then reduce to that of the underlying disks and a substantial and sudden drop in performance may occur. The effect is quite remarkable – an abrupt and drastic reduction in disk throughput and massive degradation in service times.

Do It Yourself Arrays

If you have multiple devices directly attached to your host server, you may wish to stripe and/or mirror them yourself. The procedure varies a little bit from system to system, but on most Linux systems, you can use the mdadm command.

Here, we create a stripe volume /dev/md0 from two raw devices /dev/sdh and /dev/sdi. The –level=0 parameter indicates a RAID 0 device.

```
[root@Centos8 etc]# # Make the array
[root@Centos8 etc]# mdadm --create --verbose /dev/md0 --level=0
      --name=raid1a --raid-devices=2 /dev/sdh /dev/sdi
mdadm: chunk size defaults to 512K
mdadm: Defaulting to version 1.2 metadata
mdadm: array /dev/md0 started.

[root@Centos8 etc]# # create a filesystem on the array
[root@Centos8 etc]# mkfs -t xfs /dev/md0
meta-data=/dev/md0                  isize=512    agcount=16, agsize=1047424
blks
         =                          sectsz=4096  attr=2,
 ...
[root@Centos8 etc]# # Mount the array
[root@Centos8 etc]# mkdir /mnt/raid1a
[root@Centos8 etc]# mount /dev/md0 /mnt/raid1a
Filesystem      Type 1K-blocks   Used Available Use% Mounted on
/dev/md0        xfs  67002404 501408  66500996   1% /mnt/raid1a
```

If we created multiple RAID 0 devices, we could combine them using RAID 1 to create a RAID 10 configuration.

Hardware Storage Arrays

Many MongoDB databases use directly attached storage devices – the server which runs the mongod instance has complete and exclusive access to the storage devices which are directly attached to the server using SATA, SAS, or PCIe interfaces. However, it's at least as common for storage and IO to be provided by an external storage device often referred to as a *storage array*.

A storage array provides shared access to a pool of devices which are normally structured in some sort of RAID configuration to provide high availability. There is often a non-volatile memory cache which ensures that data in the cache is still written to disk even in the event of a power failure.

A storage array connects to the server over a local – usually dedicated – network interface and provides the server with a block device that provides all the functionality of a directly attached disk drive.

There's a wide variety of storage array configurations provided by various hardware vendors. For a MongoDB server, the critical considerations for storage arrays are as follows:

- No matter how good the hardware storage arrays internal configuration, you are adding network latency to each IO request. When compared to optimized direct-attached IO, a hardware storage array may have higher latency.

- The internal configuration of the storage array matters – recommendations regarding HDD vs. SSD, PCI vs. SATA, and SLC vs. MLC all apply to hardware storage arrays.

- Hardware storage array vendors will generally try to convince you that their RAID 5 configuration is more economical than RAID 10. However, decades of experience in database IO argue against this point – RAID 5 is a false economy which will generally increase the cost of IOPS, even if it lowers the dollar cost per GB of storage.

> **Tip**   When considering an IO subsystem, remember that you have to pay for IOPS as much as GB of storage. RAID 5 might seem more cost-effective per GB, but will make it much harder – and ultimately more expensive – to achieve a desired write IO rate.

Cloud Storage

In a cloud environment, the underlying hardware architecture is normally obscured. Instead, the cloud vendor provides a variety of block store devices, each of which is associated with specific latency and throughput service levels.

Table 12-2 describes some of the volume types available on the Amazon AWS cloud. Google Cloud Platform (GCP) and Microsoft Azure offer very similar offerings.

Table 12-2. *Amazon AWS volume types*

Volume Type	Description
General Purpose SSD	These volumes are based on commodity SSDs, and the IO limits depend on the amount of GB storage requested. The number of SSDs used to provision the volume is determined by the amount of storage requested. A 100 GB volume provides a 300 IOPS baseline.
Provisioned IOPS SSD	These SSD volumes provide a specific IO level independent of the amount of storage provisioned. Under the hood, this implies that the number of SSD devices is determined by the IO requirement, not the storage requested.
Throughput Optimized HDD	High-performance magnetic disk volumes optimized for sequential reads and write operations.
Cold HDD	Cheap magnetic disks optimized for low cost of storage.
Instance Store	Instance store – or ephemeral disks – are HDD, SATA SSD, or NVMe SSD devices that are directly attached to the physical machine hosting the EC2 VM. Ephemeral NVMe disks are the fastest of all device types, but as with all ephemeral disks, data is lost in the event of an instance failure, so these should not be used for MongoDB datafiles.

Our guiding principle for optimizing IO is to provision disks based on IO rates, not storage capacities. Therefore, if provisioning a cloud-based VM for a MongoDB installation, you would generally choose a provisioned IOPS SSD disk type. In AWS this would mean choosing a *provisioned IOPS SSD*, in GCP the *SSD persistent disk (pd-ssd)* type, and in Azure *premium SSD* disks.

Each of the preceding disk types is implemented from disks in external disk arrays attached to the virtual machines by dedicated networks. If you need the very high performance of a directly attached device, such as an NVMe-attached SSD, you can consider the *AWS Nitro* configuration which offers high-speed directly attached disk devices in a high-performance EC2 virtual machine.

Tip   When configuring a cloud-based VM for a MongoDB server, use provisioned IOPS SSDs (Amazon), premium SSD disks (GCP), or SSD persistent disks (GCP). Choose your devices based on the required IO capacity, not on the storage capacity.

Disk Devices in MongoDB Atlas

When configuring a MongoDB Atlas cluster, you configure the maximum IOPS required for the cluster. Behind the scenes, Atlas attaches provisioned SSD devices with the required IOPS capacity from the cloud platform you have selected.

MongoDB IO

Now that we have reviewed the performance characteristics of various types of storage devices, let us take a look at how MongoDB uses these devices.

In a standard configuration of MongoDB with WiredTiger as the storage engine, MongoDB performs three major types of IO operations:

- **Temporary file IO** involves reads and writes to the "_tmp" directory within the dbPath directory. These IOs occur when a disk sort or disk-based aggregation operation occurs. We discussed these operations in Chapters 7 and 11. These IOs are generally sequential read and write operations.

- **Datafile IO** occurs when WiredTiger reads from and writes to collection and index files in the dbPath directory. Reads and writes to index files tend to be random accesses (though index scans can be sequential), while reads and writes to collection files may be random or sequential.

- **Journal file IO** occurs as the WiredTiger storage engine writes to the "write-ahead" journal file. These are sequential write IOs.

Figure 12-7 illustrates the various types of MongoDB IO.

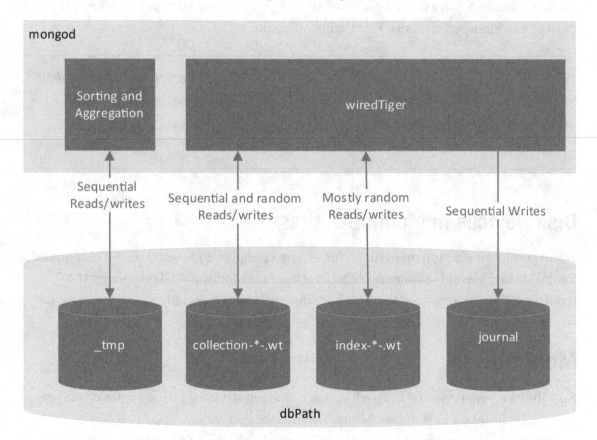

Figure 12-7. *MongoDB IO architecture*

Temporary File IO

Temporary file IO occurs when a MongoDB aggregation request cannot be performed in memory, and the allowDiskUse clause has been set to true. In this case, excess data will be written to temporary files in the "_tmp" directory within the dbPath directory.

For example, here we see that there are three disk sorts in progress, each writing to a unique file in the _tmp directory:

```
$ ls -l _tmp
total 916352
-rw-------. 1 mongod mongod 297770960 Sep 26 05:19 extsort-sort-executor.3
-rw-------. 1 mongod mongod 223665943 Sep 26 05:19 extsort-sort-executor.4
-rw-------. 1 mongod mongod  99258259 Sep 26 05:19 extsort-sort-executor.5
```

The amount of IO read and written to these files is not directly exposed in db. serverStatus() or from monitoring tools so it can easily "fall under the radar." Indeed, practically the only place that you might find evidence of disk sorts is in the MongoDB log and only then if you have set the slow query setting (see Chapter 3):

```
[root@Centos8 mongodb]# tail mongod.log |grep '"usedDisk"'|jq
{
 <snip>
   "msg": "Slow query",
   "attr": {
     "type": "command",
     "ns": "SampleCollections.baseCollection",
     "appName": "MongoDB Shell",
     "command": {
       "aggregate": "baseCollection",
<snip>
     "planSummary": "COLLSCAN",
     "keysExamined": 0,
     "docsExamined": 1000000,
     "hasSortStage": true,
     "usedDisk": true,
<snip>
     "protocol": "op_msg",
     "durationMillis": 28011
   }
}
```

When this IO becomes extreme, it can disrupt IO to the datafiles and the journal. So as well as creating slow aggregation pipelines, disk sorts can easily create a generalized performance bottleneck.

If you suspect that IO to temporary files is an issue, you should consider increasing the `internalQueryMaxBlockingSortMemoryUsageBytes` configuration parameter. This change may allow these operations to be satisfied within memory and avoid IO to the _tmp directory.

Alternatively, because these IOs are to temporary files only, you might consider locating the "_tmp" directory on a fast volatile medium. This might be a dedicated SSD or a cloud-based ephemeral disk. As we discussed in a previous section, in a cloud-hosted VM, you can usually configure fast, directly attached disks which do not persist across VM restarts. These devices may be suitable for the "_tmp" directory.

Unfortunately, in the current implementation of MongoDB, it is not possible to map "_tmp" directly to a dedicated device. Your only option would be to map everything else to dedicated devices – this is possible, but probably impractical in most cases. See section "Splitting Up Datafiles Across Multiple Devices" later in this chapter for the procedure.

The Journal

When MongoDB changes a document image in the WiredTiger cache, the modified "dirty" copy is not written to disk immediately. The modified pages are only written to disk when a *checkpoint* occurs. We discussed checkpoints in the previous chapter.

To ensure that data is not lost in the event of a server failure, WiredTiger writes all changes to a *journal* file. The journal file is an example of the *write-ahead log (WAL)* pattern, which has been common in database systems for many decades. The advantage of a write-ahead log is that it can be written to sequentially, and for most devices (particularly magnetic disk), sequential writes can achieve greater throughput than random writes.

MongoDB exposes WiredTiger journal statistics through the "log" sub-section of the "WiredTiger" section within `db.serverStatus()` output:

```
rs1:PRIMARY> db.serverStatus().wiredTiger.log
{
        "busy returns attempting to switch slots" : 1318029,
        "force archive time sleeping (usecs)" : 0,
        "log bytes of payload data" : 83701979208,
```

```
    "log bytes written" : 97884903040,
    ...
    "log sync operations" : 415082,
    "log sync time duration (usecs)" : 47627625426,
    "log sync_dir operations" : 936,
    "log sync_dir time duration (usecs)" : 331288246,
    ...
}
```

Within this section, the following statistics are the most useful:

- **log bytes written**: The amount of data written to the journal.

- **log sync operations**: The number of log "sync" operations. A sync occurs when journal information held in memory is flushed to disk.

- **log sync time duration (μsecs)**: The number of microseconds spent in sync operations.

By monitoring these metrics, we can determine the rate of data writes to the journal and the delay incurred when flushing that data to disk. The time spent in flush operations is particularly relevant since MongoDB sessions must wait for these flushes to occur.

The following command calculates the average journal sync time since the server has been started:

```
rs1:PRIMARY> var journalStats = db.serverStatus().wiredTiger.log;
rs1:PRIMARY> var avgSyncTimeMs =
...    journalStats['log sync time duration (usecs)'] / 1000 /
       journalStats['log sync operations'];
rs1:PRIMARY> print('Journal avg sync time (ms)', avgSyncTimeMs);
Journal avg sync time (ms) 114.07684435539662
```

The average log sync time is probably the most sensitive measure of journal disk contention. However, the expected time does depend on the nature of the workload. In the case of small document updates, we'd expect the log sync time to be very short, since the average amount of data to be written is small. On the other hand, bulk loading of massive documents might result in a higher average time. Nevertheless, we generally don't feel comfortable with sync times over 100ms, and the preceding sync time of 114ms probably demands attention.

Within our tuning script (see Chapter 3), we calculate some journal-related statistics, all of which start with "log". For instance, in the following example, we retrieve journal statistics over a 5-second period:

```
rs1:PRIMARY> mongoTuning.monitorServerDerived(5000,/^log/)
{
  "logKBRatePS": "888.6250",
  "logSyncTimeRateMsPS": "379.9926",
  "logSyncOpsPS": "6.2000",
  "logAvgSyncTime": "61.2891"
}
```

In this example, we see that the server is writing about 888KB of journal data per second and flushes that data to disk about six times per second, and each flush takes about 61ms.

Unfortunately, there's no "right" value for the log sync time. Workloads that perform the same logical amount of work can result in very different journal activity depending on the amount of work that is "batched" into each statement. For instance, consider this update:

```
db.iotData.find({ _id: { $lt: limit } }, { _id: 1 }).
    forEach(id => {
    var rc = db.iotData.update(
      { _id: id['_id'] },
      { $inc: { a: 1 } },
      { multi: false }
    );
  });
```

This statement generates a lot of individual updates and hence a large number of small journal writes. However, the following statement performs the same work but in a single statement. It results in fewer journal writes, but each journal write is larger.

```
    db.iotData.update(
      { _id: { $lt: limit } },
      { $inc: { a: 1 } },
      { multi: true }
    );
```

Figure 12-8 illustrates the effect. A single bulk update results in fewer journal writes but with each write operation taking longer. Note that the total amount of journal time taken was lowest for the bulk update.

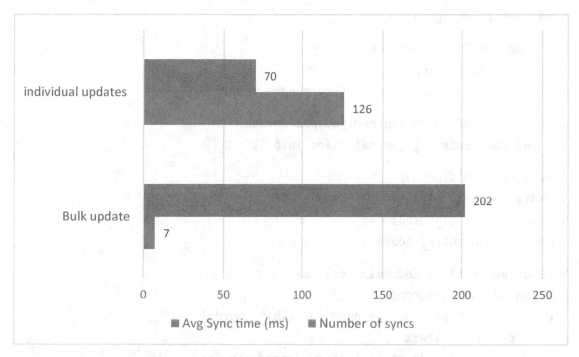

Figure 12-8. *Bulk updates result in fewer, but larger journal sync writes*

Note   The average journal "sync" time is your best indication of the IO contention for journal writes. However, the average time is heavily dependent on workload, and there is no "correct" value for this latency.

Moving the Journal to a Dedicated Device

Because the IO to the journal is fundamentally different in nature to the IO to the other datafiles, and because database modifications usually have to wait on journal writes to complete, in some circumstances, you might want to mount the journal on a dedicated high-speed device. This procedure involves mounting a new external disk device and moving the journal files to that device.

Here's an example in which we move the journal files to a dedicated device located on /dev/sde:

```
$ # go to the dbpath directory
$ cd /var/lib/mongodb

$ # Stop the Mongod service
$ service mongod stop
Redirecting to /bin/systemctl stop mongod.service

$ # Mount /dev/sde as the new journal device
$ # and copy existing journal files into it

$ mv journal OldJournal
$ mkdir journal
$ mount /dev/sde journal
$ cp -p OldJournal/* journal

$ # Set permissions including selinux
$ chown -R mongod:mongod journal
$ chcon -R -u system_u -t mongod_var_lib_t journal
$ service mongod start
Redirecting to /bin/systemctl start mongod.service
```

You would also need to make sure that this new device was mounted permanently, by adding the appropriate entry to /dev/fstab.

Moving the journal file is not an activity to be undertaken lightly, and you should only do so if you have very strong motivation to optimize write performance. Nevertheless, the effect can be significant. In Figure 12-9, we compare journal latency when mounted on external HDD or SSD compared to the default in which the journal is placed on the same filesystem as the datafiles.

Moving the journal file to a dedicated magnetic disk increased the average time taken to write log entries. However, moving the journal to a dedicated high-speed device reduced the average sync time significantly.

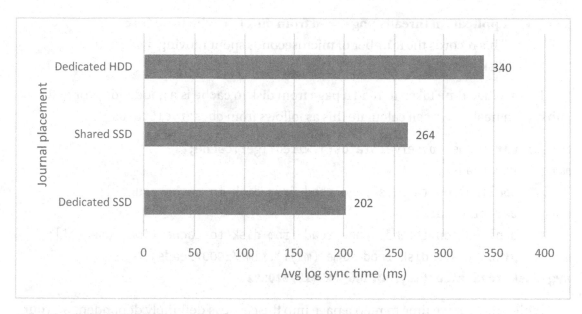

Figure 12-9. *Effect of moving the journal file to a dedicated device*

Tip   Because the journal IO is fundamentally different in nature to datafile IO, it can be worthwhile moving the journal to a dedicated high-speed device.

Datafile IO

For most databases, reads greatly outnumber writes. Even when a system is update-intensive, data has to be read before it can be written. Only when a workload consists almost entirely of bulk inserts does write performance become the dominant factor.

In the previous chapter, we discussed at length the role of the WiredTiger cache in avoiding disk reads. If a document can be found in the cache, it does not need to be read from disk, and for a typical workload, more than 90% of documents reads can be expected to be found in the cache.

However, when data cannot be found in the cache, it must be read from disk. Read IO into the cache is recorded in the following two statistics within the `wiredTiger.cache` section of `db.serverStatus()` output:

- **application threads page read from disk to cache count**: This records the number of reads from disk into the WiredTiger cache.

- **application threads page read from disk to cache time (usecs)**:
  This records the number of microseconds spent moving data from
  disk to cache.

The average time taken to read a page from disk to cache is a good indicator of IO
subsystem health. We can calculate this as follows from `db.serverStatus()`:

```
mongo> var cache=db.serverStatus().wiredTiger.cache;
mongo> var reads=cache
    ['application threads page read from disk to cache count'];
mongo> var time=cache
    ['application threads page read from disk to cache time (usecs)'];
mongo> print ('avg disk read time (ms):',time/1000/reads);
avg disk read time (ms): 0.10630484187820192
```

While the average time to read a page into the cache is definitely dependent on your
hardware configuration and somewhat dependent on workload, this is one metric where
we have a good basis for rules of thumb. If the time exceeds the normal read time for a
disk device, then something is wrong!

Generally, your average disk to cache read time should be less than 10ms – even if
you are using a magnetic disk. If your disk subsystem is on Solid State Disk devices, then
the average read time should generally be below 1ms.

Tip   If the average time taken to load a page from disk to cache exceeds 1–2ms,
then your IO subsystem may be overloaded. If you are using magnetic disk, then
average times approaching 10ms may be expected.

Datafile Writes

As we discussed in Chapter 11, WiredTiger writes to the datafiles asynchronously, and
most of the time, the application does not need to wait for these writes. As discussed
earlier, the application will normally wait only for the write to the journal to complete.

However, should write IO become a bottleneck, then the eviction process will block
operations until the cache is sufficiently cleared of dirty (modified) data. These waits are
hard to monitor, but we did discuss options in Chapter 11 for optimizing checkpoint and
eviction processing in an attempt to reduce these waits.

Writes from cache to disk are recorded in the `WiredTiger.cache` sections of the `db.serverStatus()` output in the following metrics:

- **application threads page write from cache to disk count:** The number of writes from the cache to disk

- **application threads page write from cache to disk time (usecs):** The time spent writing from cache to disk

However, while we can calculate an average write time from these metrics, it's harder to interpret the result. A page read from the disk should generally be predictable, but writes to disk can vary in size markedly, and, therefore, you may see variations in the average write time based on workload fluctuations. It is, therefore, best to use the average *read* time as your primary indicator of datafile IO health.

Splitting Up Datafiles Across Multiple Devices

The normal practice for disk layout is to place all the datafiles on a single filesystem backed by a disk array which is configured as RAID 10 – striped and mirrored. However, in some cases, it might be worth mapping specific elements of the datafiles to dedicated devices.

For instance, your server might contain a database that consists of very large quantities of "cold" archived data, together with smaller quantities of very "hot" data which is subject to frequent modifications. It might be economical and sensible to host the cold data on cheap magnetic disk and the hot data on premium SSDs.

Splitting datafiles across multiple devices is possible. However, it's a lot easier if it is planned for during initial database creation. The `directoryPerDB` and `directoryForIndexes` configuration parameters result in each database's datafiles being stored in their own directory and with indexes and collection files in separate subdirectories.

Here's an example of a configuration file in which these two parameters are set:

```
# Where and how to store data.
storage:
  dbPath: /mnt/mongodb/mongoData/rs1
  directoryPerDB: true
  journal:
    enabled: true
```

```
wiredTiger:
  engineConfig:
    cacheSizeGB: 16
    directoryForIndexes: true
```

The dbPath directory for this server looks something like this:

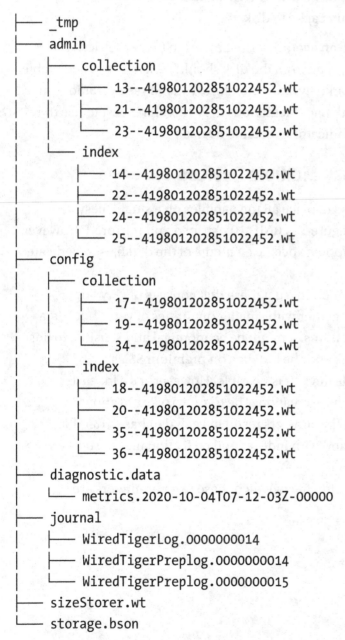

```
├──── _tmp
├──── admin
│     ├──── collection
│     │     ├──── 13--419801202851022452.wt
│     │     ├──── 21--419801202851022452.wt
│     │     └──── 23--419801202851022452.wt
│     └──── index
│           ├──── 14--419801202851022452.wt
│           ├──── 22--419801202851022452.wt
│           ├──── 24--419801202851022452.wt
│           └──── 25--419801202851022452.wt
├──── config
│     ├──── collection
│     │     ├──── 17--419801202851022452.wt
│     │     ├──── 19--419801202851022452.wt
│     │     └──── 34--419801202851022452.wt
│     └──── index
│           ├──── 18--419801202851022452.wt
│           ├──── 20--419801202851022452.wt
│           ├──── 35--419801202851022452.wt
│           └──── 36--419801202851022452.wt
├──── diagnostic.data
│     └──── metrics.2020-10-04T07-12-03Z-00000
├──── journal
│     ├──── WiredTigerLog.0000000014
│     ├──── WiredTigerPreplog.0000000014
│     └──── WiredTigerPreplog.0000000015
├──── sizeStorer.wt
└──── storage.bson
```

As you can see, each database now has its own directory with subdirectories for the collection and index files. To shift a database to a dedicated device, we can follow the same procedure we used earlier to move journal files to a dedicated device. For instance, if we had a database that contained infrequently accessed archives, we could mount it on a cheap HDD rather than on the fast SSDs that might back the rest of the server.

Detecting and Solving IO Problems

As you've seen by now, there's a lot of variation in IO subsystem types, in MongoDB IO operations, and in the workloads that create IO. Now that we've reviewed each of these dimensions, it's time to confront the two key questions of IO tuning:

1.   How do I know if my IO subsystem is overloaded?

2.   What can I do about an overloaded IO subsystem?

We've already reviewed a few symptoms of IO overloading. For instance, we saw that the average time to read a page of data from disk into cache should not exceed 1–2ms (for SSD-based IO).

We can also look to operating system statistics for evidence of IO overload. You may remember from earlier in this chapter, an IO subsystem that is overloaded will exhibit *queuing*. This queuing is visible from operating system commands.

In Linux, we can use the iostat command to view disk statistics. Here, we look at aggregate statistics for the sdc device (which is the device hosting the MongoDB dbPath directory on this server)[5]:

```
# iostat -xm -o JSON sdc 5 2 |jq
        {
            "avg-cpu": {
              "user": 45.97,
              "nice": 0,
              "system": 3.63,
              "iowait": 1.81,
```

---

[5]You may need to install the sysstat package to enable the iostat command.

```
            "steal": 0,
            "idle": 48.59
        },
        "disk": [
            {
                "disk_device": "sdc",
                "r/s": 0.4,
                "w/s": 49.2,
                "rkB/s": 15.2,
                "wkB/s": 2972,
                "rrqm/s": 0,
                "wrqm/s": 0.4,
                "rrqm": 0,
                "wrqm": 0.81,
                "r_await": 15.5,
                "w_await": 42.55,
                "aqu-sz": 2.08,
                "rareq-sz": 38,
                "wareq-sz": 60.41,
                "svctm": 0.87,
                "util": 4.32
            }
        ]
    }
```

In this output, the aqu-sz statistic indicates the length of the disk queue. Higher values indicate longer queues and are an indication that the device is overloaded. The r_await statistic indicates the average time to service a read IO requests in milliseconds. Values above 10ms may indicate that the device is either overloaded or underconfigured. In the case of a network-attached device, it may indicate that the network transit time is excessive.

In Windows, raw performance counters are available from PowerShell:

```
PS C:\Users\guy> Get-Counter -Counter '\\win10\physicaldisk(_total)\% disk
time'
```

```
Timestamp                    CounterSamples
---------                    --------------
4/10/2020 4:11:56 PM         \\win10\physicaldisk(_total)\% disk time :
                             0.201584556251408
PS C:\Users\guy> Get-Counter -Counter '\\win10\physicaldisk(_total)\current
disk queue length'

Timestamp                    CounterSamples
---------                    --------------
4/10/2020 4:12:24 PM         \\win10\physicaldisk(_total)\current disk queue
length :
                             0
```

Tip   Your best indication of a disk IO bottleneck is higher than usual average wait times for reading pages into the WiredTiger cache. At the operating system level, high queue lengths are also an indication of trouble.

When an IO bottleneck is indicated, there are two remedies:

1. Reduce the demand on the IO subsystem.

2. Increase the bandwidth of the IO subsystem.

The first option – reducing the demand on the IO subsystem – has been the subject of almost every previous chapter of this book. Creating indexes, optimizing schemas, tuning aggregations, and so on all work to reduce the amount of logical IO requests and consequently to reduce the demand on the physical IO subsystem. Configuring the WiredTiger cache serves to reduce the amount of logical IO that turns into physical IO.

The focus of this chapter is on optimizing physical IO. However, before you do any restructuring of your IO subsystem, make absolutely sure that you've done everything to reduce demand. In particular, can you spare any more memory for the WiredTiger cache? Is there a single query that is dominating IO that could be optimized? If not, then time to consider increasing the IO subsystem capacity.

Increasing IO Subsystem Bandwidth

In the "old days" – when databases ran on dedicated hardware devices – the solution to an IO subsystem bottleneck was relatively simple: add more disks or get faster disks. This is still the fundamental solution, though it may be obscured by the layers of abstraction provided by disk arrays, cloud storage devices, and so on.

Let's consider the measures you can take to increase IO bandwidth, depending on the nature of your hardware platform.

Dedicated Server with Dedicated Disks

If your MongoDB server is hosted on a dedicated server with directly attached disks, then you have the following options:

- If your directly attached disks are multi-level cell (MLC) SSDs or (shudder) magnetic disks, then you should consider replacing them with high-speed single-level cell (SLC) devices. SLC devices can have significantly lower latency than MLC devices, particularly for write operations. Cheap MLC devices can often exhibit poor sustained write throughput due to simplistic garbage collection algorithms.

- You might also consider using NVMe/PCI-attached SSDs in preference to SATA- or SAS-based devices.

- If your server has free slots for additional disks, you can add additional devices and either stripe the data across all of the disks or segment your IO by relocating your journal file or datafiles to dedicated devices as discussed in the earlier sections.

Each of these operations involves data movement and significant downtime. So if there is an easier alternative (such as adding more RAM to the server), you should definitely make sure that you've exhausted these options.

Tip   On a dedicated server with directly attached devices, you can consider replacing slower SSDs or HDD with high-performance devices or attach more devices and distribute your data across the additional devices.

Storage Arrays

If your IO services are provided by a storage array and you are experiencing an IO bottleneck, then you should check the following:

- What sort of devices are inside the array? Some storage arrays mix magnetic disk and SSD to provide economies of storage. However, such hybrid arrays provide unpredictable performance, especially for database workloads. If possible, your storage array should contain only high-speed SSDs.

- Are there enough devices in the array? The maximum IO bandwidth for the array will be determined by the number of devices in the array. Most arrays allow additional devices to be added without downtime: this might be the easiest way to increase the IO capacity of the array.

- What RAID level is being used in the array? For database workloads, RAID 10 ("Stripe And Mirror Everything) is almost always the correct RAID level and RAID 5 or 6 is almost always the wrong level. Be very skeptical if a vendor tries to tell you that their RAID 5 has some sort of magical technology that avoids the RAID 5 write penalty – RAID 5 is almost always bad news for database workloads.

Tip   For a database server which relies on IO from a storage array, ensure that the devices used are high-speed SSDs, that there are enough SSDs to meet the IO requirements, and that the RAID configuration is RAID 10 and never RAID 5 or RAID 6.

Cloud Storage

If your server is running in a cloud environment such as AWS, Azure, or GCP, then the usual way to increase IO bandwidth is to reconfigure the virtual disk. You can change the type and provisioned IOPS for any of the attached disks with just a few clicks. In some cases, a reboot of the VM will be required to implement the change.

Figure 12-10 shows just how easy it is to resize an AWS volume. Here, we modify the maximum IOPS for a EBS volume attached to a EC2 virtual machine.

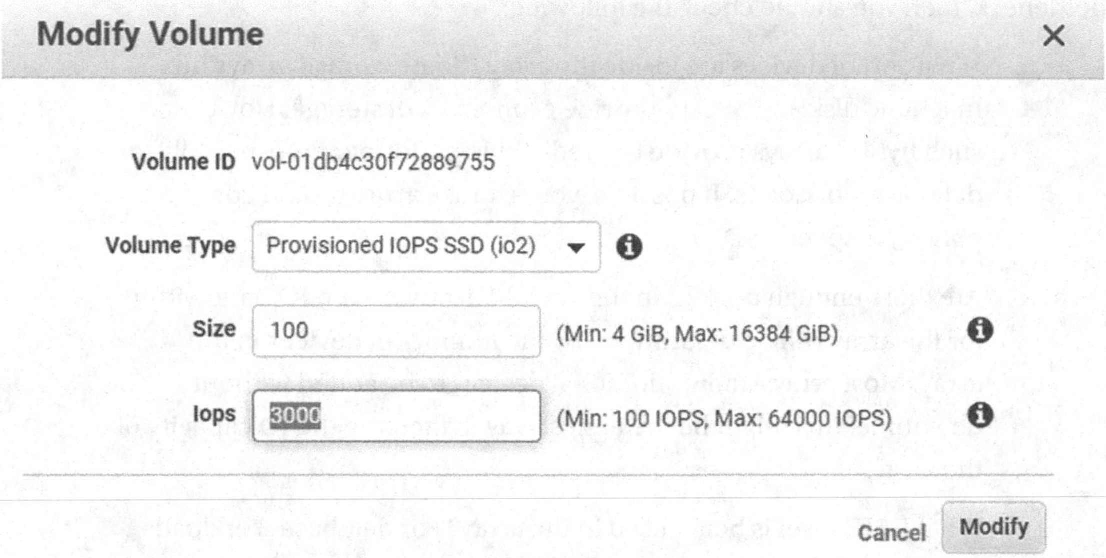

Figure 12-10. *Changing the IOPS for an AWS volume*

MongoDB Atlas

It's even easier to change the IO levels for an Atlas-based server. The Atlas console allows you to choose the IOPS level that you require. No reboot of the server is required, though a series of primary step-downs will occur as the changes are migrated through the replica set. The interface for configuring IO in Atlas can be seen in Figure 12-11.

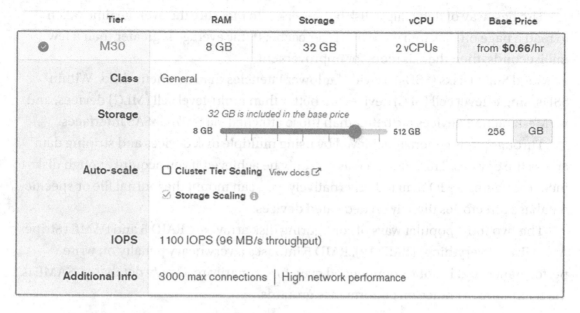

Tier	RAM	Storage	vCPU	Base Price
● M30	8 GB	32 GB	2 vCPUs	from $0.66/hr

Class	General
Storage	*32 GB is included in the base price* 8 GB ●————————● 512 GB 256 GB
Auto-scale	☐ Cluster Tier Scaling View docs ☑ ☑ Storage Scaling ❶
IOPS	1 100 IOPS (96 MB/s throughput)
Additional Info	3000 max connections | High network performance

Figure 12-11. *Adjusting IO for an Atlas server*

Tip   For cloud-based MongoDB servers on AWS, Azure, GCP, or Atlas, changing IO bandwidth can be done with a couple of clicks, sometimes without downtime!

Summary

Once you've made all reasonable efforts to avoid physical IO – by reducing workload and optimizing memory – it's time to configure the IO subsystem so that it can meet the resulting IO demand.

The delay for an individual IO is referred to as *latency* or *service time* and is typically measured in milliseconds. The amount of IO that can be done in a unit of time is referred to as *throughput* and is usually expressed in IO operations per second (IOPS).

There's an inverse relationship between latency and throughput – the higher the throughput, the worse the latency. Be aware that even if you succeed in pushing more work through your database, you may be causing unacceptable delays for individual transactions.

The best way of detecting a disk bottleneck is to measure the average time taken to read a page off disk into the WiredTiger cache. If this average is greater than a few milliseconds, then there is room for improvement.

Solid State Disks (SSDs) provide far lower latencies than magnetic disks. Within SSDs, single-level cell (SLC) devices are better than multi-level cell (MLC) devices, and NVMe-attached devices are better than those attached via SATA or SAS interfaces.

Throughput is generally achieved by using multiple disk devices and striping data across the devices. Throughput goals can only be achieved if you acquire enough disks to meet the aggregate IO demand. Alternatively, you can mount the journal file or specific database directories directly on dedicated devices.

The two most popular ways of configuring disk arrays are RAID 5 and SAME (Stripe And Mirror Everything) (RAID 10). RAID 5 imposes a very heavy penalty on write performance and is not recommended even for primarily read-only databases. SAME is the technique of choice on performance grounds.

CHAPTER 13

Replica Sets and Atlas

So far, we have considered performance tuning singleton MongoDB servers – servers that are not part of a cluster. However, most production MongoDB instances are configured as replica sets, since only this configuration provides sufficient high availability guarantees for modern "always-on" applications.

None of the tuning principles we have covered in previous chapters are invalidated in a replica set configuration. However, replica sets provide us with some additional performance challenges and opportunities which are covered in this chapter.

MongoDB Atlas provides us with an easy way to create cloud-hosted, fully managed MongoDB clusters. As well as offering convenience and economic advantages, MongoDB Atlas contains some unique features that involve performance opportunities and challenges.

Replica Set Fundamentals

We introduced replica sets in Chapter 2. A replica set following best practice consists of a *primary node* together with two or more *secondary nodes*. It is recommended to use three or more nodes, with an odd number of total nodes. The primary node accepts all write requests which are propagated synchronously or asynchronously to the secondary nodes. In the event of a failure of a primary, an election occurs to which a secondary node is elected to serve as the new primary and database operations can continue.

In a default configuration, the performance impact of a replica set is minimal. All read and write operations will be directed to the primary, and while there will be a small overhead incurred by the primary in transmitting data to secondaries, this overhead is rarely critical.

© Guy Harrison, Michael Harrison 2021
G. Harrison and M. Harrison, *MongoDB Performance Tuning*, https://doi.org/10.1007/978-1-4842-6879-7_13

However, if a higher degree of fault tolerance is required, then write performance can be sacrificed by requiring writes to complete on one or more secondaries before being confirmed. This is controlled by the MongoDB *write concern* parameter. Additionally, the MongoDB *read preference parameter* can be configured to allow secondaries to service read requests, potentially improving read performance.

Note   In order to clearly illustrate the relative effects of read preference and write concern, we've used a replica set with widely geographically distributed nodes – in Hong Kong, Seoul, and Tokyo, with application workloads originating in Sydney. This configuration has much higher latencies than are typical but allows us to show the relative effects of various configurations more clearly.

Using Read Preference

By default, all reads are directed to the primary node. However, we can set a *read preference* which directs the MongoDB drivers to direct read requests to secondary nodes. There are a couple of reasons why reading from secondaries might be preferable:

- The secondary nodes are likely to be less busy than the primary and, therefore, able to respond more quickly to read requests.

- By directing reads to secondary nodes, we reduce load on the primary, possibly increasing the write throughput of the cluster.

- By spreading read requests across all the nodes of the cluster, we improve overall read throughput since we are taking advantage of the otherwise idle secondaries.

- We might be able to reduce network latency by directing read requests to a secondary which is "nearer" to us – in terms of network latency.

These advantages need to be balanced against the possibility of reading "stale" data. In a default configuration, only the master is guaranteed to have up-to-date copies of all information (though we can change this by adjusting *write concern* as described in the next section). If we read from a secondary, we might get out-of-date information.

Warning   Secondary reads may result in stale data being returned. If this is unacceptable, either configure write concern to prevent stale reads or use the default `primary` read concern.

Table 13-1 summarizes the various read preference settings.

Table 13-1. *Read preference settings*

Read Preference	Effect
primary	This is the default. All reads are directed to the replica set primary.
primaryPreferred	Direct reads to the primary, but if no primary is available, direct reads to a secondary.
secondary	Direct reads to a secondary.
secondaryPreferred	Direct reads to a secondary, but if no secondary is available, direct reads to the primary.
nearest	Direct reads to the replica set member with the lowest network round trip time to the calling program.

If you have decided to route reads to a non-primary node, `secondaryPreferred` or `nearest` are the recommended settings. `secondaryPreferred` is generally better than `secondary`, because it allows reads to fall back to the primary if no secondaries are available. When there are multiple secondaries to choose from and some are "further away" (have greater network latencies), then `nearest` will route requests to the "closest" node – secondary or non-secondary.

Figure 13-1 provides an example of the effect of read preference settings on queries issued from different locations. Queries were issued from each of the nodes hosting a replica set member (Tokyo, Hong Kong, and Seoul) and from a remote node in Sydney which was not part of the replica set. Except when queries were issued directly on the primary, `secondaryPreferred` reads were faster than `primary` reads. However, the `nearest` read preference always resulted in the best read performance.

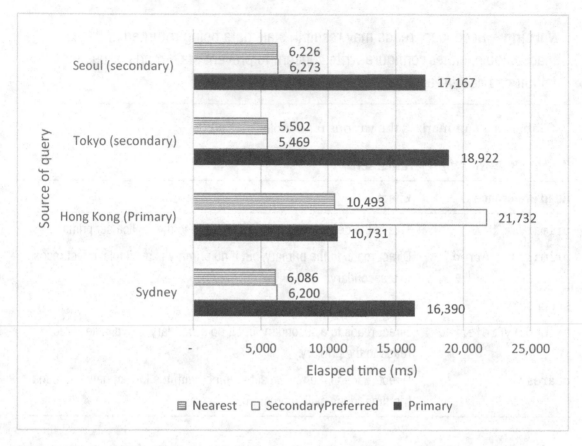

Figure 13-1. *Effect of read preference on read performance (reading 411,000 documents)*

Tip   Secondary reads will usually be faster than primary reads. The `nearest` read preference can help pick the replica set node with the lowest network latency.

Setting Read Preference

Read preference can be set at the connection level or at the statement level.

To set it when connecting to MongoDB, you can add the preference to the MongoDB URI. Here, we set the readPreference to secondary:

```
mongodb://n1,n2,n3/?replicaSet=rs1&readPreference=secondary
```

To set the read preference for a specific statement, include the read preference within the options document associated with each command. For instance, here, we set the read preference to nearest for a find command in NodeJS:

```
const client = await mongo.MongoClient.connect(myMongoDBURI);
const collection=client.db('MongoDBTuningBook').
    collection('customers');
const options={'readPreference': mongo.ReadPreference.NEAREST};
await collection.find({}, options).forEach((customer) => {
  count++;
  });
});
```

See your MongoDB driver documentation for guidance in setting read preference in your programming language.

maxStalenessSeconds

maxStalenessSeconds can be added to a read preference to control the tolerable lag in data. When picking a secondary node, the MongoDB driver will only consider those nodes who have data within maxStalenessSeconds seconds of the primary. The minimum value is 90 seconds.

For instance, this URL specified a preference for secondary nodes, but only if their data timestamps are within 5 minutes (300 seconds) of the primary:

```
mongodb://n1,n2,n3/?replicaSet=rs1\
    &readPreference=secondary&maxStalenessSeconds=300
```

Tip   maxStalenessSeconds can protect you from seriously out-of-date data when using secondary read preferences.

Tag Sets

Tag sets can be used to fine-tune read preference. Using tag sets, we can direct queries to specific secondaries or sets of secondaries. For instance, we could nominate a node as a business intelligence server and another node for web application traffic.

Here, we apply "location" and "role" tags to the three nodes in our replica set:

```
mongo> conf = rs.conf();

mongo> conf.members.forEach((m)=>{print(m.host);});
mongors01.eastasia.cloudapp.azure.com:27017
mongors02.japaneast.cloudapp.azure.com:27017
mongors03.koreacentral.cloudapp.azure.com:27017

mongo> conf.members[0].tags={"location":"HongKong","role": "prod" };
mongo> conf.members[1].tags={"location":"Tokyo","role":"BI" };
mongo> conf.members[2].tags={"location":"Korea","role": "prod" };

mongo> rs.reconfig(conf);
{
   "ok": 1,
   ...
}
```

We can now use either of the tags in a read preference string:

```
db.customers.
   find({ Phone: 40367898 }).
   readPref('secondaryPreferred', [{ role: 'prod' }]);
```

If we want to set up a specific secondary as a read-only server for analytics, tag sets are a perfect solution.

We can also use tag sets to distribute workload evenly across the nodes in a server. For instance, consider a scenario in which we are reading data from three collections in parallel. With the default read preference, all the reads will be directed to the primary. If we choose secondaryPreferred, then we might get more nodes participating in the work, but it's still possible that all the requests will go to the same node. However, with tag sets, we can direct each query to a different node.

For instance, here we direct a query to Hong Kong:

```
db.getMongo().setReadPref('secondaryPreferred', [{
    "location": "HongKong"
}]);

db.iotData1.aggregate(pipeline, {
    allowDiskUse: true
});
```

Queries against collections iotData2 and iotData3 could similarly be directed to Korea and Japan. Not only does this allow every node in the cluster to participate simultaneously, it also helps with cache effectiveness – since each node is responsible for a specific collection, all of that node's cache can be dedicated to that collection.

Figure 13-2 shows elapsed time for three simultaneous queries against different collections using various read preferences. Using secondaryPreferred improved performance, but the best performance was achieved when tag sets were used to distribute load across all nodes.

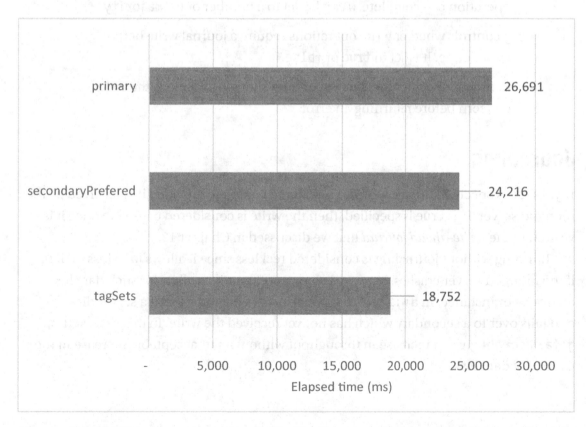

Figure 13-2. *Using tag sets to distribute work across all nodes in a cluster*

> **Tip** Tag sets can be used to direct read requests to specific nodes. You can use tag sets to nominate nodes for special purposes such as analytics or to distribute read workload more evenly across all nodes in the cluster.

Write Concern

Read preference helps MongoDB decide *which* server should service a read request. *Write concern* tells MongoDB *how many* servers should be involved in a write request.

By default, MongoDB considers a write request complete when the change has made its way into the journal file of the primary. Write concern allows you to vary this default. Write concern takes three settings:

- w controls how many nodes should receive the write before the write operation can complete. w can be set to a number or to "majority".

- j controls whether write operations require a journal write before completing. It is set to true or false.

- wtimeout specifies the amount of time allowed to achieve the write concern before returning an error.

Journaling

If j:false is specified, then a write is considered complete provided it is received by the mongod server. If j:true is specified, then the write is considered complete once it is written to the *write-ahead journal* that we discussed in Chapter 12.

Running without journaling is considered reckless since it allows for a loss of data if the mongod server crashes. However, some configurations allow for such data loss anyway. For instance, in a w:1,j:true scenario, data might be lost if a server dies and fails over to a secondary which has not yet received the write. In this case, setting j:false might give an increase in throughput without an unacceptable increase in the chance of data loss.

The Write Concern w Option

The w option controls how many nodes in the cluster must receive a write before the write operation completes. The default setting of 1 requires that only the primary receives the write. Higher values require the write to propagate to a larger number of nodes.

The w:"majority" setting requires that a majority of nodes receive the write operation before the write completes. w:"majority" is a sensible default for systems in which data loss is deemed unacceptable. If the majority of nodes have the update, then in any single-node failure or network partition scenario, the newly elected primary will have access to that data.

Of course, the impact of writing to multiple nodes has a performance overhead. You might imagine that your data is being written to multiple nodes simultaneously. However, the write is made to the primary and only then propagated to the other nodes through the replication mechanism. If there is already a significant replication lag, then the delay may be much higher than expected. Even if the replication lag is minimal, the replication can only commence after the initial write has succeeded, so the performance lag is always greater than w:1.

Figure 13-3 shows the sequence of events for a write concern of {w:2,j:true}. Only after the write is received on the primary and synced to the journal will it be transmitted via replication to a secondary. The write must then sync to the journal on the secondary nodes before the write operation can complete. These operations occur sequentially, not in parallel. In other words, the replication delay is added onto the primary write delay, rather than occurring at the same time.

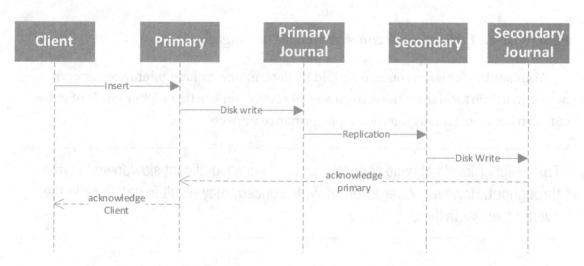

Figure 13-3. *Sequence of events for* w:2, j:true *write concern*

Figure 13-4 shows the time taken to insert 50,000 documents with various levels of write concern. Higher levels of write concern result in significantly lower throughput.

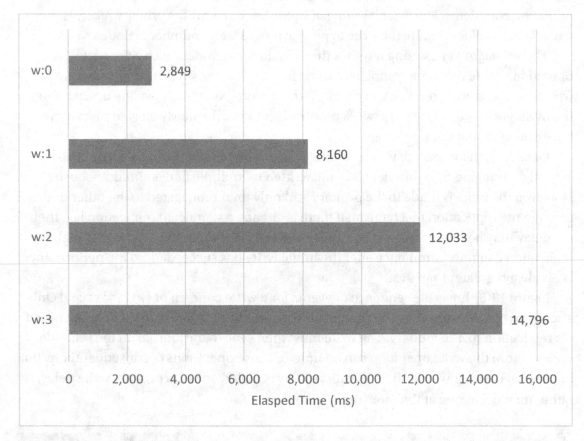

Figure 13-4. *Effect of write concern on write throughput*

Your setting for write concern should be determined by fault tolerance concerns, not by write performance. However, it's important to realize that higher levels of write concern have potentially significant performance impacts.

Tip   Higher levels of write concern can result in a significant slowdown in write throughput. However, lower levels of write concern may result in data loss in the event of server failure.

As we can see, `w:0` provides the absolute best performance. However, a write with `w:0` can succeed even if the data doesn't make it to the MongoDB server. Even a transitory network failure might result in a loss of data. In almost all circumstances, `w:0` is just too unreliable.

Warning   A write concern of `w:0` might result in a performance boost, but at the cost of completely unreliable data writes.

Write Concern and Secondary Reads

Although higher levels of write concern slow down modification workloads, there may be a pleasant side effect if your overall application performance is read-dominated. If the write concern is set to write to all members of the cluster, then secondary reads will *always* return the correct data. This might allow you to use secondary reads even if you cannot tolerate stale queries.

However, be aware that if you manually set the write concern the number of nodes in the cluster, any failures In the cluster may result in reads timing out.

Warning   Setting w to the number of nodes in the cluster will result in secondary reads always returning up-to-date data. However, write operations might fail if a node is unavailable.

MongoDB Atlas

MongoDB Atlas is MongoDB's fully managed database-as-a-service (DBaaS) offering. Using Atlas, you can create and configure MongoDB replica sets and sharded clusters from a web interface without having to configure your own hardware or virtual machines. Atlas takes care of most of database operational considerations including backups, version upgrades, and performance monitoring. Atlas is also available in the three major public clouds: AWS, Azure, and Google Cloud.

When it comes to deploying a MongoDB cluster, Atlas offers a lot of convenience by handling much of the dirty work behind the scenes. However, as well as the operational advantages, Atlas boasts additional features not available for other deployment types. These features include advanced sharding and query options that can be highly appealing when creating a new cluster.

Although implementing these options may be as simple as clicking a button, it is essential to remember that they can also require careful planning and design to meet their full potential. In the following, we will go through a number of these Atlas features along with their performance implications.

Atlas Search

Atlas Search (formerly known as Atlas Full-Text Search) is a feature built upon *Apache Lucene* to provide a more powerful text search functionality. Although all versions of MongoDB support text indexes (see Chapter 5), the Apache Lucene integration provides far more powerful text search capabilities.

The strength of Apache Lucene is provided through *analyzers*. Simply put, analyzers will determine how your text index is created. You can create a custom analyzer, but Atlas provides built-in options that will cover the majority of use cases.

Choosing an appropriate analyzer during index creation is one of the easiest ways to improve the results of your Atlas Search queries.

Note   When we talk about improving the performance of text search, we are not always referring to query speed. Some analyzers may improve the "performance" of a query by providing more relevant scoring results, but may also lead to slower queries.

The five prebuilt analyzers include

- **Standard**: All words are converted to lowercase and punctuation is ignored. Additionally, the standard analyzer can correctly interpret special symbols and acronyms and will discard joining words like "and" to provide better results. The standard analyzer creates index entries for each "word" and is the most commonly useful index type.

- **Simple**: As you might guess, the simple analyzer is like the standard analyzer but with less advanced logic when determining a "word" for each index entry. All words are converted to lowercase. A simple analyzer will create an entry by finding a word between any two characters that are not a letter. Unlike the standard analyzer, the simple analyzer will not handle joining words.

- **Whitespace**: If the simple analyzer is a dumbed-down version of the standard analyzer, the whitespace analyzer takes this even further. Words will not be converted to lowercase, and entries are created for any string divided by a whitespace character with no additional handling of punctuation or special characters.

- **Keyword**: The keyword analyzer takes the entire value of the field as a single entry, requiring exact matches to return the result in a query. This is the most specific analyzer provided.

- **Language**: The language analyzer is where Lucene is particularly powerful, as it provides a series of presets for each language you might encounter. Each preset will create index entries based on the typical structure of text written in that language.

When creating Atlas Search indexes, there is no single best analyzer to choose, and making a choice will not be about query speed alone. You will have to consider the shape of your data and the type of queries users are likely to send.

Let's look at an example based upon a property rental marketplace dataset. In this dataset, large amounts of text data exist in various attributes. Names, addresses, descriptions, and property metadata are all stored as strings for each listing, along with reviews and comments.

Each of these attributes is best suited to different types of search indexes based on which analyzer most fits the matching query. Descriptions and comments may best be served by a language index which interprets language-specific semantics. Property types like "house" or "apartment" match a keyword analyzer best as we want exact matches. Other fields are probably indexed correctly by the standard analyzer or may not need indexing at all.

Another factor to consider when selecting an analyzer will be the size of the index created. Figure 13-5 is a comparison of index size for each analyzer on a small text field (property name) and a large text field (property description).

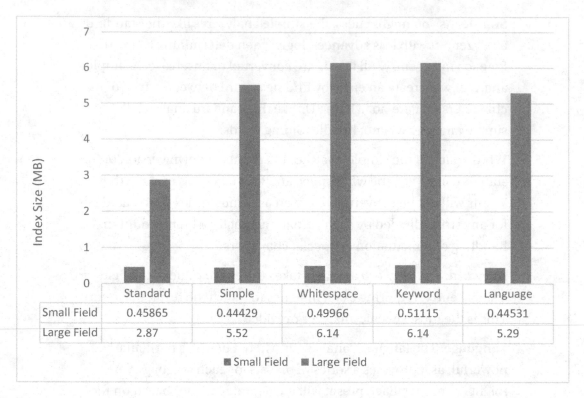

	Standard	Simple	Whitespace	Keyword	Language
Small Field	0.45865	0.44429	0.49966	0.51115	0.44531
Large Field	2.87	5.52	6.14	6.14	5.29

■ Small Field   ■ Large Field

Figure 13-5. *Index size by analyzer and field length (5555 documents)*

Although these results will vary greatly depending on the text data itself, this chart primarily indicates two things.

Firstly, a smaller text field will produce little to no variation in index size (and thus the time taken to scan that index). This makes sense, since a smaller number of words or characters can be subdivided into a smaller number of ways and are less likely to require complex rules to create the index.

Secondly, on larger, more complex text data, the size of the index can vary significantly between analyzer types. Sometimes a larger index will be a good thing, providing superior results and performance. However, it's still something worth considering when creating Atlas Search indexes.

So now we know how the different analyzer types will affect index size, but what about query time? Figure 13-6 shows execution time for an identical query executed against the five different index analyzer types.

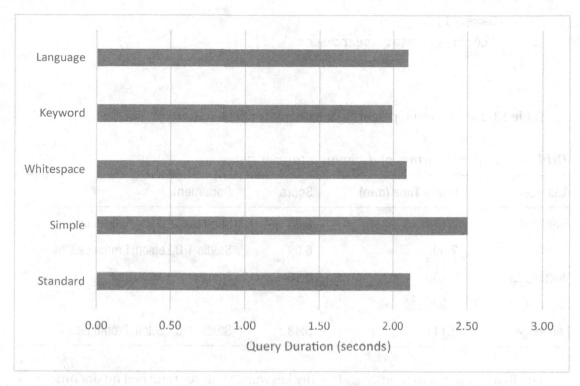

Figure 13-6. *Query duration by index analyzer type (5555 documents, 1000 queries)*

If we were to look at this data alone, we would assume that the keyword analyzer will provide us with the best performance for our query. However, with any text search, we also need to take into account the scoring of our results.

For instance, consider this query:

```
db.listingsAndReviews.aggregate([
    {
      $search: {
        text: {
          query: ["oven", "microwave", "air conditioning"],
          path: "notes",
        },
      },
    },
    {$limit: 3,},
    {$project: {
```

```
        name: 1,
        score: { $meta: "searchScore" },},
    },
  ]);
```

Table 13-2 shows our top-scoring document for each index type.

Table 13-2. *Performance of different analyzer types*

Analyzer	Query Time (min)	Score	Document
Standard	2.13	6.25	Studio 1 Q Leblon, Promo de…
Simple	2.50	6.09	Studio 1 Q Leblon, Promo de...
Whitespace	2.10	6.16	Tree Fern Garden Appt,…
Keyword	1.99		
Language	2.11	5.48	Studio 1 Q Leblon, Promo de...

The first thing you may notice is that the keyword analyzer returned no documents (and thus a 0 score) for our query, despite having the lowest query time. This is expected, as the keyword index requires an exact match to the entire value of the field. So although it's fast, it doesn't necessarily return the best results.

You may also notice that for our remaining analyzers, only the whitespace index returned a different result. The other types found the same document, but with varying levels of confidence. Figure 13-7 shows a scatter plot of these results.

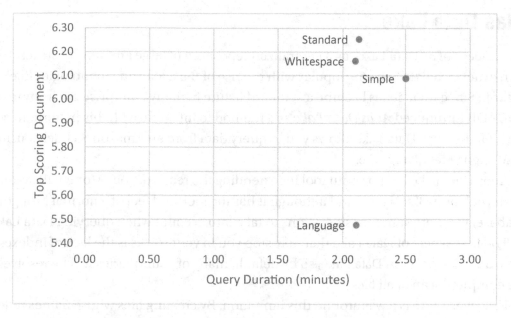

Figure 13-7. *Query duration, document score, and document by analyzer (5555 documents, 1000 queries)*

These results correspond roughly to our created index size, with the larger indexes taking longer to return a result. Interestingly, although the standard analyzer is not the quickest, it does provide the best combination of high confidence results for only a fraction more query time. You may have expected a language-specific analyzer to perform better than the standard analyzer. In this case, there are multiple languages both in the indexed field and across many other fields. When it comes to user input, it's hard to guarantee a single unified language.

You could repeat this analysis on your dataset to try and find the right analyzer for your Atlas Search. It is integral to think about the type of data, as well as the types of queries when creating an Atlas Search index. Although there is no always-right or always-wrong answer, the standard analyzer is likely to provide you with good overall performance. However, be aware that different analyzers can return different results, and it's generally not good practice to make a query faster if doing so returns the wrong results.

Tip   The various Atlas Search text search analyzers have different performance characteristics. However, the fastest analyzer might not return the best results for your application. Make sure you balance the accuracy of results with the speed of the text search.

Atlas Data Lake

The concept of a "Data Lake" as a centralized repository of large amounts of structured or unstructured data became popular with the rise of Big Data and technologies like Hadoop. Since then, it has become a standard fixture in many enterprise environments. MongoDB introduced *Atlas Data Lake* as a method to integrate with this pattern. In a nutshell, the Atlas Data Lake allows you to query data from an Amazon S3 bucket using the Mongo Query Language.

Atlas Data Lake is a powerful tool for extending the reach of your MongoDB system to external, non-BSON data, and although it has the look and feel of a normal MongoDB database, there are some considerations to take into account when querying Data Lake.

The first aspect of Data Lake that may stop you in your tracks is the lack of indexes. There are no indexes in Data Lake, so by default, many of your queries will be resolved by a complete scan of all files.

However, there is a way around this limitation. By creating files whose names reflect a key attribute value, we can restrict the file accesses to only relevant files.

For example, let's say you have your Data Lake set up with one file per collection. A single `customers.json` file contains all your customers, and this is mapped to the `customers` collection, as in the following example:

```
databases: {
  dataLakeTest: {
    customers: [
      {
        definition: '/customers.json',
        store: 's3store'
      }
    ],
  }
}
```

We can't index these files; however, we can instead define the collection with multiple files, one file for each customer, where the name of the file is the `customerId` (the field we would want to index):

```
customers: [
  {
    definition: '/customers/{customerId string}',
```

```
      store: 's3store'
    }
  ],
```

Our new collection is now defined by the union of all the files in the /customers folder. Each file in the customers folder will be named by the customerid value; for example, the file /customers/1234.json will have all data with a customerId of 1234. The Data Lake will now only need to scan files for the customer IDs concerned in a query, rather than all of the files in the directory. You can see this in action by viewing the explain plan:

```
> db.customersNew.find({customerId:"1234"}).explain("queryPlanner")

{
    "ok": 1,
    "plan": {
        "kind": "mapReduce",
        "map": [{
            "$match": {
                "customerId": {
                    "$eq": "1234"
                }
            }
        }],
        "node": {
            "kind": "data",
            "partitions": [{
                "source": "s3://datalake02/customers/1234?delimiter=/&regio
                n=ap-southeast-2",
                "attributes": {
                    "customerId": "1234"
                }
            }]
        }
    }
}
```

We can see that only a single file (partition) was accessed along with the name of the matching partition.

Tip   We can avoid having to scan all files in an Atlas Data Lake by creating files whose contents and file names correspond to a particular key value.

Another area where a lack of indexes can cause problems is in the case of $lookup. As we discussed in Chapter 7, indexes are absolutely essential when optimizing joins with $lookup.

If we are joining between two collections in an Atlas Data Lake, we will definitely want to make sure that the collection referred to in the $lookup section is partitioned based on the join condition. We can see how this improves $lookup performance in Figure 13-8.

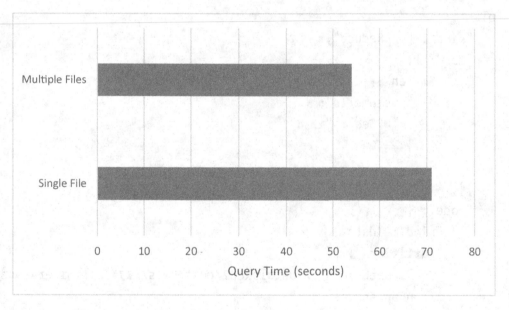

Figure 13-8. *$lookup performance by file structure in Data Lake (5555 documents)*

Additionally, this method is far more scalable. With a $lookup against a single file, the file must be repeatedly scanned for each customer we join. However, with separate files for each customer, a much smaller file is read for each $lookup operation. With a single large file, performance will steeply degrade as documents are added to the file, whereas with multiple files, performance will scale more linearly.

There are some downsides to splitting your data into multiple files. As you might expect, when scanning the entire collection, there is overhead on opening each file. For example, a simple aggregation that counts all the documents in a collection completes almost instantly on a single file but takes significantly longer when each document exists in its file. The overhead of opening each file dominates the performance of the query. We can see this illustrated in Figure 13-9.

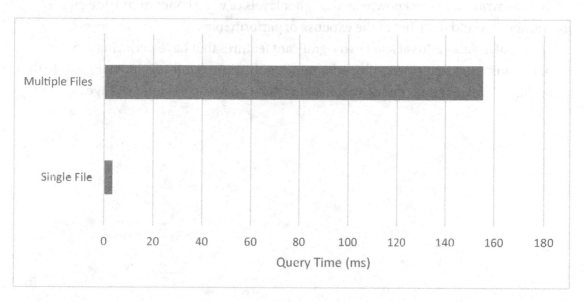

Figure 13-9. *Full collection query duration by file structure in Data Lake (254,058 documents)*

In summary, while you can't index files directly in Data Lake, you can make up for some of the lost performance by manipulating file names. The file name can become a sort of high-level index, which is particularly useful when using $lookup. However, if you are always accessing the complete dataset, your scan performance will be best on a single file.

Summary

Most MongoDB production implementations incorporate replica sets to provide high availability and fault tolerance. Replica sets are not intended to solve performance problems, but they definitely have performance implications.

In a replica set, *read preference* can be set to allow reads from secondary nodes. Secondary reads can distribute work across more nodes in the cluster, reduce network latency in geographically distributed clusters, and allow for parallel processing of workloads. However, secondary reads can return out-of-date results which won't always be acceptable.

Replica set *write concern* controls how many nodes must acknowledge a write before the write can be acknowledged. Higher levels of write concern provide greater guarantees around data, but at the expense of performance.

MongoDB Atlas adds at least two significant features that have performance implications. Atlas text search allows for more sophisticated full-text indexing, while the Atlas Data Lake allows for queries against data held on low-cost cloud storage.

CHAPTER 14

Sharding

In the previous chapter, we covered the most commonly deployed MongoDB configuration: replica sets. Replica sets are essential for modern applications requiring availability that a single MongoDB instance cannot provide. As we've seen, replica sets can do some limited scaling of reads through secondary write. But, for large applications, particularly where the write workload exceeds the capability of a single cluster, sharded clusters may be deployed.

Everything we have covered in previous chapters is entirely applicable to sharded MongoDB servers. Indeed, it's probably best not to consider sharding until you have optimized your application workload and individual server configuration using the techniques covered in previous chapters.

However, there are some significant performance opportunities and challenges presented by sharded MongoDB deployments, and these will be covered in this chapter.

Sharding Fundamentals

We introduced sharding in Chapter 2. In a sharded database cluster, selected collections are partitioned across multiple database instances. Each partition is referred to as a "shard." This partitioning is based on a shard key value.

While replica sets are designed to provide high availability, sharding is designed to provide greater scalability. When your workload – particularly your write workload – exceeds the capacity of your server, then sharding provides a way to spread that workload across multiple nodes.

© Guy Harrison, Michael Harrison 2021
G. Harrison and M. Harrison, *MongoDB Performance Tuning*, https://doi.org/10.1007/978-1-4842-6879-7_14

Scaling and Sharding

Sharding is an architectural pattern developed to allow databases to support the massive workloads of the world's largest websites.

As application load grows, at some point the workload exceeds the capability of a single server. The capability of the server can be extended by shifting some read workload to secondary nodes, but eventually the amount of write workload to the primary becomes too great. We can no longer "scale up."

When "scaling up" becomes impossible, we turn to "scaling out." We add more primary nodes and split the workload across those primaries using sharding.

Sharding at scale was critical to the establishment of the modern Web – Facebook and Twitter were both early adopters of large-scale sharding using MySQL. However, it's not universally loved – sharding with MySQL involves a huge amount of manual configuration and breaks some of the core database capabilities. However, sharding in MongoDB is fully integrated into the core database and is relatively easy to configure and manage.

Sharding Concepts

Sharding is a big topic, and we can't provide a tutorial for all sharding considerations here. Please consult the MongoDB documentation or the book *MongoDB Topology Design* by Nicholas Cottrell (Apress, 2020) for a full review of sharding concepts.

The following sharding concepts are particularly significant:

- **Shard key**: The shard key is the attributes which determine into which shard any given document will be placed. Shard keys should have high cardinality (lots of unique values) to ensure that the data can be evenly distributed across shards.

- **Chunks**: Documents are contained within chunks, and chunks are allocated to specific shards. Chunking avoids MongoDB having to laboriously move individual documents across shards.

- **Range sharding**: With range sharding, contiguous groups of shard keys are stored within the same chunk. Range sharding allows for efficient shard key range scans but can result in "hot" chunks if the shard value is monotonically increasing.

- **Hash sharding**: In hash-based sharding, keys are distributed based on a hash function applied to the shard key.

- **The balancer**: MongoDB tries to keep the data and workload attributed to each shard equal. The balancer periodically moves data from one shard to another to maintain this balance.

To Shard or Not to Shard?

Sharding is the most sophisticated MongoDB configuration topology, and sharding is used by some of the world's largest and most performant websites. So sharding must be good for performance, right? Well, it is not quite that simple.

Sharding adds a layer of complexity and processing on top of your MongoDB database that – as often as not – makes individual operations a little slower. However, it allows you to throw more hardware resources at your workload. If – and only if – you have a hardware bottleneck involving operations to a replica set primary, then sharding might be the best solution. However, in most other circumstances, sharding adds complexity and overhead to your deployment.

Figure 14-1 compares the performance for sharded and unsharded collections for a few simple operations on equivalent hardware.[1] In most cases, operations against sharded collections are slower than against unsharded collections. Of course, every workload will be different, but the point is that sharding alone does not make things go faster!

---

[1]To make it a fair comparison, the shards were located on the same host as the single replica set option. Each node had an equivalent cache size, and there was no memory bottleneck.

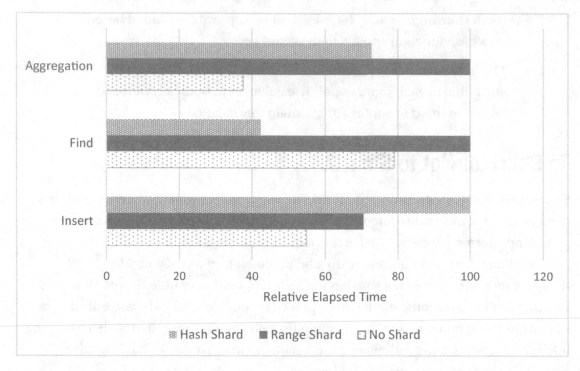

Figure 14-1. *Sharding doesn't always help performance*

Sharding is expensive in terms of dollar costs for the hardware and in terms of operational overhead. It should truly only be a recourse of last resort. Only when you have exhausted all other tuning measures, and all "scale-up" options, should you consider sharding. In particular, make sure that the disk subsystem on your primary is optimized before considering sharding. It's much cheaper and easier to buy and deploy some new SSDs than to shard a primary!

Warning   Sharding should be the last resort for scaling a MongoDB deployment. Make sure your workload, server, and replica set configuration are optimized before commencing a sharding project.

Even if you believe that sharding is inevitable, you should still thoroughly tune your database before commencing the sharding project. If your workload and configuration are creating unnecessary load, then you may end up creating more shards than are necessary. Only when your workload is tuned can you make a rational determination of your sharding requirements.

Shard Key Selection

Sharding occurs at the collection level. While the number of shards in a cluster is the same for all collections, not all collections need be sharded and collections need not all have the same shard key.

Collections should be sharded if the aggregate IO write demand on the collection exceeds the capacity of a single primary. We then choose the shard key based on the following criteria:

- The keys should have a **high cardinality** so that data can be divided into small chunks if necessary.

- The keys should have an **even distribution** of values. If any single value is particularly common, then the shard key may be a poor choice.

- The key should be **frequently included in queries** so that queries can be routed to specific shards.

- The key should be **non-monotonically** increasing. When a shard key value increases monotonically (e.g., always increases by a set value), then the new documents appear in the same chunk, causing a hot spot. If you do have a monotonically increasing key value, consider using a hashed shard key.

Tip   Choosing the correct sharding key is critical to the success of your sharding project. A shard key should support a good balance of documents across shard and support as many query filter conditions as possible.

Range- vs. Hash-Based Sharding

Distribution of data across shards can be either *range-based* or *hash-based*. In range-based partitioning, each shard is allocated a specific range of shard key values. MongoDB consults the distribution of key values in the index to ensure that each shard is allocated approximately the same number of keys. In hash-based sharding, keys are distributed based on a hash function applied to the shard key.

There are advantages and compromises involved in each scheme. Figure 14-2 illustrates the performance trade-offs inherent in range and hash sharding for inserts and range queries.

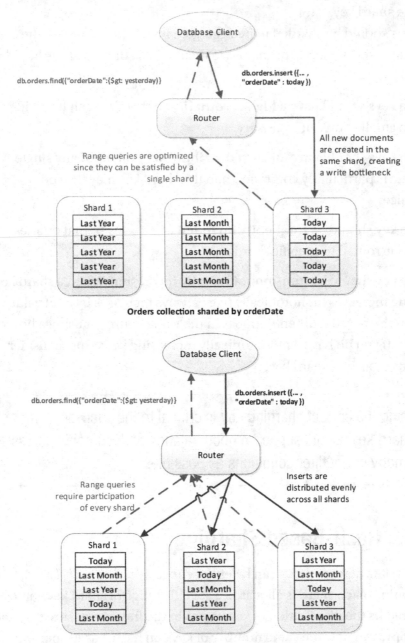

Figure 14-2. *Range- and hash-based sharding compared*

Range-based partitioning allows for efficient execution of shard key range scans since these queries can often be resolved by accessing a single shard. Hash-based sharding requires that range queries be resolved by accessing all shards. On the other hand, hash-based sharding is more likely to distribute "hot" documents (unfilled orders or recent posts, for instance) evenly across the cluster, thus balancing load more effectively.

Tip   Hashed shard keys result in more evenly distributed data and workload. However, they result in poor performance for range-based queries.

Hashed shard keys do result in a more even distribution of data. However, as we'll soon see, hashed shard keys do create significant challenges for a variety of query operations, particularly those which involve sorting or range queries. Furthermore, we can only hash on a single attribute, while our ideal shard key is often composed of multiple attributes.

However, there is one use case in which a hashed shard key is clearly indicated. If we must shard on an attribute which is constantly increasing – often referred to as *monotonically increasing* – then a range sharding strategy will result in all new documents being inserted into a single shard. This shard will become "hot" in terms of inserts and probably in terms of reads as well since recent documents are often more likely to be updated and read than older documents.

Hashed shard keys come to the rescue here because the hashed values will be evenly distributed across the shards.

Figure 14-3 illustrates how monotonically increasing shard keys affect inserts into collections using hashed or range shard keys. In this example, the shard key is the orderDate which is always increasing as time moves forward. With hash sharding, inserts are distributed evenly between shards. In the range sharded scenario, all documents are inserted into a single shard. The hashed shard key not only distributes the workload across multiple nodes, it also results in greater throughput since there is less contention on that single node.

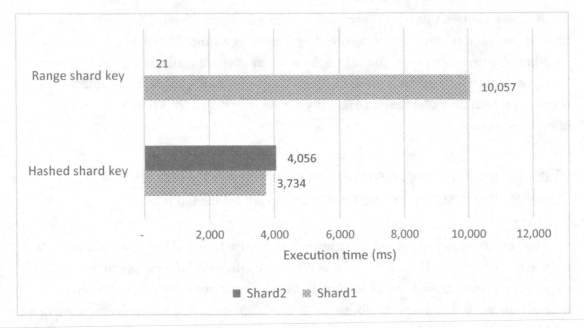

Figure 14-3. *Time to insert 120,000 documents into a sharded collection – hash vs. range monotonically increasing key*

Tip   If your shard key must be a perpetually (monotonically) increasing value, then a hashed shard key is preferable. However, consider the possibility of sharding on another attribute if range queries on the shard key are required.

Zone Sharding

Most of the time, our sharding strategy is to distribute documents and workload evenly across all shards. Only by distributing the load evenly can we hope to gain effective scalability. If one shard is responsible for a disproportionate amount of the workload, then that shard may become a limiting factor in our overall application throughput.

However, there's another possible motivation for sharding – to distribute workload across shards so that data is close, in network terms, to the applications that want that data or to distribute data so that "hot" data is on expensive high-powered hardware, while "cold" data is stored on cheaper hardware.

Zone sharding allows the MongoDB administrator to fine-tune the distribution of documents to shards. By associating a shard with a zone and associating a range of keys within a collection within that zone, the administrator can explicitly determine the shard on which these documents will reside. This can be used to archive data to shards on cheaper, but slower storage or to direct particular data to a specific data center or geography.

To create zones, we first allocate shards to zones. Here, we create one zone for the United States and another zone for the rest of the world:

```
sh.addShardToZone("shardRS2", "US");
sh.addShardToZone("shardRS", "TheWorld");
```

Even though we have only two zones, we can have as many shards as we want – each zone can have multiple shards.

Now we assign shard key ranges to each zone. Here, we have sharded by Country and City, so we use minKey and maxKey as proxies for the high and low City values within a Country range:

```
sh.addTagRange(
  "MongoDBTuningBook.customers",
  { "Country" : "Afghanistan", "City" : MinKey },
  { "Country" : "United Kingdom", "City" : MaxKey },
  "TheWorld");

sh.addTagRange(
  "MongoDBTuningBook.customers",
  { "Country" : "United States", "City" : MinKey },
  { "Country" : "United States", "City" : MaxKey },
  "US");

sh.addTagRange(
  "MongoDBTuningBook.customers",
  { "Country" : "Venezuela", "City" : MinKey },
  { "Country" : "Zambia", "City" : MaxKey },
  "TheWorld");
```

We would then locate the hardware for the "US" zone somewhere in the United States and the hardware for "TheWorld" somewhere in the rest of the world (Europe maybe). We would also deploy mongos routers in each of these regions. Figure 14-4 illustrates what this deployment might look like.

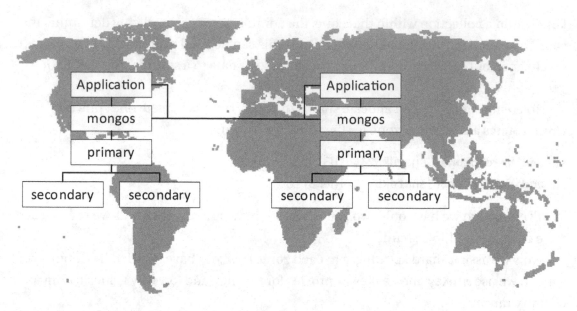

Figure 14-4. *Zone sharding to reduce geographic network latency*

The end result is lower latency for US queries issued from the US router and similarly for other geographies. Of course, if you issue a query for US data from Europe, your round trip time would be higher. But if queries issued from a region are mainly for data zoned to that region, then overall performance is improved.

We could add more zones in other regions as our application grows.

Tip   Zone sharding can be used to distribute data across geographies, reducing latencies for region-specific queries.

Another use of zone sharding is to create archives of old data on slow but cheap hardware. For instance, if we have decades of order data, we could create a zone for older data which is hosted on VMs or servers with less CPU, memory, and maybe even using magnetic disk rather than premium SSD. Recent data could be kept on high-speed servers. This might result in a better overall performance for a given hardware budget.

Shard Balance

The getShardDistribution() method can show the breakdown of data across shards. Here's an example of a well-balanced sharded collection:

```
mongo> db.iotDataHshard.getShardDistribution()
```

```
Shard shard02 at shard02/localhost:27022,localhost:27023
  data : 304.04MiB docs : 518520 chunks : 12
  estimated data per chunk : 25.33MiB
  estimated docs per chunk : 43210

Shard shard01 at shard01/localhost:27019,localhost:27020
  data : 282.33MiB docs : 481480 chunks : 11
  estimated data per chunk : 25.66MiB
  estimated docs per chunk : 43770

Totals
  data : 586.38MiB docs : 1000000 chunks : 23
  Shard shard02 contains 51.85% data, 51.85% docs in cluster, avg obj size
  on shard : 614B
  Shard shard01 contains 48.14% data, 48.14% docs in cluster, avg obj size
  on shard : 614B
```

In a well-balanced sharded cluster, there are approximately the same number of chunks and the same amount of data in each shard. If the number of chunks between shards is inconsistent, then the balancer should be able to migrate chunks to return balance to the cluster.

If the number of chunks is roughly equivalent, but the amount of data in each shard varies significantly, then it may be that your shard key is not evenly distributed. A single shard key value cannot span chunks, so if some shard keys have massive document counts, then massive "jumbo" chunks will result. Jumbo chunks are sub-optimal, as the data within cannot be effectively distributed across shards and thus a larger proportion of queries may be sent to a single shard.

Rebalancing Shards

Let's say you have selected an appropriate shard key type (range or hashed) and the key possesses the right attributes – high cardinality, even distribution, frequently queried, non-monotonically increasing. In that case, your chunks will likely be well balanced across shards, and consequently, you will achieve a well-distributed workload. However, several factors may cause the shards to fall out of balance, with many more chunks existing on one shard than another. When this occurs, that single node will become a bottleneck until the data can be evenly redistributed across multiple nodes – as shown in Figure 14-5.

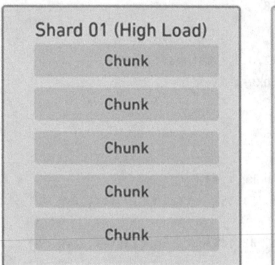
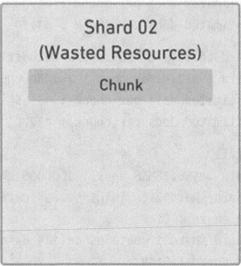

Figure 14-5. *A set of poorly balanced shards, most queries will go to Shard 01*

If we can maintain an appropriate balance among our shards, query load is more likely to be divided evenly among the nodes – as shown in Figure 14-6.

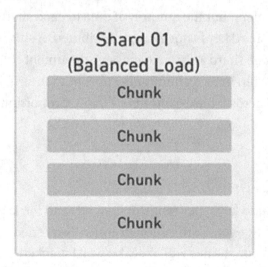
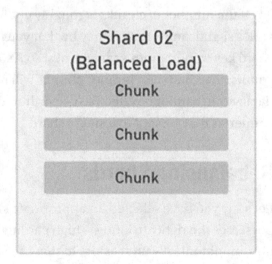

Figure 14-6. *A set of well-balanced shards: query load will be evenly distributed*

Fortunately, MongoDB will automatically rebalance a sharded collection whenever a large enough disparity is detected between shards. The threshold for this disparity depends on the number of total chunks. For example, if there are 80 or more chunks, the threshold will be a difference of eight between the most chunks on a shard and the least. For between 20 and 80, the threshold is four, and if there are fewer than 20 chunks, the threshold is two.

If this disparity is detected, the shard balancer will begin to migrate chunks to rebalance the distribution of data. This migration might be triggered by large amounts of new data being inserted within a specific range or simply by the addition of a shard. A new shard is initially empty and therefore causes a large disparity in chunk distribution that requires rebalancing.

The `balancerStatus` command allows you to see the current balancer status:

```
mongos> db.adminCommand({ balancerStatus: 1})
{
        "mode" : "full",
        "inBalancerRound" : false,
        "numBalancerRounds" : NumberLong(64629),
        "ok" : 1,
        "operationTime" : Timestamp(1604706062, 1),
        . . .
}
```

In the preceding output, the `mode` field indicates that the balancer is enabled, and the `inBalancerRound` field indicates the balancer is not currently distributing chunks.

Although MongoDB automatically handles the rebalancing, rebalancing does not come without performance implications. Bandwidth, workload, and disk space usage will all increase during chunk migration. To mitigate this performance hit, MongoDB will only migrate a single shard at a time. Additionally, each shard can only participate in one migration at a time. If the impact of chunk migrations is affecting your application performance, there are a few things to try:

- Modifying the balancer window

- Manually enabling and disabling the balancer

- Changing the chunk size

We'll discuss each of these options in the following few pages.

Modifying the Balancer Window

The balancer window defines the time periods during which the balancer will be active. Modifying the balancer window will prevent the balancer from running outside of a given time window; for example, you may only want to balance chunks when application load is at its lowest. In this example, we limit rebalancing to a 90-minute window starting at 10:30 PM:

```
mongos> use config
switched to db config
mongos> db.settings.update(
... { _id: "balancer" },
... { $set: {activeWindow :{ start: "22:30", stop: "23:59" } } },
... { upsert: true })
WriteResult({ "nMatched" : 1, "nUpserted" : 0, "nModified" : 1 })
```

Note   When selecting a balancing window, you must ensure that enough time is provided to balance all the new documents from that day. If your window is too small, there will be a cumulative effect of leftover chunks which will increasingly unbalance your shards.

Disabling the Balancer

It is possible to disable the balancer and re-enable it later. You could, for instance, disable the balancer during a nightly batch window that modifies lots of documents because you don't want the balancer to "thrash" during the process.

Be careful when using this approach, however, as failing to re-enable the balancer could cause shards becoming heavily out of balance. Here's some code showing the balancer being stopped and restarted:

```
mongos> sh.getBalancerState()
true
mongos> sh.stopBalancer()
{
        "ok" : 1,
```

```
            "operationTime" : Timestamp(1604706472, 3),
            . . .
}
mongos> sh.getBalancerState()
false
mongos> sh.startBalancer()
{
        "ok" : 1,
        "operationTime" : Timestamp(1604706529, 3),
        . . .
        }
mongos> sh.getBalancerState()
true
```

Note   Migrations may still be in progress after the balancer is disabled. You may need to wait until sh.isBalancerRunning() returns false to be sure that the balancer has completely stopped.

Changing the Chunk Size

The chunksize option – 64MB by default – will determine how large a chunk will grow before being split. By reducing the chunksize option, you will have a larger number of small chunks. This will increase migrations and query routing time, but also provide a more even distribution of data. By increasing the chunk size, you will have fewer, larger chunks; this will be more efficient in terms of migrations and routing but may result in a larger proportion of your data sitting in a single chunk. This option won't take effect immediately, and you will have to update or insert into an existing chunk to trigger a split.

Note   Once chunks are split, they cannot be recombined by increasing the chunksize option, so be careful when reducing this parameter. Additionally, sometimes a chunk may grow beyond this parameter but cannot be split because all the documents have the same shard key. These unsplittable chunks are known as jumbo chunks.

Each of these rebalancing options involves a trade-off between maintaining cluster balance and optimizing the overhead of rebalancing. Continual rebalancing might create a noticeable drag on your throughput, while allowing a cluster to become out of balance may create a performance bottleneck on a single shard. There's no "one-size-fits-all" solution, but establishing a maintenance window for rebalancing operations is a low-risk and low-impact way of ensuring that rebalancing operations do not cause performance degradation during peak periods.

Tip   Establishing a maintenance window for rebalancing operations is often the best way to maintain cluster balance while avoiding excessive rebalancing overhead.

Before using any of these methods to control the balancer directly, try to avoid the shards getting out of balance in the first place! Careful selection of a well-distributed shard key is a good first step. Hashed shard keys might also be worth considering if a cluster is experiencing a continually high rebalancing overhead.

Changing Shard Keys

If you have determined that a poorly chosen shard key is creating performance overheads, there are ways to change that shard key. Changing or recreating your shard key is not an easy or quick process in MongoDB. There is no automatic process or command you can run. The process of changing the shard key for a collection is even more work than creating it in the first place. The procedure to change an existing shard key is to

1.   Back up your data

2.   Drop the entire collection

3.   Create a new shard key

4.   Import the old data

As you can imagine, with large datasets, this can be a prolonged and tedious process.

This awkward procedure makes it even more important to consider, design, and implement a good shard key from the beginning. If you're not sure you have the right shard key, it can be useful to create a test collection with a smaller subset of the data.

You can then create and recreate the shard keys while observing the distribution. Just remember, when selecting the subset of data to test on, it must be representative of the whole dataset, not just a single chunk.

Although MongoDB does not explicitly support changing shard keys, starting in version 4.4, it does support a method for improving existing sharded collection performance without fully recreating it. In MongoDB, this is called *refining* a shard key.

When refining a shard key, we can add additional fields to the shard key, but not remove or edit the existing fields. These suffix fields can be added to increase the granularity and reduce the size of our chunks. Remember, the balancer cannot split or move jumbo chunks (chunks larger than the chunksize option) consisting of documents for a single shard key. By refining our shard key, we may be able to break a jumbo chunk into many smaller chunks which can then be rebalanced.

Imagine our application was relatively small, and initially, sharding by the country field was good enough. However, as our application grew, we have a lot of users in a single country, creating jumbo chunks. By refining this shard key with the district field, we have increased the granularity of our chunks and thus removed the permanent imbalance created by jumbo chunks.

Here is an example of refining the country shard key with the district attribute:

```
mongos> db.adminCommand({
    refineCollectionShardKey:
        "MongoDBTuningBook.customersSCountry",
        key: {
            Country: 1, District: 1}
})
{
        "ok" : 1,
        "operationTime" : Timestamp(1604713390, 40),
        . . .
}
```

Note   To refine a shard key, you must ensure that a matching index exists on the new shard key attributes. For example, in the preceding code snippet, an index must exist on {Country: 1, District: 1}.

Keep in mind that refining a shard key will not have an immediate effect on the data distribution: it will merely increase the ability for the balancer to split and rebalance existing data. Furthermore, newly inserted data will be of finer granularity, and this should lead to fewer jumbo chunks and more balanced sharding.

Sharded Queries

Sharding might help you escape a write bottleneck, but if critical queries are negatively affected, then your sharding project is unlikely to be deemed a success. We want to be sure that sharding is not causing any degradation in queries.

Sharded Explain Plans

As usual, we can use the explain() method to see how MongoDB will execute a request – even if the request is executed across multiple nodes of a sharded cluster. Generally, we'll want to use the executionStats option when looking at a sharded query, since only that option will show us how work was distributed across the cluster.

Here's an example of the executionStats section for a sharded query. Within the output, we should see a shards step, which has child steps for each shard. Here's a truncated version of explain output for a sharded query:

```
var exp=db.customers.explain('executionStats').
    find({'views.title':'PRINCESS GIANT'}).next();

mongos > exp.executionStats {
    "nReturned": 17874,
    "executionTimeMillis": 9784,
    "executionStages": {
        "stage": "SHARD_MERGE",
        "nReturned": 17874,
        "executionTimeMillis": 9784,
        "shards": [
            {"shardName": "shard01",
             "executionStages": {
                "stage": "SHARDING_FILTER",
                "inputStage": {
```

```
               "stage": "COLLSCAN"}}},
         {"shardName": "shard02",
          "executionStages": {
              "stage": "SHARDING_FILTER",
                "inputStage": {
                    "stage": "COLLSCAN"}}}}}
```

This plan shows that the query was resolved by performing collection scans on each shard, then merging the results – SHARD_MERGE – before returning the data to the client.

Our tuning script (see Chapter 3) generates an easy-to-read execution plan for a sharded query. Here's an example of this output which shows the plans on each shard:

```
mongos> var exp=db.customers.explain('executionStats').
    find({'views.title':'PRINCESS GIANT'}).next();

mongos> mongoTuning.executionStats(exp)
```

```
1    COLLSCAN ( ms:4712 returned:6872 docs:181756)
2    SHARDING_FILTER ( ms:4754 returned:6872)
3   Shard ==> shard01 ()
4    COLLSCAN ( ms:6395 returned:11002 docs:229365)
5    SHARDING_FILTER ( ms:6467 returned:11002)
6   Shard ==> shard02 ()
7  SHARD_MERGE ( ms:6529 returned:17874)

Totals:  ms: 6529  keys: 0  Docs: 411121
```

The SHARD_MERGE step occurs when we combine output from multiple shards. It indicates that the mongos router received data from multiple shards and combined them into unified output.

However, if we issue a query filtered against the shard key, then we may see a SINGLE_SHARD plan. In the following example, the collection was sharded on LastName, so the mongos was able to retrieve all the needed data from a single shard:

```
mongos> var exp=db.customersShardName.explain('executionStats').
    find({'LastName':'HARRISON'})

mongos> mongoTuning.executionStats(exp)
```

```
1       IXSCAN ( LastName_1_FirstName_1 ms:0
                    returned:730 keys:730)
2     SHARDING_FILTER ( ms:0 returned:730)
3    FETCH ( ms:149 returned:730 docs:730)
4   Shard ==> shard01 ()
5  SINGLE_SHARD ( ms:158 returned:730)

Totals:  ms: 158  keys: 730  Docs: 730
```

Shard Key Lookups

As we've seen, when a query contains the shard key, MongoDB may be able to satisfy the query from a single shard.

For instance, if we have sharded on LastName, then a query on LastName resolves as follows:

```
mongos> var exp=db.customersSLName.explain('executionStats').
                find({LastName:'SMITH','FirstName':'MARY'});

mongo> mongoTuning.executionStats(exp);
1       IXSCAN ( LastName_1 ms:0 returned:711 keys:711)
2     FETCH ( ms:93 returned:9 docs:711)
3    SHARDING_FILTER ( ms:93 returned:9)
4   Shard ==> shardRS ( ms:97 returned:9)
5  SINGLE_SHARD ( ms:100 returned:9)

Totals:  ms: 100  keys: 711  Docs: 711
```

However, note that in the preceding example, we lack a combined index on LastName and FirstName so the query is less efficient than it might be. We should refine the shard key to include the FirstName, or we can simply create a new compound index on both attributes:

```
mongo> var exp=db.customersSLName.explain('executionStats').
                find({LastName:'SMITH','FirstName':'MARY'});

mongo> mongoTuning.executionStats(exp);

1       IXSCAN ( LastName_1_FirstName_1 ms:0 returned:9 keys:9)
```

```
2      SHARDING_FILTER ( ms:0 returned:9)
3      FETCH ( ms:0 returned:9 docs:9)
4    Shard ==> shardRS ( ms:1 returned:9)
5   SINGLE_SHARD ( ms:2 returned:9)

Totals:  ms: 2  keys: 9  Docs: 9
```

Tip   If a query contains the shard key and additional filter conditions, you can optimize the query by creating an index that includes both the shard key and those additional attributes.

Accidental Shard Merge

Wherever possible, we want to send queries to a single shard. To achieve this, we should make sure that our shard key is aligned with our query filters.

For instance, if we shard by Country, but query by City, MongoDB will need to do a shard merge, even though all the documents for a given City will be in the shard that contains that City's Country:

```
mongo> var exp=db.customersSCountry.explain('executionStats').
           find({City:"Hiroshima"});

mongo> mongoTuning.executionStats(exp);

1      IXSCAN ( City_1 ms:0 returned:544 keys:544)
2     FETCH ( ms:0 returned:544 docs:544)
3    SHARDING_FILTER ( ms:0 returned:0)
4    Shard ==> shardRS ( ms:2 returned:0)
5      IXSCAN ( City_1 ms:0 returned:684 keys:684)
6     FETCH ( ms:0 returned:684 docs:684)
7    SHARDING_FILTER ( ms:0 returned:684)
8    Shard ==> shardRS2 ( ms:2 returned:684)
9   SHARD_MERGE ( ms:52 returned:684)

Totals:  ms: 52  keys: 1228  Docs: 1228
```

It may have been better to shard by City, not Country – since City has a higher cardinality. However, in this case, it's equally effective to simply add Country to the query filter:

```
mongo> var exp=db.customersSCountry.explain('executionStats').
          find({Country:'Japan',City:"Hiroshima"});

mongo> mongoTuning.executionStats(exp);

1      IXSCAN ( City_1 ms:0 returned:684 keys:684)
2     FETCH ( ms:0 returned:684 docs:684)
3    SHARDING_FILTER ( ms:0 returned:684)
4   Shard ==> shardRS2 ( ms:2 returned:684)
5  SINGLE_SHARD ( ms:55 returned:684)

Totals:  ms: 55  keys: 684  Docs: 684
```

> **Tip** Whenever it makes sense, add the shard key to queries that execute against a sharded cluster. If the shard key is not included in a query filter, then the query will be sent to all shards even if the data is only present in one of the shards.

Shard Key Range

If the shard key is range sharded, then we can use the key to perform an index range scan. For instance, in this example, we have sharded orders by orderDate:

```
mongo> var startDate=ISODate("2018-01-01T00:00:00.000Z");
mongo> var exp=db.ordersSOrderDate.explain('executionStats').
          find({orderDate:{$gt:startDate}});

mongo> mongoTuning.executionStats(exp);

1      IXSCAN ( orderDate_1 ms:0 returned:7191 keys:7191)
2     SHARDING_FILTER ( ms:0 returned:7191)
3    FETCH ( ms:0 returned:7191 docs:7191)
4   Shard ==> shardRS2 ( ms:16 returned:7191)
5  SINGLE_SHARD ( ms:68 returned:7191)

Totals:  ms: 68  keys: 7191  Docs: 7191
```

However, if hash sharding is implemented, then collection scans in every shard are required:

```
mongo> var exp=db.ordersHOrderDate.explain('executionStats').
       find({orderDate:{$gt:startDate}});
mongo> mongoTuning.executionStats(exp);
```

```
1     COLLSCAN ( ms:1 returned:2615 docs:28616)
2     SHARDING_FILTER ( ms:1 returned:2615)
3   Shard ==> shardRS ( ms:17 returned:2615)
4     COLLSCAN ( ms:1 returned:4576 docs:29881)
5     SHARDING_FILTER ( ms:1 returned:4576)
6   Shard ==> shardRS2 ( ms:20 returned:4576)
7   SHARD_MERGE ( ms:72 returned:7191)

Totals:  ms: 72  keys: 0  Docs: 58497
```

Tip   If you frequently perform range scans on the sharding key, range sharding is preferable to hash sharding. However, remember that range sharding can lead to hot spots if the key values are constantly incrementing.

Sorting

When sorted data is retrieved from more than one shard, the sort operation occurs in two stages. First, data is sorted on each shard and then returned to the mongos where a SHARD_MERGE_SORT combines the sorted inputs into a consolidated, sorted output.

Indexes that exist to support the sort – including the shard key index if appropriate – can be used on each shard to facilitate the sort, but even if you are sorting by shard key, a final sort operation must still be performed on the mongos.

Here's an example of a query which sorts orders by orderDate. The shard key is used to return data in sorted order from each shard before a final SHARD_MERGE_SORT is performed on the mongos:

```
1     IXSCAN ( orderDate_1 ms:22 returned:527890 keys:527890)
2     SHARDING_FILTER ( ms:58 returned:527890)
```

```
3    FETCH ( ms:87 returned:527890 docs:527890)
4   Shard ==> shardRS2 ( ms:950 returned:527890)
5     IXSCAN ( orderDate_1 ms:29 returned:642050 keys:642050)
6    SHARDING_FILTER ( ms:58 returned:642050)
7   FETCH ( ms:102 returned:642050 docs:642050)
8   Shard ==> shardRS ( ms:1011 returned:642050)
9  SHARD_MERGE_SORT ( ms:1013 returned:1169940)

Totals:  ms: 1013  keys: 1169940  Docs: 1169940
```

If there is no appropriate index to support the sort, then blocking sorts will need to be performed on each shard:

```
1     COLLSCAN ( ms:37 returned:564795 docs:564795)
2    SHARDING_FILTER ( ms:70 returned:564795)
3   SORT ( ms:237 returned:564795)
4  Shard ==> shardRS ( ms:1111 returned:564795)
5     COLLSCAN ( ms:30 returned:605145 docs:605145)
6    SHARDING_FILTER ( ms:78 returned:605145)
7   SORT ( ms:273 returned:605145)
8  Shard ==> shardRS2 ( ms:1315 returned:605145)
9  SHARD_MERGE_SORT ( ms:1363 returned:1169940)

Totals:  ms: 1363  keys: 0  Docs: 1169940
```

The normal considerations for optimizing sorts apply to each of the shard sorts. In particular, you need to make sure you don't exceed the sort memory limit on each shard – see Chapter 6 for more details.

Non-Shard Key Lookups

If a query does not include a shard key predicate, then the query is sent to each shard, and the results merged back on the mongos. For instance, here we perform a collection scan on each shard and merge the results in the SHARD_MERGE step:

```
mongo> var exp=db.customersSSCountry.explain('executionStats').
                  find({'views.filmId':637});

mongo> mongoTuning.executionStats(exp);
```

```
1      COLLSCAN ( ms:648 returned:10331 docs:199078)
2     SHARDING_FILTER ( ms:648 returned:10331)
3   Shard ==> shardRS ( ms:1602 returned:10331)
4      COLLSCAN ( ms:875 returned:4119 docs:212043)
5     SHARDING_FILTER ( ms:882 returned:4119)
6   Shard ==> shardRS2 ( ms:1954 returned:4119)
7   SHARD_MERGE ( ms:2002 returned:14450)

Totals:  ms: 2002  keys: 0  Docs: 411121
```

There's nothing wrong with a SHARD_MERGE – we should totally expect that many queries will need to resolve in this manner. However, you should make sure that the query that runs on each shard is optimized. In the preceding example, a need for an index on views.filmId is clearly indicated.

Tip   For queries that must be executed against every shard, ensure that each shard's workload is minimized using the indexing and document design principles outlined in previous chapters.

Aggregations and Sorts

When performing aggregation operations, MongoDB tries to push as much work as possible to the shards. The shards are responsible not just for the data access portions of the aggregation (such as $match and $project) but also pre-aggregations necessary to satisfy $group and $unwind operations.

The explain plan for a sharded aggregation includes unique sections to illustrate how the aggregation was resolved.

For instance, consider this aggregation:

```
db.customersSCountry.aggregate([
  { $unwind:  "$views" },
  { $group:{     _id:{ "views_title":"$views.title" },
          "count":{$sum:1}
     }
  },
]);
```

An execution plan for this aggregation contains a unique section showing how the work will be split across the aggregation:

```
"mergeType": "mongos",
"splitPipeline": {
  "shardsPart": [
    {
      "$unwind": {
        "path": "$views"
      }
    },
    {
      "$group": {
        "_id": {
          "views_title": "$views.title"
        },
        "count": {
          "$sum": {
            "$const": 1
          }
        }
      }
    }
  ],
  "mergerPart": [
    {
      "$group": {
        "_id": "$$ROOT._id",
        "count": {
          "$sum": "$$ROOT.count"
        },
        "$doingMerge": true
      }
    }
  ]
},
```

The `mergeType` section tells us which component will perform the merge. We expect to see `mongos` here, but in some circumstances, we might see the merge allocated to one of the shards, in which case we'd see "`primaryShard`" or "`anyShard`".

The `splitPipeLine` shows the aggregation stages that are sent to the shards. In this example, we can see that the `$group` and `$unwind` operations will be performed on the shards.

Finally, `mergerPart` shows us what operations will occur in the merging node – in this case, on the `mongos`.

For the most commonly used aggregate steps, MongoDB will push down the majority of work to the shards and combine output on the `mongos`.

Sharded $lookup Operations

Join operations using `$lookup` are only partially supported on sharded collections. The collection referenced in the `from` section of the `$lookup` stage *cannot* be sharded. Consequently, The work of the `$lookup` cannot be distributed across the shard. All the work will occur on the master shard that contains the lookup collection.

Warning   `$lookup` is not fully supported on sharded collections. A collection referenced in a `$lookup` pipeline stage cannot be a sharded collection, although the initiating collection may be sharded.

Summary

Sharding provides a scale-out solution for very large MongoDB implementations. In particular, it allows the write workload to be spread across multiple nodes. However, sharding adds operational complexity and performance overhead and should not be implemented lightly.

The most important consideration for sharded cluster implementation is to pick a shard key with care. The shard key should have a high cardinality to allow for chunks to split as data grows, should support queries that can operate against individual shards, and should distribute workload evenly across shards.

Rebalancing is a background operation that MongoDB performs to keep shards balanced. Rebalancing operations can cause performance degradation: you may wish to tweak rebalancing to avoid this or limit rebalancing to a maintenance window.

Query tuning on a sharded cluster is driven by most of the same considerations that exist for single node MongoDB – indexing and document design are still the most important factors. However, you should make sure that queries that can include the shard key do include that key and that indexes exist to support the queries that are routed to each shard.

Index

© Guy Harrison, Michael Harrison 2021
G. Harrison and M. Harrison, *MongoDB Performance Tuning*, https://doi.org/10.1007/978-1-4842-6879-7

Printed in the United States
by Baker & Taylor Publisher Services